C000259357

Critical **I**nven

General Editor: John Schad
University of Lancaster

"a creative intellectual enterprise as rare as it is necessary in an academy which is now over-institutionalised and deadened by bureaucracy."
Jonathan Dollimore

John Schad is Professor of Modern Literature at the University of Lancaster. He is the author of *The Reader in the Dickensian Mirrors, Victorians in Theory, Arthur Hugh Clough*, and the editor of *Dickens Refigured*, Thomas Hardy's *A Laodicean*, and *Writing the Bodies of Christ*; and co-editor of *life.after.theory*. His recent work, *Queer Fish: Christian Unreason from Darwin to Derrida*, was published by Sussex Academic in 2004.

Oxford Town in the afternoon
Ev'rybody singin' a sorrowful tune
Two men died 'neath the Mississippi moon
Somebody better investigate soon.

Someone Called Derrida

Derrida

An Oxford Mystery

JOHN SCHAD

sussex
ACADEMIC
PRESS

BRIGHTON • PORTLAND

2 4 6 8 10 9 7 5 3

First published 2007 in Great Britain by
SUSSEX ACADEMIC PRESS
PO Box 139
Eastbourne BN24 9BP

and in the United States of America by
SUSSEX ACADEMIC PRESS
920 NE 58th Ave   Suite 300
Portland, Oregon 97213-3786

British Library Cataloguing in Publication Data
A CIP catalogue record for this book is available from the British Library.

Library of Congress Cataloging-in-Publication Data
Schad, John, 1960–
    Someone called Derrida : an Oxford mystery / John Schad.
    p. cm. — (Critical inventions)
    Includes bibliographical references and index.
    ISBN 978-1-84519-030-9 (alk. paper) —
    ISBN 978-1-84519-031-6 (pbk. : alk. paper)
    1. Derrida, Jacques. I. Title.

B2430.D484S33 2007
194—dc22
[B]
                                                    2007028249

Typeset and designed by SAP, Brighton & Eastbourne.
Printed by TJ International, Padstow Cornwall.
This book is printed on acid-free paper.

Contents

Illustrations

Jacket / cover illustrations: Jacques Derrida, Paris, 1949–1950, reproduced by kind permission of Marguerite Derrida; John Richard Schad, Oxford, 1951.

Figures on pages 6, 14 and 16 are from Matthew Paris, *Prognostica Socratis basilei* (a fortune-telling book. English, thirteenth-century, the work of Matthew Paris) and are reproduced by kind permission of the Bodleian Library, University of Oxford.

A Rather Dull but Important Note

This book is an experiment in which I am often attempting a style that is, in many ways, novelistic; however, I am also attempting that equally difficult thing – to tell the truth. To be more precise, every factual detail is, as I far as I can tell, correct. The same applies to every quotation; on the few occasions when I adapt a quote it is made clear in the notes. Just occasionally I invent some dialogue but the context makes clear, I hope, that this is invention rather than quotation.

As you will see, I quote extensively from someone called Jacques Derrida – his words are always italicised and the vast majority are from a book called *The Post Card: From Socrates to Freud and Beyond*; all extracts are fully referenced in the notes. I also quote my father throughout; most of his words come from a transcript that is included as an appendix.

Acknowledgments

I am, in the first instance, indebted to the generous help of a whole number of Oxford scholars, archivists and administrators – among them: Anthony Kenny (formerly of Balliol College); Emma Leeson of Linacre College for her help with the Gilbert Ryle Papers; Blair Worden and Judith Curthoys for their help with the Dacre Papers at Christ Church; Thomas Moore of the Faculty of Philosophy; Clare Stevenson of the Maison Française; and, finally, Martin Kaufmann, Bruce Barker-Benfield and their colleagues in the Duke Humfrey Room of the Bodleian Library.

I am also indebted to Chris Woolgar and his colleagues at the Parkes Library, University of Southampton; the librarians at the British Library Newspapers Reading Rooms in Colindale; and the immensely kind teachers and archivist at my father's school.

A number of Jacques Derrida's closest friends were also extremely helpful. Among them: Jonathan Culler, Geoffrey Hartman, Peggy Kamuf, J. Hillis Miller, Jean-Michel Rabaté, David Wood, and (above all) Alan Montefiore.

I must also mention Marguerite Derrida who very kindly sent me the photograph of the young Jacques Derrida which appears on the cover. I shall never, of course, know what Derrida himself might have made of this book; though he did once kindly say (in his characteristically generous way) that he liked the idea of it.

The following very kindly read and advised on early drafts of part or all of this book: Katy Cohen, Steve Cohen, Roger Ebbatson, Mark Knight, Willy Maley, Kevin Mills, Peter Nicholls, Adam Roberts, Jonathan Taylor, and Simon Morgan Wortham, and (above all) Anthony Grahame.

A number of folk kindly offered more occasional or informal advice and help – among them: Arthur Bradley, Jo Carruthers, Valentine Cunningham, David Crossley, Frederic Dalmasso (who once played the voice of JD), Matthew Edmonds, Philip Griffin, James Holden, Simon King (who once played the voice of my father), Daniel Ogden, and Christina Ujma.

An earlier version of chapter one appeared in *Textual Practice*. I am very grateful to them for permission to re-publish here.

Finally: thank you Katie, again (not to mention Thomas, Bethan and . . . Rebecca!).

The Critical Inventions Series

Do I dare / Disturb the universe?
(T. S. Eliot, 'The Love Song of J. Alfred Prufrock', 1917)

In 1961 C. S. Lewis published *An Experiment in Criticism*; over forty years later, at the beginning of a new century, there is pressing need for a renewed sense of experiment, or invention in criticism. The energies unleashed by the theoretical movements of the 1970s and 1980s have been largely exhausted – many now say we are experiencing life after theory; some, indeed, say we are experiencing life after criticism. Criticism, we might say, is in crisis. But that is where it should be; the word 'criticism' comes, as we know, from the word 'crisis'.

Talk of crisis does not, though, fit easily within the well-managed contemporary academy; with its confident talk of 'scholarly excellence', there is a presumption that we all know, and are agreed upon, what scholarship and criticism is. However, to echo Paul de Man, 'we don't even know what reading is'; and what is, potentially, exciting about our present crisis is that now we really know that we don't know what reading is. It is, then, in a spirit of learned ignorance that we propose 'critical inventions', a series which will feature books that, in one way or another, push the generic conventions of literary criticism to breaking point. In so doing the very figure of the critic will shift and change. We shall, no doubt, glimpse something of what Oscar Wilde famously called 'the critic as artist', or what Terry Eagleton called 'the critic as clown'; we may even glimpse still more unfamiliar figures – the critic as, for example, autobiographer, novelist, mourner, poet, parodist, detective, dreamer, diarist, flaneûr, surrealist, priest, montagist, gambler, traveller, beggar, anarchist... or even amateur. In short, this series seeks the truly critical critic – or, to be paradoxical, the critic as critic; the critic who is a critic of criticism as conventionally understood, or misunderstood. He or she is the critic who will dare to disturb the universe, or at least the university – in particular, the institutionalisation of criticism that is professional, university English.

Establishment English is, though, a strange institution that is capable of disestablishing itself, if only because it houses the still stranger institution of literature – which, as Jacques Derrida once wrote, 'in principle allows us to say everything/ anything [*tout dire*]'. We, therefore, do not or cannot yet know of what criticism may yet be capable – capable of being, capable of doing. 'Critical inventions' will be a series that seeks to find out.

Read the text right and emancipate the world.
(Robert Browning, 'Bishop Bloughram's Apology', 1855)

JOHN SCHAD, Series Editor

To Mum, and Dad

CHAPTER ONE

'Si puer vivet'

It is late, later than I think, and I am reading; but even while reading I keep drowsing and dreaming, and often I am dreaming that I am still reading. The book in question, the one I'm supposed to be reading, was written by someone called Jacques Derrida, a philosopher, a strange one. And his book is also strange – strange, I would say, in about a thousand ways; in fact it is, he says, a book of *inaudible murmurs . . . deformed names, displaced events {and} real catastrophes.* One particular catastrophe, or strangeness, is that this philosopher does not seem to know the someone of whom he somehow writes. He murmurs, *I truly believe that I am singing someone who is dead and that I did not know.* Still more strange is that, as I read this book (and as, from time to time, I drowse) I have become persuaded that this someone is my father. After all, he is dead and the philosopher did not know him.

This, I confess, is absurd. But I just can't help dreaming that the philosopher's book has me in mind. *Suppose that at the end of reading something, one of the voices of the book murmurs to you . . . I was thinking of you.* And that's what it's like when I read this book; the philosopher, I do think he sees me coming, knows how I will read. *'That's me.' I can hear it said by so and so who by chance falls upon this letter.* I am not, I suppose, quite saying 'That's me' but I am saying, *Why am I thinking . . . of my father?* These too are words stolen from the philosopher's book.

So, why *am* I thinking of my father while reading a book by someone called Derrida? They are, or were, so very different. Jacques Derrida was famous and even glamorous, a celebrated Parisian intellectual; my father, John Richard, was a minister of religion who lived and worked on a council estate near Watford. But he is most definitely dead, and Derrida most certainly did not know him. *They did not know each other, but according to me, they form a couple . . . just because of that.* Philosopher and pastor, *an odd couple,* it is true; but the philosopher says that *haunting has no limit,* that we may all (all of us) be haunted by each other. I shall, therefore, clutch at straws and point to anything that might just possibly link the two men. I shall say, firstly, that they were both born in 1930; secondly, that both were known to me – albeit, not very well; and thirdly, that both died on a Friday somewhere in October. I consider it no accident that, way back in October 1978, the philosopher should whisper: *I hadn't noticed it was a Friday.*

Still clutching at straws, at *these interlaced lines of life,* I shall also point, like a mute, to the fact or facts that both pastor and philosopher had sons called John or Jean, were related to a woman called Esther, and wrote censored love letters from somewhere called Oxford. Finally, I must add this: that both suffered, or seemed to have suffered, some kind of childhood calamity in the middle of the Second World War.

Allow me to explain, or begin to explain. In September 1942, on the very first day of the new school year, someone called Derrida into his study. *The only school officer whose name I remember today, he has me come into his office: 'you are going to go home, my little friend, your parents will get a note.'* The boy, just twelve years old, is told he will be leaving his school because he is Jewish; after all, this is French Algeria, a place where (the boy must understand) Nazi writ now runs, runs in jack-boots. No Germans have walked on the Algerian earth, but they occupy most of France and that is enough. So the Jewish boy leaves school for home.

Exactly one year later, in England, another boy goes the other way, leaving home for school. He is, or will be, my father. He is thirteen, has finished preparatory school, and is beginning at boarding-school, in Sussex. Here, at some early stage, something happens, something quite terrible; or rather, it may have happened. We don't know. Or at least not yet.

All we have to go on is that, at around the age of 60, after several years of a cruel, premature and mysterious dementia (it was never diagnosed) my father slowly disappeared. He took the slowest possible train out into the dark, into a dark room of his own. In the black-out that followed he was like a man dispossessed, a kind of beggar. Everyday he simply sat, folded in a chair or, worse still, poised precariously on the very edge of a bed that had been brought downstairs, into the living room – he could no longer climb the carpeted Alp that the rest of us mistook for a staircase.

He would hang his head, his face would be agitated, and his thinning body would be afflicted with a whole school of alien pains, both real and phantom. My father seemed to understand almost nothing that we said, just as we understood almost nothing that he said; but then, we did not really want to understand, since his words and cries seemed to describe a series of appalling events.

Well, perhaps not events. Perhaps I should purloin yet more of the philosopher's words and ask: *Disaster – we have dreamed of it, no?* My father, he may have dreamed of it. In the living room. If so, he was dreaming of it every day and every night for the last five or six years of his life, his death; in the living room.

Perhaps his dream was what those Freudians love to call 'false memory.' I see the philosopher nods at this, as if to say 'yes'; he then asks, very gently: *Is it what the child says or is it what says the child?* The philosopher is right, there may have been something scripting my father, working him like a ventriloquist's doll. It is, I accept, quite possible that my father was duped by the memory of something that never happened; but if so, that is still more alarming, a memory from somewhere called nowhere or nowhere called somewhere.

It certainly seemed to come from nowhere, my father having never spoken like this before. It is true that he had, from time to time, talked of not being particularly happy at school, but there had been no prologue to the dramatic monologue of his final years. I heard much of it myself, but my mother, she heard it all, and set it down, even as he spoke.

For instance, he said and she wrote: 'Tell my mother about the teacher. Don't make me go back mother. It was lethal . . . He was hanging there, they were kicking him . . . at school.'

Another time, he said and she wrote: 'Hanging. I said "Turn on the light you can't see anything." They were just kicking him. Just shut the door. 666.'

Yet another time (I recall) he said and she wrote: 'I must telephone. He is murdering me.'

The boy did, finally, telephone. I think he meant to make the call in or soon after 1943, but it took him fifty years to do so, fifty years before he could get through. (*I tried to call you but it was busy, then no answer, you must have gone out*). When he did get through it was not just my mother who picked up the phone; anyone who sat with my father would have heard him. I did. And I am now beginning to think that the philosopher heard as well, that he too heard what (and I quote) *my 'poor father' said.*

I should perhaps explain that the philosopher was well used to peculiar phone calls, calls even from the dead. For example, in the summer of 1979 someone called Derrida, someone called Martin Heidegger, even though he, Heidegger, had died three years before.

On the morning of 22 August 1979, 10 a.m. while typing {the words, 'from Freud and from Heidegger'} . . . the telephone rings . . . The American operator asks me if I accept a . . . 'call' from Martin . . . Heidegger. . . . I know that I will be suspected of making it all up, since it is too good to be true. But what can I do? It is true, rigorously, from start to finish, the date, the time, the content etc. . . . All this must not lead you to believe that no telephonic communication links me to Heidegger's ghost, as to more than one other. Quite the contrary, the network of my hookups . . . is on the burdensome side, and more than one switchboard is necessary in order to digest the overload.

With messages coming in from the dead as well as the living, the philosopher's switchboards are overloaded, burdened with crossed-wires, interference, noises off. And these are terrible noises: the noise of *all the cruelty in the world,* even (he says) *the worst concentration of evil.* Indeed, this concentration is itself concentrated when the philosopher begins to curse and to damn: *To the devil with the child . . . the child, the child.* You can, perhaps, see why I have thought that the philosopher got my father's call, my father's 666 call. I am now thinking all this again as, of a sudden, the philosopher pauses, looks round, and tenderly asks: *Who is he afraid of, this child?*

This, I guess, is an inquiry worthy of Dr Freud, but it is also a detective's question. *The police,* you know, *are not far off;* and they are never far off, not as long as there is what you call 'literature.' As our philosopher insists, *in literature everything . . . is a . . . police affair.* The philosopher would like to evade the police but he can't, he is too much in love with literature, particularly detective literature. That is why he is forever pursued by *all those cops always on my path,* even cops and detectives from long-ago books, from his reading as a boy. Hence, from nowhere, his long-ago friends *Dupont and Dupond* whom you may remember as 'Thomson and Thompson,' the hapless bowler-hatted sleuths from Hergé's *Amazing Adventures of Tintin.* These two resemble, it is said, 'twins who are constantly lost, running to catch up, beside the question, always on the wrong trail.' What on earth they are doing here, in the philosopher's open and wounded book, heaven only knows; but even more unlikely detectives appear to the philosopher as, in 1979, he drowses in his hotel room whilst watching the television: *I have just fallen asleep, as I do every day, watching . . . Charley's Angels (four female private detectives).*

Hold it there. Charley (or rather Charlie) has only three angels; the nodding philosopher must have dreamt a fourth into existence, a fourth and phantom angel. This fourth TV detective is, I think, the philosopher himself. And, in fact, I have a friend who has always insisted that Jacques Derrida was, in reality, none other than Peter Falk in the part of that celebrated seventies TV cop, 'Columbo.' I can see the physical resemblance but I think it unlikely that they are one and the same person, or detective, if only because the philosopher receives his calls from the dead. *Charley's Angels,* he observes, get *their orders . . . on the telephone, . . . and {as I watched on TV} in passing I caught this: ' . . . the dead don't talk.'* This, though, is folly (thinks the philosopher) who immediately shouts at his hotel television, bellowing: *That's what you think! They are the most talkative . . . .* And he should know; with the late Martin Heidegger on the line, our philosopher's case opens with a phone-call from a dead man.

He said and she wrote: 'I must telephone, he's murdering me.' And the philosopher does seem to get this call too, this call from my father as a child. I know this, because his book is stuffed full with dead children, hundreds of thousands of them. *For the children,* he writes, *the holocaust has already begun . . . Holocaust of the children.* As if this, or they, were not enough, there is also *Norbert, my dead younger brother,* he who died in March 1940 of tubercular meningitis at the age of two. And as if *he* were not enough, there is also *Paul . . . the little brother dead before me, a year before I think, and they have never wanted to know or to say of what.*

He said and she wrote: 'Poor boy, dead boy . . . .' But which boy is this now? Which boy are we mourning? The boy erased by meningitis? The boy they had called Paul? The boy expelled for being a Jew? The thousands of boys that were lost in the Holocaust? Or simply the boy that was my father? Or, perhaps, the boy my father says he saw being killed; if there ever was such a boy, such a never never boy.

He said and she wrote: 'The last time. This is the place where . . . . Poor lad . . . only one little lad . . . He's dead! That poor little boy . . . I saw them bring him out screaming. His poor mum. . . . He was hanging . . . chairs and a plank. I had to get him down.'

The boy, if ever he was, did he survive? Did he live? This question, it happens, is a question our philosopher asks; or rather it is a question which confronts him in a book from the thirteenth century, a book called *Prognostica Socratis basilei.* The philosopher found it one day in Oxford's Bodleian Library. It is a mysterious fortune-telling book that includes a series of thirty-six questions, or half-questions, and each time you open the book you are invited to choose one. I do not know why, but the philosopher chose: *Si puer vivet* – 'If the boy lives.'

Once you have chosen your question you are then referred to a bird: a Goose, a Peacock, a Quail, and so on. Beside the name and picture of each bird is a different text, with each text including an answer to your question. And if you are asking about the boy, you are advised to see the Dove, *Columba.* The Dove gives the answer of an unnamed judge, but the philosopher does not tell us the answer. Or rather, the answer is censored.

Forgive me, I forgot (as I do these days) to explain something. I forgot to explain that the philosopher's book consists of a vast collection of messages written to an unnamed 'you,' a far-away lover that is someone close: *give ear closely, come near to my lips.* This lover may be someone best called no-one, but whoever she is (or *whoever you are, my love*) the philosopher does not want us to see all he has written. Whole passages have completely disappeared, many words have gone as if *destroyed by fire,* and *whatever their original length, the passages that have disappeared are indicated, at the very place of their incineration, by a blank of 52 signs.* And here, here at the very point at which we are referred to the bird that is the Dove, the bird that gives us the judge's answer to the question of the boy, the question 'does he live?', what we have is: . . . nothing, or rather 52 nothings, a blank of 52 no-signs, one for each week of your year.

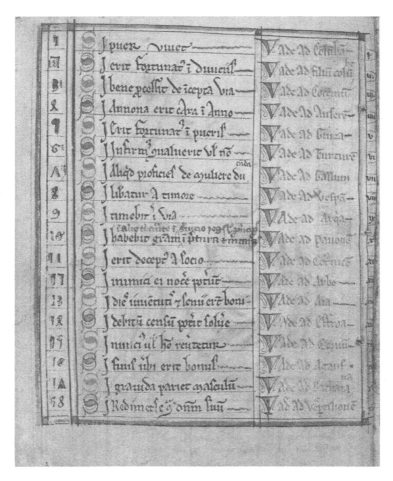

Si puer vivet (MS Ashmole 304, fol. 42 v).

To find the answer you must, therefore, take the last train to Oxford, a city that is home (as someone once said) to lost causes, forsaken beliefs, unpopular names, and impossible loyalties. Once in Oxford, in amongst the lost, forsaken, unpopular and impossible, you must descend into that *labyrinth between the . . . colleges.* At last, you must follow the philosopher to the dead centre of the labyrinth. There you will find the oldest part of the Bodleian Library, a room they call the Duke Humfrey Room, *sanctuary of the most precious manuscripts.* The philosopher asks, *Are you following?* Perhaps not, but you should. You owe it to a boy, and perhaps even to a philosopher. So, listen well as he tells your future, as he says:

One day I will be dead, {and} you will come all by yourself into the Duke Humfrey Room . . . {to} look for the answer in this book {and} . . . you will find a sign that I am leaving in it.

The philosopher *is* now dead. He died on Friday, October the 8th 2004; I heard it on the radio, a day later, a day late (*the radio transmits . . . no one understands*); but the philosopher is now dead, of that I am certain. It is, then, time for you to go, at last, *all by yourself,* into the Duke Humfrey Room *to look for the answer.*

Before you do, however, you must perform two solemn rituals. First, you must take the Bodleian oath. Second, you must buy a sharp new pencil from the Bodleian gift shop, for Duke Humfrey does not allow ink to be spilt within the walls of his Room. I don't know if our philosopher bought a pencil, but he certainly took the oath.

Did I tell you, the oath that I had to swear out loud . . . stipulated . . . that I introduce neither fire nor flame into the premises: 'I hereby undertake . . . not to bring into the Library or kindle therein any fire or flame.' . . . The librarian seemed to know me . . . but this did not get me out of the oath. . . . Therefore I read it and handed her back the cardboard covered with transparent paper that she had tendered me. At this point she starts to insist that I had not understood: no, you have to read it out loud. I did so, with the accent you make fun of all the time, you can see the scene.

The Duke Humfrey Room is an ancient, T-shaped library, nearly cruciform, but not quite; it is a room shaped not so much by prayer as concentration, the concentration of all the knowing world. *Letters, knowledge wall them up in their crypt.* The ceiling of the crypt is like an inverted chess-board, each square a coat of arms; history in code borne up by history in wood, a frozen procession of ornate oak beams. And here everything seems to be made of oak – not just the beams but the desks, the book-cases, even the books and, above all, the light. What once was fire here takes on the pale aspect of all this oak and all these books. Or so it seemed on the day I myself visited the Room. As I stood there I thought the books so splendid, so imperious, that they seemed not to need the light any more than they needed readers – certainly not this rough reader. With my head stuffed full of sleep and distraction I knew I did not belong here, in this concentration room.

As for the philosopher, he remarks, of his visit, that, *I felt myself watched*; and so he too just stood there. This I was told by a man who had emerged, like a holy father, from the latticed confessional box that they call 'The Reserve.' The man, himself reserved, was an archivist, and explained that it was he who, twenty-six years before, had assisted the philosopher. The archivist was French and the very last person I had expected to meet in such a place, for this last person looked at once too savage and too noble to be an archivist. He was not, I felt, one of those *archivists {who} . . . with . . . their imperturbable assurance . . . will kill us with their taste.* No, this man was more anarchist than archivist. His ungovernable hair was a Paris revolt and his beard an outrage, whilst his loose-fitting shirt was un-tucked, open-necked and collarless. And if he did not look like an archivist neither did he walk like one, his gait seeming almost recalcitrant — as if, after all these years, he was still ever so slightly at odds with his wooden cage. I would accept that he spoke with the diffidence and care of one who had lived forever among precious books, but even as he spoke he seemed to nod to himself at almost every word, as if to check each one for fire or flame, as if, just occasionally, he suspected himself of wanting to burn the whole place down.

After all, this is the kind of thing that the French will do, at least when in Paris. Like in 1970, when rioting students, infuriated at being too late for the famous events of May '68, set fire to part of the library at the École Normale Supérieure, the philosopher's own institution at that time. As it happens, this belated storm brought to a fiery end a series of academic exchanges between Oxford and the ENS, a series that had, more than once, smuggled our philosopher across the Channel and into England. It is said that the funds which had once supported this human contraband were now consumed by the need to replenish the fired Parisian library. However, if the Bodleian's noble anarchist was to be believed, there were some in Oxford who felt that 1970 was not quite the right time to be sharing fine wines with French Structuralists. In the late-sixties anyone suspected of being a radical Parisian philosopher was also suspected of being more interested in sedition than sherry; inspired by near-revolution in Paris, there was considerable student activism in Oxford and much fear as to 'Where It Would All Lead.'

My noble friend was very keen that I should be aware of this historical tension, even hostility. At times, as we stood half-hidden in an alcove, he seemed to be looking over his shoulder, as if ever-so-slightly afraid to be seen talking with me. The more we talked the more I dreamt that within this kind and learned man I could see a mute Parisian rage. Indeed, I begin now to think that he was himself the sign that the philosopher had left, a sign of nameless anger, a sense that even here, in the Bodleian, something is wrong, or someone is dead.

So: does the boy live? The omens are not good. I am beginning to suspect there may be a body in the library. Any reader of detective fiction would feel the same, and that includes the philosopher. I say this because another archivist kindly showed me what the philosopher had hand-written, using bold and blue ink, in a special copy of his book, a copy which he had sent to old Duke Humfrey way back in 1980; there, on the frontispiece, I read *To the soul and body of the Bodleian* ('à l'âme et au corps de la Bodleian'). For some reason, my quiet French anarchist had never seen this inscription before, but he immediately got the long-delayed message, the inter-linguistic news – 'I am,' he joked, 'the *corpse* of the Bodleian.'

He is right, there is a stiff in Jacques Derrida's Bodleian; however (and this must be stressed) it has not yet been finally identified. *I arrived {at the Room} at opening time, just now, still dragging along with me a dream: all around someone sick and visibly in danger of death, several doctors. The patient . . . is stretched out, passive, immobile. . . . The death sentence won't be long now, everyone appears to be waiting for it. The disease is visibly at chest level (my father) . . . .*

If there *is* a body in the Room then, at first glance, it is (the philosopher dreams) *my father*. Several years before, the philosopher's father, someone called Aimé (*he was well loved*) had died of cancer at the age of seventy-four. One day, the philosopher would also die of cancer at seventy-four, in hospital, during an operation. The passive and immobile patient is, I now fear, Jacques as well as Aimé, son as well as father. If so, the philosopher is addressing himself when he writes: *You are my fortune teller, the seer and indi-cator of my {own} death.* The body in the Bodleian may yet turn out to be the philosopher's.

Six months before, in January 1979, he had declared: *I intend to go back to Oxford, to take {the} investigation to its end.* The philosopher's investigation is, ostensibly, into that book from the thirteenth-century, but I have always believed that it secretly doubles as an enquiry into his own death. In his late 40s, his own middle-ages, the philosopher has come to Oxford in order to die. *It would be good*, he breathes, *if I died tonight, in the college.*

The college is Balliol. And it is a place where the thought of the philoso-pher's death had, in fact, already been entertained, even proposed:

June 6th 1977 . . . seminar (at Balliol) . . . Afterward, on the lawn where the discussion continued . . . a young student (very handsome) thought he could provoke me and, I think, seduce me . . . by asking why I didn't kill myself. In his eyes this was the only way to 'forward' (his word) my 'theoretical discourse.' . . . Instead of arguing . . . I answered with a pirouette.

If, two years later, when the philosopher returned to pirouette once more on the lawn, he had then died overnight (as was his morbid fancy) the handsome student may himself have faced some awkward questions; the pirouettist's Balliol death might have looked somewhat suspicious.

Balliol, you see, is particularly adept at murder. I first learnt this valuable lesson when, about three hundred years ago, I came across an old issue of *The Spectator*. Here I read a letter from Oxford that had somehow been intercepted by the magazine's editor. The letter was written by an Oxford don who went by the name, or pseudonym, of 'Mercurius Oxoniensis' and seemed, by his diction, to be living deep in the seventeenth century. The letter was, nevertheless, somehow concerned with student activism in 1970, and revealed that the Master of Balliol was now dead. According to Mercurius, whom I have no reason to doubt, 'The late Master was hustled to his grave at midnight very obscurely . . . The Proctors have, though, forgiven the young men who hanged their Master, as they were doubtless ignorant of the statutes against murther.'

You or I might find this somewhat alarming, but Oxford did not; for the Master in question was Christopher Hill, the Marxist historian, and Oxford tends to overlook the murther of Marxists, or indeed trouble-makers of any hue. If our trouble-making philosopher from trouble-making Paris were aware of this (which is possible, since he returned to Balliol in 1970) he must have slept uneasily in his college bed.

He would, in fact, have barely slept at all if had ever read Thomas de Quincey's famously famous essay, 'On Murder Considered as one of the Fine Arts,' written one day in 1827. 'Gentlemen,' de Q. declares, 'it is a fact that every philosopher of eminence . . . has either been murdered or at least been very near it, – insomuch that, if a man calls himself a philosopher and never had his life attempted, rest assured there is nothing in him . . . .'

Quite so. A sentiment shared, one feels, by our philosopher, particularly whenever in Balliol. But then, where better to be murdered than glorious Oxford? Indeed, where else are you so likely to have your murderer identified than in a city which, despite all its lost causes and forsaken beliefs, also boasts a host of brilliant detectives. Who could ever forget such as Gervase Fen, sometime Professor of English Literature, or Lord Peter Wimsey the Balliol alumnus, or indeed our beloved Inspector Morse? I do realise that all three, even Morse, are dead now, but perhaps that helps when it comes to solving a murder.

I was, in fact, reminded of dear Morse even whilst researching this book of mine. I was slouching along Catte Street roughly heading for the Bodleian, when who should I see plodding toward me but Morse's doughty assistant, Lewis. (I swear this is true.) However, I scuttled past, head down, clutching my brief-case, all the while pretending not to recognise this latter-day Dr Watson. I did not, you see, wish to inflate still further the ego of the celebrity sleuth. But it was also, I must confess, that I did not wish to involve the police in my investigation. It is true that my desperate father once said, 'We must tell the police,' but I would really rather not. I might, now and then, make as if to call them, but it will only be a ruse.

That is, by the way, exactly what the amateur detective does in a wonderful novel I once read called *Which Way Came Death?* I love this book; it's a 1936 murder-mystery that is set in (of all places) my father's school. As ever, this is true. The novel was written by one Faith Wolseley, the *nom-de-plume* of the then-Headmaster's wife. At the novel's climax, a scene set in her study, the Headmaster's wife (the fictional one, that is) confronts the murderer, or at least the man who thinks he is the murderer. This man (he is called 'Floyd Burney') was, until fired, a master at the school; he is, though, described by a fellow master as 'that bounder with the Homburg hat, Bohemian tie and Nazi manner.' A somewhat conspicuous figure, one might feel, in an English public school – but then again . . . . Whatever, the Headmaster's wife (one 'Petronella Cary') threatens to call the police unless Burney persuades a certain benefactor to endow the school.

'"I see – blackmail," said Burney, with a sudden sneer.

"Exactly," she replied, looking at her clock.

"I can't," he said.

"Then you'll hang," retorted Petronella, as she put out a tentative hand towards the telephone. Burney was silent, there were beads of sweat on his forehead.'

So, what will the master with the Nazi manner do? Will he give in to Petronella's blackmail or will he call her bluff? As the Headmaster himself observes, 'No school could stand up against the sort of scandal a prosecution for murder would bring. . . . Death from natural causes is bad for a school, but, if a suspicion of unnatural causes leaks out, it's – damnation.'

He has a point, any school, any college, would be tempted to keep a murder silent, mute; a slight hand may reach towards the telephone but the police may not, in the end, be called. Yes, let us keep this in-house, in-school, within the academy; we must, like weary caryatids, bear this heavy load ourselves. Let us return to our libraries, our learning, and our books to help us deal with the very worst things we could possibly imagine, or even do. Some things are just too strange for the police. Let us see what books can tell us, what books might know, or even fore-know.

This, perhaps, is madness, or even dementia; but if so, it is shared by the philosopher. *I will look up*, he says, *what has happened to us . . . in this . . . book from the 13th century.* He is, for some reason, certain that this fragile book *secretly recounts . . . our history.* And that is precisely why I must find the fading page that will tell me, once and for all, if the boy lives, *Si puer vivet*. It is also why I turn, and turn, to this murder-mystery called *Which Way Came Death?* It too whispers our history. And what it first whispers is that the one who investigates murder must himself be a suspect. You see, the headmaster's wife might herself be the murderer; after all, she is the first to discover the body, she has a motive, and she is (remember?) reluctant to call the police. The detective must always be a suspect. He must even suspect himself.

My father certainly suspected himself, suspected that he was in some way complicit in the beating and killing of which he spoke, in particular the beating and killing of a girl and her child.

'The girl . . . I had to hold her head . . .They took turns . . . I could not kill her. . . . I had to drag her. She gave birth. I had to see the dead boy. I could not kill him. . . . I didn't kill the girl. I never hurt her. Kill her . . . My gun. . . . Shoot!'

So, which way came this particular death? Did my father shoot the girl? Was it his gun that killed her? The philosopher, he cries: It's *a firing squad . . . someone gives the order to fire, and . . . everyone goes to it.* I now remember how, one day, my mother told my father, 'You didn't kill her'; to which my father, who hardly ever responded, astonished us by replying (after the longest possible sigh of relief) 'Oh good.'

This 'good' moment means much to my mother; but the trouble is, when you're shooting in the dark it's difficult to know who shot whom. Friendly fire, you call it. The point is made in the school magazine, in a report on an army cadet camp of August 1947, a camp my father attended. As the boys themselves recall, 'We had the thrill of night ops on the Saturday; blackened faces and lowered voices helped towards realism, but the problem of "who shot whom" was never solved.'

It may never be. Not that it matters; I do realise that these were only operations, that the cadets were only play-shooting. Bang-bang, he is dead. It's like when, as children, we would go to the fair, and my father would so impress us at the shooting-booth and say that he'd learnt to shoot at school. Fitting, then, that at school he should have played the part of a character called Pistol in Shakespeare's *Henry V.* That was June 1947, just a couple of months before the cadet camp.

So, to resume, to summarise: Whom did Pistol shoot? And if it wasn't Pistol that did the killing, who was it? It is, I think, too early to say, and too late; but no-one can be ruled out. Everyone of us is a suspect; not just the school-master, the Headmaster's wife and the army cadet but also the scholar, even the philosopher.

I say this because Jacques Derrida openly confesses to murder; he says, with blackened voice and lowered face, *Right here I kill you . . . there is someone in me who kills.* Bang-bang, you are dead.

I accept that confession is not proof, but it is evidence; as is the philosopher's astonishing claim that Socrates had (and I quote) a *revolver-pocket*. This pocket is detected by the philosopher as he stares at the picture of Socrates that he finds in the fortune-telling book. Have a look for yourself on the page that follows. Can you see it, the revolver-pocket? Can you? . . . No, neither can I; but perhaps anything is possible in a picture that reverses the one thing everybody knows about Socrates – namely, that he spoke and Plato wrote. Here, in this Oxford looking-glass, Socrates is no longer the dictator, the great dictator; here it is the finger-pointing Plato who dictates and Socrates (the one in the ludicrous hat) who is busy transcribing.

I should perhaps add that our philosopher, who may yet emerge as something of a milliner, once remarked that Socrates' hat is *rather like a condom*. This I do see; though I should not say it to Socrates' face lest he really does have a gun in his pocket. Or, perhaps, he is just glad to see someone? Mind you, I get from our philosopher the impression that Socrates would know how to use a gun.

. . . you know the end of the detective story: Socrates knocks off all of them . . . he remains alone, the gangbusters take over the locale, he sprays gas everywhere, it's all ablaze in a second, and behind the cops the crowd presses forward somewhat disappointed that they didn't get him alive.

I knew that Socrates was tried and found guilty of perverting the youth of Athens, and I knew he was condemned to take hemlock, but what I did not know was that, like Samson, he took everyone else down with him. Again, we are in the dark as to who shot whom, but I have now learnt that the first-man of Western philosophy is not so much a martyr as a suicide-bomber with a condom on his head.

This particular Socrates is funny, even dead funny. But I guess that's because he writes, and writing, as every philosopher knows, is odd, or queer, and fatally so. St Paul once said that 'The letter killeth,' but so too do all philosophers, for philosophers (I have learnt) are always writing, always killing, even when just thinking, just using their brains. 'The brains, kill, quick!' said my father. 'The brains, kill, quick!' The brain, I think, is another unusual suspect. Let it be noted: thinking may not be trusted.

'Think! Think!' cried my father, 'Think! Think!' And think-think is exactly what Socrates does, *that devil of a Socrates*, that perverter of youth, that philosophical celebrant of the beautiful boy. Everyone knows that the father of metaphysics cannot be trusted with boys, or at least not his thinking, his brains, his mind. Indeed, I shall here insist that if philosophy

Plato and Socrates (MS Ashmole 304, fol. 31 v).

were personified, were someone (as she so often is), she might well be saying,
'Hell is in my father's head.'

'Hell is in my father's head.' These are words that my own father heard, in
Oxford, at the University Church, on April 23rd 1951, in the first-ever

production of Christopher Fry's play *A Sleep of Prisoners*. It is, I have found, a verse-drama about four British soldiers held in a church that has been turned into a prison camp. I am not sure why they are prisoners, or who is holding them, or even where they are, but their hell somehow mirrors the hell that, one day, would be in *my* father's head.

He said and she wrote: 'Oh, someone take me out . . . The door, smash it . . . He came back. To get to church. . . . I know where to get blessed, the cross. A little church . . . I don't want to go and sing. . . . It was the Sergeant. . . . He was wearing uniform. . . . In the army. . . . You're coming with me. . . . Trapped.'

The boy that was my father is trapped in a church with men who look like soldiers. Or so his blackened story goes. If the boy then lives, lives to become a young man who, in 1951, watches a play about soldiers caught in a church, what happens in the young man's lowered head? Did the play awaken a memory, or create a memory? 'The boy's dead. / You might as well be told: I say / The boy's dead' – these are words from the play, first spoken forty years before it is staged within my father's head.

Writing at the time, my father remarks: 'It was a very fine play.' And so it is. In fact, it is a fine play finely entangled with the history of my father's school; and this is despite Christopher Fry himself having no connections with the school. The play was, though, performed there in 1960 – an unusual choice I would have thought, except perhaps that the play opens with one of the imprisoned soldiers playing, at the organ, the opening bars of 'Now the Day is Over,' a hymn that happens to have been written by a long-dead master at the school.

Strange this, or these, these coincidences; but perhaps they begin to explain why my father remarks that 'the play, though fine, was rather too mystical, by which I mean that I found it rather hard to get hold of the meaning and the moral.'

I should like now to shake him and say: 'Think! Think! Is not the meaning and moral what you suffered as a boy, whilst away at school? Don't you recall – the church? the soldiers? being trapped?'

But he would not listen. He was never one to look back and, besides, April 1951 was not a time to walk backwards. This was Oxford in springtime and he is in love, has just turned twenty-one, and is busy finding ways not to revise for Schools. His letters, at this time, speak of choirs and cocktails, of dancing like the Scottish and playing canasta like the smart set, of chasing the college eight on the river and singing madrigals from a punt in the evenings. The philosopher whispers: *'madrigal'* . . . *a song with 4,5,6, 7 voices.*

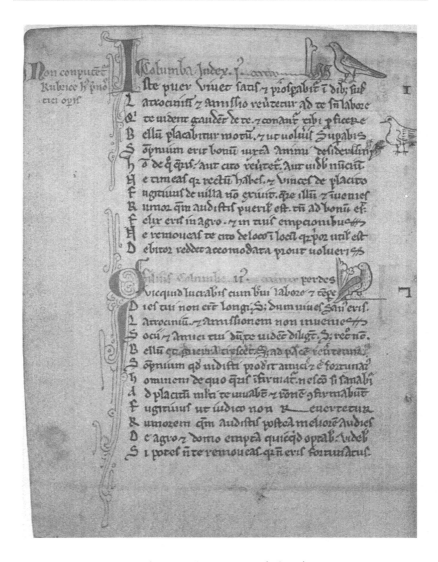

Columba (MS Ashmole 304, fol. 43 v).

My father's Oxford letters transcribe, I suppose, a dream of Oxford, a dream of Oxford-past. But it is also a dream of Oxford-future. For in March 1951, he declares, 'Somehow I am sure that the summer is going to be a fine one.' And it was. The young woman who would become his wife will return from a year of America; and, once Schools are over, she will go up to Oxford for a Commemoration Ball, and that night, at Christ Church, within the Dean's garden, he will propose to her. She will answer with a pirouette and, come the dawn, they will drive in a 1926 Morris Cowley to Woodstock for breakfast. The summer is going to be fine, and so too the world.

The philosopher, he pleads, *Promise me that one day there will be a world*; but he need not worry, the young Oxonian will make sure that there is. In February 1951 he writes, 'Though I haven't become a socialist yet, I am very much in sympathy with pacifist ideals.' Just a month later he *has* become a socialist, and is already impatient for the millennium: 'I have now swallowed socialist clap-trap hook, line and sinker; however, it does not seem to make our meat rations any larger.'

War was slow to leave hungry Oxford, but Pistol-the-pacifist will still set down his gun, declaring himself a conscientious objector to National Service. He once said (and she wrote): 'We don't fight . . . .'

In *Henry V*, when Pistol exits stage-right a character simply known as 'Boy' is left, all alone; looking around at the deserted English camp, he declares that 'there is none to guard it but boys.' In 1951 there is one boy less to guard camp England. Not that England needs saving any more; war is finally over, the summer will be fine, so too England. And my father is sure of this, for his world is one of pure prediction, pure prognostication. In the summer of 1951 his world is the world of the Oxford fortune-telling book.

Time then to turn, at last, to the page to which the philosopher points, Columba's page, the page that will reveal if the boy lives, *Si puer vivet*. Like the headmaster's wife, I put out a tentative telephonic hand, and hesitate. A moment later and the page is turned, another page from our thirteenth century, but I cannot read it, *I have to get some help*. Then, someone transcribes, someone translates, and what is transmuted is: someone familiar; for the text before me reads like a dream-text that has somehow come straight from my father, the post-war, pacifist man-boy who was so much in love. It reads:

That boy will live long in the land . . .

Wars initiated will be rendered peaceful . . .

You will have good sleep by the side of your heart's desire.

CHAPTER TWO

A Sleep of Prisoners

There *was* good sleep, the good sleep of love. I know because, when in Rome, they say 'amor vincit omnia' but, when in Oxford, where Christopher Fry's prisoners are forever sleeping, they say: 'amor vincit *ins*omnia.' My father liked this pun or 'Fry-ism,' as he calls it in a letter to his love, my mother to-be. Good sleep. Good night. Or, as he used to whisper to me at bedtime, gently stealing Horatio's words to dead Hamlet, 'Good night, sweet prince. And flights of angels sing thee to thy rest.'

For Hamlet, 'the rest is silence,' the silence of death; for my father, the silence that mattered was the silence of forgetting, or even of remembering to forget. But the problem is that we can't always do this; in the end, at the end, we will forget to forget, and our sleep will be rough sleep.

Tell this to our philosopher who, in the spring of 1951, is busy struggling to sleep; whilst my father dreams in Oxford, the philosopher lies awake in Paris, and beside him lies the murdered body of sleep. These were weeks, he recalls, of *nervous collapse, sleeplessness, sleeping tablets . . . amphetamines.* But what is it that keeps the young philosopher awake? Some say it is the examination he is about to take, an examination to gain entrance to one of the Grandes Écoles, but I shall say it is the sheer distance between Paris and the family home in Algeria. In 1949 when the philosopher follows his beloved St Augustine and takes the voyage out from Algiers harbour it is the very first time he leaves home. When his ship reaches Marseilles he is (within his own words) *alone on the other shore.* The philosopher's sleeplessness is, I think, a kind of homesickness, the kind that could beset anyone separated from home by the sea. It is a trick of the sea. *I hope to perceive you when I land.* This, all this, is a trick of the sea.

And this trick, the trick that strangles sleep, is also played upon my father, just one year later, in the long, slow Fall of 1952. He, my father, is now crossing the Atlantic as a merchant seaman, or rather 'Assistant Steward,' on a Cunard liner called *RMS Samaria* – twenty-thousand tons in pursuit of pleasure. Just eight years before, in November 1944, when going the other way, the liner had carried hundreds of young Americans to old Europe, senile and demented with war – these young hundreds were the 7th Battalion of the 8th Amoured Division. Now in 1952 the boys of war are gone and the *Samaria* once more carries people who are, by cruel contrast, sublimely pointless.

But the pointless are generally rich, which is why, I think, my father and his mates called them 'Bloods' – they were there to be bled for tips. And my father could certainly do some bleeding whenever he got to carry luggage, run baths, or wait at tables in the saloon. There were, though, many bloodless tasks, like washing-up, scrubbing the floor, and the all-night fire-watch. There was also the cleaning of toilets, a role which earned John Richard the sobriquet 'Richard the Turd,' something of which he was always justly proud. I think he was also known as 'Dick the Shit,' and all his life he happily answered to either. This was useful in Watford.

However, I have digressed, have abandoned the sleepless. What I had meant to say was that, in March 1952, whilst returning from Quebec, my father writes, 'I had one bad night when I was sick three times; for once, it was not due to the weather or the beer.' Merchant Seaman Schad does not go on to say from which way this bad night had come, but the same letter mentions that he has recently heard that his mother, back in England, after months of 'dreadful depression,' has had 'a nervous breakdown.'

Again something is not right, something is disturbing the sleep of our boys across the water; theirs is not the good sleep foretold by Columba but the bad sleep of prisoners, those prisoners forever trapped in Oxford's University Church.

'This is,' they say, 'no place for lying awake.'

Nor for sleeping, I think; for when Fry's soldiers do sleep it is, they say, the sleep of madmen.

They say, 'We're mad boys. Sleep has gone to our heads.'

I think that *our* boys (the philosopher, my father) are mad boys too; bad sleep goes to their heads, and there it stays. Even late in life my father is still sleeping the mad, bad sleep of war, world war, total war, everybody's war.

Dreaming, I ask my father: 'What nightmare's this you're dragging me into?'

Dreaming, he replies: 'Humanity's. Everybody's.'

I must confess that I gathered this last fragment of dialogue from *A Sleep of Prisoners*; but there is no other way to talk with my father. If I pick lines from the pocket of Christopher Fry (and he will never miss them) at least I can be sure that my father did once hear the words. So, let me also murmur, in purest ventriloquy: 'A dream has got you prisoner . . . Don't let it take you in.'

It is, though, too late, for my father was taken in long ago – the dream, the nightmare began way back in 1943, 1944, 1945. And I shall soon be dialling these numbers, if only to see whether war and its rumours could have put a Sussex public school under such strain that a boy of thirteen or fourteen, away from home for the first time in his life, might see or imagine things that only no-one should see or imagine.

I now recall that Karl Marx says somewhere that Hegel says somewhere that history happens twice: the first time as tragedy, the second time as farce. And, at my father's school, the war certainly happened twice: the first time as air-raids, rifles, evacuees, land-girls, night-watches, missing masters, weak tea, and the school's own Home Guard platoon; the second time as films, newsreels, radio broadcasts, letters from home, prize-day speeches, and, above all, a school magazine so beautifully written that it seems to have been composed not by boys but angels.

These boy-angels take flight most brilliantly whenever they write about what they call the 'Disadvantages of the Place,' the beloved cage in which, by day and by night, they beat their scruffy wings.

'We will never forget,' they say, 'the wind howling through the unglazed cloisters, whistling under doors and through keyholes; the raw chill of the unheated rooms; the gas jets with their asthmatic wheeze, casting a dim, but far from religious light; the harsh cry of the peacocks in the summer dawn . . . and that peculiar aroma . . . compounded apparently of escaping gas, ink, and damp clothes.'

These same damp angels tend to spill their boyish ink on such mortal ground as the Inter-House PT Competition, the Gramophone Society, and the Jazz Club (led, I note, by one who signs himself 'Pistol-Packing Mama'). But they also tread immortal ground, writing, as they must, of boys (now 'old boys') who have gone to war and are not returning – wrestling angels all now fallen. One such boy is posted as missing after a flight to Egypt, another is lost in action at Dunkirk, another has been killed in the famous raid on the Möhne Dam, another has died in northern waters off Iceland, another is now a prisoner of war in Germany, and still another is lost forever somewhere over the English Channel – 'he died in the way he would have most desired.' We can write, we are told, to the prisoner of war, his address is: Stalag Camp, XIIC, Germany, Kriegsgefanegenpost. For the boy lost over the Channel no postal address is given.

Old boys, however, are boys old enough to kill as well as to be killed. And this is suddenly remembered when one particular alumnus writes to the school magazine from France, in September 1944.

'I thought you would like to know,' he says, 'how the Liberation of Europe appears through the eyes of an old boy. . . . It is a great game of

"Jerry Chasing" and Liberating with a spot of "Chap-Shooting." Like the Panzer lunatic who stood up in his tank and shouted "I want to die for the Führer" – the tank chaps, obliging fellows, I have always found, promptly shot him.'

I feel sure I know this Panzer lunatic, this would-be martyr who speaks such good English – he is, I think, that bounder with the Nazi manner, the one who is blackmailed by the Headmaster's wife. The school has clearly done for him a second time, this time as farce, as a spot of chap-shooting. The old boy who writes, however, knows it is farce, a bloody farce, and he knows this far better than any philosopher: 'It's all,' he adds, 'a fantastical, nightmare.'

The bad sleep of war has clearly gone to everybody's head. They're all mad boys now, even those still at school. They too cannot sleep for war. When the boy-angels who edit the school magazine look back to D-Day they recall how 'we lay in bed listening to the Lancaster bombers overhead as they thundered south to the coast.' How could the pupils sleep when they knew that so many of the thundering boys overhead would not be thundering back? Besides, to sleep is perhaps to dream, and to dream is to risk nightmare, to risk becoming the enigmatic and tormented figure that, to my astonishment, suddenly appears in a mock-Shakespearean flourish at the end of the same editorial.

'But who,' say the editors, 'is this whose dreams are nightmares? Who is this so pale and wan? No fond lover! Muttering, frowning, pacing pleading. Pity and do not condemn. For all your easy pleasures, here is one in torment . . . one who will . . . collapse through sheer exhaustion and pass on to quiet insanity. Not until then will his fellows cease their mournful litany.'

For a moment, I see the tormented figure of the old, old boy in our living-room. With his elsewhere-body almost as restless as his wasted mind, he forever paced, or rather shuffled – his timid and aimless feet barely moving him. *I less and less know where my body is.* Just beneath his hanging head one hand would clutch the top of his shirt; meanwhile, with his waist being so thin, his trousers would threaten to fall, as if in a farce, or rather a show-trial when they take away the prisoner's belt. Now and then his wide and frightened eyes would sweep the room like headlamps, before fixing on a terrible faraway place in, say, the corner of the living-room. He would be muttering, frowning, pacing, pleading. 'Go home,' he once said, 'and lock the door!' Day by day, he was delivering to someone a final, unfinished, and unruly sermon.

I apologise, I have been thinking of 1994, not 1944. So, I look again at the editorial, and again at its tormented figure; this time I see the figure of the Headmaster, a man who took up his post in 1937 but who, by 1943, was already close to exhaustion. He had finally discovered that any decision he made could be overruled by the Church of England 'Chapter' that had final responsibility for the school; frustrated and impotent, the Headmaster once dared to wonder with whom he was working: 'Is it,' he asked, 'a body I never meet?'

But some bodies are like that, particularly when the world's clocks all chorus: 'Time for War.' In August of 1943 the Headmaster writes, in a letter, 'I cannot cope with this, I am too worn with the struggle of war-time difficulties. My average for the last eight days of term was getting to bed between 2.30 and 3.00 a.m., finishing up with an all-night show with the Home Guard.'

Two years later, with war finally over, this worn and sleepless Head is, quite suddenly, gone. And the angels write this:

'At the beginning of the school year there were two bombshells to set tongues wagging. The first was the atomic disintegration of Hiroshima. The second was really unexpected: a letter to say that the Headmaster had been stricken with a nervous breakdown and compelled to relinquish his post.'

This second Hiroshima, the nervous one, it catches my closing eye; particularly when the school historian writes, of the Headmaster's going, that 'the boys were *told* it was due to a nervous breakdown.' The history man discretely says no more, will say no more, and I am intrigued. In 1945 talk of a headmaster suffering 'a nervous breakdown' was bomb enough; so, if such talk were a cover, or veil, then the real reason for the Head's disappearance must have been still more of a bomb. This other Hiroshima, the secret Hiroshima, the secreted light of a thousand suns (*light, light, more light!*) is what I am after.

And it must, I think, all connect (if Hiroshimas can ever connect) with the poor boy that was my father. There is, there must be, a cryptic clue in the fact that the bomb which was dropped on Hiroshima was nicknamed 'Little Boy.' *Everything,* you see, *comes back to the child* – not just the dying but the killing. After Hiroshima, after Little Boy, the question is not just 'Does the boy live?' but 'Does the boy kill?' I sometimes worry that my father's final, demented sermon might yet prove to be a time-bomb, a long-delayed Hiroshima, a Little Boy who is still able to devastate.

But, it must not be like that; I promise right now that no one will get hurt, that there will be no accusations. For, as those boy-angels write: 'Pity and do not condemn.' It is true that my father cried, 'He was hanging there, they were kicking him,' but still the angels write: 'Pity and do not condemn.' It is, again, true that my father cried, 'Legs, hands, trunk, buried in the sand. Hanging. Legless,' but still, still the angels write: 'Pity and do not condemn.'

Echoing the angels, I plead 'Pity and do not condemn *me*.' I confess that I am not free of guilt, not free of the philosopher's hard, rhetorical questions. He asks, you know, questions like:

Who is he afraid of, this child, and who uses him in order to send terrifying signs everywhere, in order to get pleasure from it and to be absolved of it at the same time, in order to write?

I know that this is me, that I am the one who uses the child in order to write. Without my child-father I would have nothing to write: no boy, no story. Pity me, I am just a literary critic, a bloody academic, for heaven's sake; I don't normally write books like this, not with a story, not with a point. But it is too late to stop, too late to stop listening to the boy. And I know I cannot be absolved, but I must still write, still listen.

And the more I listen the more I return to the light-shocked summer of 1945, when it was not only the Headmaster who resigned but the School Sergeant. This man was an army veteran, a machine-gunner from a previous world and war, the one with the trenches and the mud. The school had employed him to run the Cadet Corps, the body that provided all older boys with basic military training – marching, camping, shooting. When recording the departure of the Sergeant, the well-drilled school magazine uses exactly the same smart right-turn of phrase as employed for the Head; each had been 'compelled to relinquish his post,' though in the case of the Sergeant there is no talk of ill-health. The Head goes on to work for the diocese, in an office; but unlike the previous Head he never returns to preach in the school chapel. Both were ordained.

So, had something somewhere gone wrong? Was something out of joint? Perhaps, just perhaps; and if so, it may be important – if only because my father did at one point whisper, 'The Master killed' and, at another, 'It was the Sergeant!'

I must go carefully into this bad night. If, all those years ago, something really did misfire within or near the school would I really want to know? What should I do with this burden of proof? Or, as the philosopher whispers, *What to do with the proper names?* I don't think there shall be any names – and no phone calls, I think, to the police. After all, who could base a case on the testimony of a man so confused, so ill, and so heavily medicated?

In those final living-room years, my father certainly saw things, heard things, and even felt things that nobody else saw, heard, or felt. *Me, I look out for the noises in the room around you, I try to surprise what you are looking at or looks at you, as if someone were hanging around, someone who might be me at times.* But nothing and, I think, no-one was really there; my father's day-mare may well have been no more than a trick of medication, just one long pharmaceutical comedy routine – each sight, each sound, and each shiver being a punch-line, or whole gag, from a host of comedy drugs. The funniest was the one they gave him to arrest the sudden onset of fits with which it all began, out of the blue, when my father first fell from the sky. The comedian that the doctors prescribed for this went by the stage-name of Benzodiazapan – a stand-up act, you might say, since it rarely allowed my father to sit down; my father's body was simply too agitated. But if we had thought that the Great Benzo was funny, we had not reckoned with what would happen when his routine was suddenly stopped – just like that, in mid-joke, without warning, in November 1991. That's when the fun really started. It was the doctors who had pulled the plug on the Benzo Show, literally overnight; it was as if there had been one too many obscenities, and so old-bugger Benzo was off the air, censored with immediate effect. One day, it's all Benzo, the next day no Benzo; no gradual withdrawal, simply sudden and immediate cease-fire.

In short: it was time for the Old Cold Turkey Show. This duly came my father's way, with all the usual side-splitting fun: cramps, paralysis, insomnia, diarrhoea, constipation, hallucinations, breathlessness, sudden pains, electric shocks, and endless pins and needles. Indeed, it was at this time that 'The Talking' began. There was no prompting, no auto-suggestion, he wasn't even listening to us. He just began, one day, all by himself, to Talk. In time, the curtain fell on The Cold And Yet Hilarious Turkey – my father's body could take no more fun; but, the Talk Show continued and did not finish until around four years later. My father (the man, the one that breathed as well as talked) he himself finished soon after that.

So, yes, medication is part of our mystery; that is certainly what the doctors would chorus. My father's Talk Show they would say was but an inevitable spin-off from the The Great Benzo Show, a regrettable side-effect of necessary treatment.

But treatment of what? What, exactly, was my father's condition? Sometimes overworked doctors would, almost casually, give it the popular name of Alzheimer's. This diagnosis was, though, never confirmed since they never got round to the autopsy. They should have; the written note attached to his corpse (to a toe, I think) formally requested a dissection, since he had always wanted that his body 'should be made,' as he would say quite grandly, 'available to science.' 'Either that,' he would add, 'or chuck me in the goldfish pond.' However, for some reason, the autopsy request did not get through. He did not reach his destination; he was, you might say, a dead letter.

But we don't know why he did not get through, did not make it to the opening ceremony. Perhaps, because it was a Friday afternoon, when time slows down. It was, in fact, that weekend in October when, in England, the clocks turn back. Time nods off, and an extra hour is invented, an hour that the clocks don't get to measure, an hour that passes behind their backs. And it is as if my father's body is still there, in the hour that the clocks did not know about, and in which the autopsy did not take place, the hour in which his brain was not opened up. I should have liked to speak to our philosopher about all this, I would have said: 'Yes, the dead may be able to talk, but they are not always given the chance to talk.'

And if this dead man, my dead man, had had the chance, would he have talked of Alzheimer's? Perhaps. The doctors sometimes said to me, 'John, if you have Alzheimer's then your brain is, quite literally, shrinking,' and it did indeed seem as if my father had been somehow shrinking. Little by little, the little boy had become ever more little. In fact, I swear that I once heard him say, 'I am tiny.' I can't, though, quite remember how he said this. Sometimes his voice was electric with terror and sometimes hollowed by the most terrible pity, but sometimes it was almost absent-minded, even nonchalant. And if anyone could say 'I am tiny' in a nonchalant manner, it was my father, a man who never needed or wanted to be big.

But, can you trust the word of a man who is shrinking? Indeed, can you trust the word of a man who, as a minister of religion, had spent thirty years listening to folk who would tell the saddest of stories; though, if he did ever counsel anyone who had witnessed murder I would not know – it would have been in confidence. I do know that he increasingly came across, albeit at second-hand, the most appalling accounts, or claims, of ritual and even Satanist abuse. Here the philosopher interjects, saying *You also showed me absolute horror*. And this you did more than ever in the early 1990s, when absolute horror was commonplace within those Christian circles where it was not deemed folly to speak of the Devil, or 'Enemy Action,' as it was sometimes called. These were circles in which my father moved, and was moved.

So, which way came his nightmare? Was it from a past that was not his own? And if so, was he remembering for someone else? Don't forget that a pastor, like his Master, is called to bear another's load, another's sorrow – perhaps even another's death. (*I am dead*, says the philosopher, *of a death that is no longer my own*.) So, was my father mad with a memory that was not his own? . . . *there is someone in me {whom} I still can't quite identify*.

At times, strange times, I wonder if this someone is the six year-old girl who on August 28th 1943 was raped by a Canadian soldier in a neighbouring village. (He said and she wrote: 'When he did it to you he would be good'). At other times, still stranger times, I wonder if the someone in question could be the seven year-old boy who, on June 27th 1945, was taken at night into a nearby wood and indecently assaulted by a repatriated prisoner of war. (He said: 'The dark. He was just a little lad! A little boy!').

Remember this: in the middle-age of the war, when the South of England became one vast military camp it also became one vast telephone exchange of both information and misinformation, intelligence and counter-intelligence; wires were easily crossed, and so too were lives. It was a time when it was all too possible to become someone else, to purloin another man's past. Just ask the man they called Major William Martin, the man whose identity was invented by MI5 and given to a corpse that, in April 1943, is allowed to wash-up on the coast of Nazi-friendly Spain. In his damp pockets were stuffed the echoes of lives lived by others: another man's theatre tickets, another man's receipts, even the photograph of another man's fiancée. . . . *metro ticket . . . movie ticket . . . wrapper of a sugar cube.*

I often go back to this corpse, this man – the real dead man, that is. His final photograph, taken just before they lowered him gently into the sea, reminds me of what I never saw: my father when dead. I was too late to see this. Major Martin (also known as 'The Man Who Never Was' – you may have seen the film) is laid out with his eyes closed, his mouth wide open, and hair swept back from his high forehead. He has, I think, a kind face. And, as with my father, the final cause of death had been pneumonia; this is because they wanted a body with water on its lungs to make him look like a man who had drowned.

Poor Major Martin, this someone who is dead (someone in me, I still can't identify) is still moving through the night, drifting South toward the open side of Spain, seduced by the tide and nursed by the waves that wash him. *I have the impression of floating in a glass coffer.* His thin manikin body is dressed in naval uniform and a trench coat; over his coat he wears a Mae West life-jacket and, as if just going to the office, his long and stiffened fingers clutch a briefcase full of misinformation. He is a human postcard, a message sent in the hope that it will be intercepted, read by the Enemy. *It falls into anyone's hands, a poor post card.* And he drifts forever on; but, despite the dark, he might just be seen by sea-going philosophers. Our philosopher is such and he does, I think, see the man, even speaks to him; for, all of a sudden, the philosopher whispers this:

You alone whose life will have been so short, the voyage short, scarcely organised, by you with no lighthouse and no book, you the floating toy at high tide and under the moon, you the crossing . . .

CHAPTER THREE

In wartime, if we are to succeed in confusing the Enemy, in ensuring he does not know who we are, it may help if we too are unsure. And, let's face it, we *are* unsure – as unsure as Christopher Fry's prisoners of war; they ask 'Who are we? . . . Who are we?' These Oxford inmates, they speak or ask on behalf of all who must endure the war, above all those who endure it in Oxford. For up in cosy Oxford we are, more than ever, lost in the fog and fug of war; up here we are unsure not just as to who we are but even as to whose side we are on. In Oxford, you see, we are not bombed. Bombs are falling like black confetti all over England, but not in Oxford; and we are beginning to wonder why. The Dean of Somerville College says it is because Hitler is keeping Oxford for himself, for the day he collects his honorary degree. Still others say that Oxford is to become the capital of Nazi England. Whatever, the virgin fact remains that in Oxford we are not bombed. In the so-called Baedeker Raids of 1942, a series of dastardly raids on English morale, a number of cathedral cities are hit, including Cambridge; but in Oxford we are still not bombed. We are certainly ready for bombs, ready for falling fire; in fact, we are quite possessed by the thought of fire. With our fire-groups, fire-captains, fire-guards, fire-parties, fire-committees, and fire-fighters we are, you might say, the University of Fire. And yet there is no fire – or at least none caused by bombing. So, we ask, what is wrong with us? Has Professor Hitler not noticed that several sections of the Secret Service have relocated to Oxford? Has the eminent Professor not realised that in the vaults of the Bodleian the Admiralty are busy planning D-Day? Perhaps not; but surely this Professor of Absolute Knowledge must know about industrial Oxford, that part we call Cowley, with its huge Morris Motors? In these days of conflict this vast, metal Bodleian is home to machines that are far deadlier than the Morris Eight; now, each day and every day, family-cars turn miraculously into tanks, sea-mines, torpedoes, and Tiger Moth fighter-planes (forty every week). But still we are not bombed.

And as our bomb-less war goes on it slowly dawns upon us, slowly falls upon us, like the gentlest imaginable bomb, that in Oxford we shall never be bombed. Thus, when the war eventually ends we, the un-bombed, feel we must speak, and we do: on May the 11th 1945 the editor of *The Oxford Times* declares that,

'We are thankful for our immunity from bombing but [our] gratitude is tinged with regret that there is no easy way to acquire the community spirit which adversity forced on other towns. . . . It is, therefore, against a background of minor inconvenience without major tragedy that Oxford's domestic war-time drama has been played.'

In Oxford, we may never have been really at war at all, or at least it may only have been a drama, a kind of theatre – a theatre of war.

But, let us limp on and observe that one Saturday, in the early summer of 1941, Oxford's theatre of war becomes a theatre of farce as, on this particular Saturday, Oxford becomes the stage for a full-scale Civil Defence exercise. Throughout this paramilitary pantomime the Fire Control Centre is to be a cellar in All Souls College, which is duly equipped with two trestle-tables, four wooden chairs, three telephones, one trailer-pump board, and an Incidents Book. This nerve-centre is then 'manned' (to use a wholly inadequate word) by no less a figure than Lord David Cecil, soon to-be Goldsmiths' Professor of English Literature. Lord David is perhaps now best known for once declaring that, as a literary critic, he 'would not advise the study of any work after 1914.' In 1941, half-buried in All Souls's cellar, Lord David is made i./c. Incidents Book – he is not, presumably, expecting any incidents of a literary kind, or at least none worthy of study.

It is perhaps fortunate, for the safety of Oxford, that Lord David is not alone; also manning the cellar is the All Souls historian Dr A. L. Rowse (i./c. trailer-pump board). Dr Rowse would, one day, fall in love with the 'lovely boy' of Shakespeare's sonnets, but at this point he is strictly an historian, a man of events and incidents, and as such is a slightly better choice for the Oxford bunker. Nevertheless, it soon turns out that most of the work at Oxford's Fire Control Centre is to be undertaken by a mere undergraduate, a young man called Bruce Montgomery. In time to come, Montgomery would compose the music for the first six *Carry On* films; however, his career within comedy arguably began on this day of imagined Oxford catastrophe.

Recalling the day, Montgomery writes: 'It started quietly enough, with five incendiaries on the roof of St Mary's, but as more calls came in reporting ever gaudier and more horrific fancies it soon became obvious that Hitler's assault on Oxford was serious and that it was coming from Balliol.' As the virtual bombs fall and panic sets in, Lord David, who cannot say his 'R's, stares wildly at the Incidents Book and cries, 'Wowse, Wowse, I cannot weed my writing!' Well might the eminent critic panic, since a phone call from Hitlerian Balliol has just informed them that All Souls has been hit and that they are all currently in the process of being incinerated. In response, Montgomery extracts a trailer-pump from the Sheldonian Theatre; this is quite an achievement given that Christopher Wren's seventeenth-century masterpiece has, technically speaking, already gone up in fire and flame. Unconcerned, however, by this latter fiction, the trailer-pump crew rushes to All Souls. Once there, the crew decide to test their shiny new hose; this they do by enthusiastically smashing one of the Warden's windows and, with ruthless efficiency, drowning a whole living-room full of antiques.

Several gallons of water later and it is very nearly tea-time. As a sodden quiet slowly spreads, Cecil and Rowse grow bored of world war and, clutching their briefcases, climb stone stairs and wander off, leaving Montgomery on his own in the besieged All Souls cave . . . *this is my crypt under the open sky.* The young man must now repel Adolf and his demons all by himself, at least for the duration of tea. Once again, as in *Henry V*, Boy stands alone. England and Oxford expects. In this momentous hour the Enemy at Balliol sends a messenger to the beleaguered Montgomery, whom we should perhaps now call 'Monty.' The messenger sent to Monty is an undergraduate distinguished not so much by his glasses as his Midlands accent and un-tucked shirttail; when not bearing messages of doom in Civil Defence exercises, this regular angel of death is busy reading Chemistry. The bespectacled angel nods affably at Monty, before leaning on a trestle-table. He carefully avoids sitting on a telephone. Pausing for Wagnerian effect, this angel of the Midlands slowly removes his glasses and wipes them on his shirt-tail; he then returns them to his abandoned nose and solemnly informs Monty that, 'This centre is now inoccupiable thanks to tear-gas.' Before Monty can reply the Midlander brings to this Oxonian fantasy a rare moment of realism by opening a large phial of genuine tear-gas. Monty is now crying uncontrollably, but alas cannot use his standard-issue respirator for it is his duty to phone 'those maniacs in Balliol' and, although one is supposed to be able to phone with a respirator on, in practice you are completely inaudible. The maniacs will not hear a bloody word you are saying. Monty has no choice but to weep down the phone, almost drowning the mouthpiece. He then staggers to the Sheldonian only to find that the telephonist, the one who had just received his martyred message, has gone off for tea without passing on the message.

In Oxford, even in 1941, history only ever happens as farce; here there is no first time, here there is no tragedy. They say that All Souls may burn (as souls so often will) but here there is no hell, not really. Fire and flame, the great Oxford terror, is only a fiction. The film now showing is *Carry On*

Not Bombing Oxford, a telephone farce of crossed wires, inaudible messages, lost calls, and (above all) unreadable writing. 'Wowse, Wowse I can't weed my witing,' says the Professor of English Literature. At the dead-centre of wartime Oxford, a cellar in All Souls, there is a panic so great as to produce a tragi-comic parody of nothing more, and nothing less, than: absolute unreadability.

But then, unreadable writing is somewhere near the strange heart of the Home for Lost Causes and Unpopular Names. It was certainly the Home's most characteristic contribution to the war effort. If asked 'What did you do in the War, Daddy?,' Oxford (were it a daddy, or father to anyone) would put down its newspaper, lean back in its armchair, puff at its pipe and talk nonchalantly of joining the Secret Service and, in particular MI5, to work on ciphers, codes and cryptograms. Staring wildly at unreadable messages was, for a number of Oxford philosophers, a way of going to war, of finally catching the train to history. There they thought for their lives, thought to the last man. For once, their cause was not lost and their names not unpopular; as long as the world was at war these philosophers mattered, they ruled. England had become Plato's republic and they were its philosopher-kings.

One such king was the Christ Church philosopher Gilbert Ryle who worked at Bletchley Park as an RSS Analyst decrypting intercepted messages from the *Abwehr*, the German Secret Service. Once the war was finally cancelled it was as 'Major Ryle' that the philosopher marched back into Oxford. Just over twenty years later, come the 1960s, the Major was again faced with unintelligible text, text that seemed to need decoding. The text took the form of a lecture given by someone called Jacques Derrida, or 'Derrida that Bloody Structuralist,' as he was known in those days. It is surprising that Ryle was in the audience; for he was by now retired and, as a former Waynflete Professor, was the grand old boy of Oxford's analytical school of philosophy – and thus profoundly suspicious of all post-war French thought. Back in 1946 he had glumly predicted that Existentialism 'may well be smuggled across in someone's warming-pan'; so when, twenty years later, he is faced with Structuralism, this latest Parisian contraband, Ryle was on his guard.

Ryle, I think, was often on his guard, a man whom only a few ever seemed to find relaxed or friendly. A younger colleague once recalled how, when he began at Oxford in 1963, he wrote a letter addressed, very formally, to 'Professor Ryle' but received back a letter insisting that such formality was quite unnecessary and that, in future, the new colleague should feel free to address him as 'Dear Ryle.' There was no writing to 'Dear Gilbert'; perhaps there was no 'Dear Gilbert' to write to. Dear Ryle never got married and never, they say, fell into love. In fact, they thought him remote, even stern;

and he knew they did – you can tell. Once upon a time, he remarked that the only completed portrait of him made him look like 'a drowned German General.' An odd remark for a landlocked British Major.

Derrida, by contrast, must have looked like an American film-star – what with his dark complexion, and his thick hair swept up high above his forehead like a wave just about to crash. I am not, therefore, surprised when I hear him mutter to himself: *Our life, barely a film.* The philosopher is right – on his birth certificate he is greeted not as 'Jacques' but 'Jackie'; his parents, as was then the fashion, had named him after a Hollywood film-star, in his case Jackie Coogan. You may once have seen this Hollywood Jackie, he is most famous for being an abandoned boy in a silent movie, a film called *The Kid.* It came out in a year like 1921. The forsaken kid, as you may now recall, is found by a tramp, a ragged figure with a hat but no name. This rag-doll of a man, who then cares for the Kid, is played by Charlie Chaplin, he who in 1940 also starred as Adolf Hitler, or rather Adenoid Hynkel in *The Great Dictator*, a comic treatment of the world-murdering tyrant.

But I have strayed from my point, which is that this celluloid Kid, the one with the big pity-me eyes, would soon be abandoned forever in black-and-white silence. As soon as films learnt to talk this child-star burnt out. Once all the talking began (talkie, talkie, talkie) the Kid Coogan very slowly vanished, very slowly slid off the slippery silver screen, that impossibly vertical stage. Not so the new Kid, the philosophic Jackie who, in 1968, arrived in Oxford in full talkie-technicolor. The Kid, you might say, had survived childhood. The child still lived, and he had done so by changing, just a touch, his name – Jackie Derrida was now Jacques Derrida.

Jacques Derrida, however, was still and forever the Kid, a philosopher made for the biggest screen. You may remember how, in lectures or when responding to questions, the more he thought or concentrated, the more his eyes would narrow and his lips would almost pout. You can see this in the various films in which he appeared, especially the final film, the one about his life, the one they barely made of him, two years before it ended. Without even trying, the filmic Kid seduced at the same time as he philosophised. *In the last analysis*, he says, *I do nothing that does not have some interest in seducing you.*

By 1968 Derrida had already romanced many in France, and still more in America, but in loveless Oxford it seems as if he could not seduce anyone. Describing the response to his lecture in Oxford he says, *If you only had seen the embarrassed silence, the injured politesse, and the faces of Ryle, Ayer, and Strawson.* The Kid (I see it now) really did die in Oxford – *the thing was not very well received: icy consternation . . . .* Jacques Derrida may have looked like a film-star but he died like a cold comedian. *Fifty minutes . . . I died several times.*

To speak frankly, this does not altogether surprise me. I don't think his stand-up routine was particularly strong; though I must admit that I do find funny his Comic Guide to Out-Arguing the Father of Western Philosophy – *Here*, he says, is *another short philosophical dialogue of my own composition*:

Myself: *Hey, Socrates!*

Socrates: *What?*

Myself: *Nothing*

Marvellous! Though not, perhaps, quite the right material for the Oxford Philosophy Faculty. *Fifty minutes . . . I died several times.* The Kid quickly discovered that *it is in the name of the serious that the Oxford people speak* – and indeed listen. That's why the Kid never forgets the faces of those that looked on as he died, in particular the drowned face of the drowned German General . . . *Ryle . . . whom I met . . . and who is dead now.* He died on October the 6th 1976.

This, in fact, is handy, Ryle's being dead, as it means you can go straight through his papers; and when I did this I fell upon a small red notebook, at the back of which were two half-finished crossword puzzles that Dear Ryle himself had devised . . . *and if one day these crosswords fall into their hands, they can always run around in order to catch up with a meaning in them.* In the second of Ryle's crosswords, I saw that three-down (seven letters) was the word 'strangle.' This, I know, means little but I feel I should mention it, if only because, over thirty years later, when in Reading (nowhere near Oxford) the Kid still wanted to talk about his early Oxford death.

I was totally mad to go to Oxford then to give that lecture! On that occasion the silence which followed it was obviously eloquent. Eloquently saying: 'there is no arguing with this man, or with this discourse.' . . . Ryle was there – didn't say a word.

Our Kid sees the silence as flat rejection, but what if he were wrong? What if it were a Secret Service silence, the grave and vigilant silence of decryption? This thought came to me the day I learnt that, just one month later, on March 21st 1968, Ryle gave a lecture called, 'The Thinking of Thoughts: What is *Le Penseur* Doing?' I have recently succeeded in persuading myself that this lecture is, in fact, a disguised response to the young French thinker, the *penseur* who had just visited Oxford. Witness, if you will, Ryle's opening philosophical exemplum: 'You hear,' he says, 'someone come out with "Today is the 3rd of February."' As I read this, I can see (if I squint) an allusion to hearing someone called Derrida. You see, according to the records of Oxford's *Maison Française*, in 1968 the Kid gave a lecture on 'Le concept de "différance"' – and the date was (wait for it) the 2nd of February. This is (you will agree) uncannily close to the 3rd of February. Indeed, the fact that it is not the very same day only strengthens my conviction, for Ryle goes on to argue that 'someone [who] comes out with "Today is the 3rd of February" might be lying'; well, clearly, had the Kid begun his Oxford lecture with 'Today is the 3rd of February' he would indeed have been lying (albeit only just, by a day – he would only have been a day late).

If I needed any more evidence that Dear Ryle is thinking of the Kid then it comes at the very end of Ryle's lecture, when he concludes his enquiry into thought, speech and writing with one final and quite dramatic philosophical exemplum, it goes like this: 'A statesmen signing his surname to a peace-treaty is doing much more than inscribe the seven letters of his surname . . . . He is bringing a war to a close.'

Do I need to point out that there are seven letters in the surname 'Derrida'? Or, indeed, that Kid Derrida is fascinated with signatures, in particular signatures that make for peace? Just glance, if you will, at the preface to his book which concludes, *I {hereby} assume without detour the responsibility for these envois . . . and that in order to make peace within you I am signing here in my proper name, Jacques Derrida. 7 September 1979.*

The seven-lettered 'Derrida' here cleverly makes sure we are counting; the trick, or prompt is in the date: the 7 is obvious but there is also the 'sept' in September as well as in '79. . . . *I can see the figure 7 reign, I can see it reign over our anniversaries.*

I can also see it reign over our investigations. As I return to my father, still in our over-lit lounge, I hear him say: 'Kill, kill! Seven. You're next . . . .Kill, kill! Seven. You're next.' The figure seven, I think, may yet help betray the secret music of what happened to my father at school as well as its long-lost twin, the secret of what happened to Jacques Derrida in Oxford. Don't forget that Derrida always dates the lecture he gave to Ryle *et al.* as nineteen sixty-*seven*. And what makes this final 'seven' so arresting is that it is almost certainly wrong; the only record of an Oxford lecture by Derrida in the late-60s is the *Maison Française* lecture of 1968, an event held at 12 Merton Street which, at that time, housed the Philosophy Sub-Faculty (as it was then).

I accept that it is just possible that Derrida also went to Oxford in 1967, as part of the same trip that took him to London for a conference on Rousseau that was held on the 3rd to the 4th of February. And this possibility does seem to increase when you look at the Oxford Philosophical Society's minute-book; there you will see that the Society did indeed meet on Friday, February the 3rd (remarkable in itself since they usually met on

Thursdays) and that Ryle was indeed in the Chair. However, Derrida was not the speaker, it was instead one Professor Chisholm. So, unless 'Chisholm' was Derrida's spectacularly canny English alias, Ryle *et al.* have a perfect alibi; it looks extremely unlikely that they would have been listening to Derrida in 1967. And yet, as I say, the Kid always says they were. Mind you, he also insists that *we have always been preoccupied with dates. Too much so . . . a very bad sign.*

It may well be a bad sign, but I am still intrigued. So, holding your breath, I stumble onto another train, this time a fast and loose one falling toward London; and there I speak to Alan Montefiore, the now-retired Balliol philosopher who, in 1977, had called Derrida back to Oxford. In the 1960s, Montefiore (let us not call him Monty, 'M' will do) had been Derrida's only real ally within occupied Oxford and so, as M himself remarked, he would certainly have known of any visit to Oxford by Derrida; and yet, as M leafed through his University-issued diary for 1967, he could find no mention of Derrida except a pencilled reference to a meal they had together in Paris toward the end of the year. (At first, M was not quite sure if he could read his own writing (an Oxford trait?), and so prised the tiny diary open for me to see, asking if I agreed that the seven-lettered scribble did indeed spell 'Derrida' – I hastily agreed). So, to conclude: it really does seem that Derrida goes off the rails whenever he talks of Oxford 1967; wittingly or not, he insists on one more seven than history will allow.

But why? Why should Derrida crash the history train when it comes to dating his Oxford trauma, his Oxford death, an event he recalls so often. About the date of one's own death one is not usually wrong. So, is it a case of false memory, a case for Vienna? Or is it a case of deliberate deception? *I will*, he says, *leave all kinds of references . . . names of persons . . . {and} identifiable events, {but} . . . with a stroke of the pen . . . will make everything derail.* But why, in heaven's name, derail the world? And why use the year 1967 to do so? I now think this is a case for the Secret Service, this case of a philosopher so in love with the figure seven that it really must be some kind of clue, some kind of numerological code. I like this idea, and am seduced still further in its direction by Ryle's suspicious response to *le penseur*'s use of dates. Regarding *le penseur*'s declaration that '"Today is the 3rd of February,"' Ryle warily remarks that *'le penseur . . .* might have been lying . . . might have been trying to get his enemy to accept a piece of misinformation.'

Ryle here takes a well-aimed hammer to *le penseur,* nailing this alien fly firmly to the wall of a Bletchley Park missen-hut – for words like 'enemy' and 'misinformation' come straight from the world of war-time deception, secrecy and code. And Ryle is right, *le penseur* is a man possessed by the codes of war, they are everywhere in his book. Indeed, he openly confesses that *this satire {is} stuffed with crypted missives*, the missives of one still fighting the war.

I will, he says, *call Sunday at the latest. If you're not there, leave them a message. Leave, for example, so that they won't understand a thing, as in the Resistance, a sentence with 'sunflower' to signify that you prefer that I come, without 'sunflower' for the opposite.*

This particular war-time code is child's play, a cut-and-dried case of disappearing sunflowers, the work of a mere florist. Our philosopher, our Kid, wants more, dreams more; he dreams, in fact, of an unbreakable war-time code, of nothing less than a *real enigma, the absolute stenography.* And that is precisely what stared Derrida in the face when he lectured to Major Ryle. During his time at Bletchley Park, Ryle had worked alongside those who had picked that most famous of German locks, the absolute stenography known as 'Enigma' . . . *enigma, the absolute stenography.* What *le penseur* encountered in late-60s Oxford was, then, a continuing Secret Service, a school of philosophy still charged with the habits of wartime suspicion. *Le penseur*, thinks Ryle, might just be trying to misinform his Oxford audience. After all, 1968 is not (as we know) a time to trust Parisian philosophers. Be careful, warns Major Ryle, *le penseur* may be seeking to double-cross Oxford.

I sometimes wonder if Derrida knew of Ryle's cryptic, Bletchley war. Could he have glimpsed it somehow pressed (a dead flower) between the pages of silence that followed the lecture? 'Probably not,' said M, very patiently, when I asked him; but Derrida's erstwhile Balliol host then kindly added, 'You could never, though, quite be sure with Jacques, since he read so much.'

One text that Derrida certainly read and that does have a coded connection with Dear Ryle's secret war is an essay that Ryle published in 1951, 'The Theory of Meaning.' You and I, we shall crack this coded connection in due course; but first allow me to explain that Ryle's essay seeks to dynamite our common-sense view that all words operate like names, and that the name Ryle plucks out of the thinnest of Oxford air (and here comes the important bit) is 'Fido.'

'We know,' he says, 'what it is for "Fido" to be the name of a particular dog . . . There, in front of us, is the dog . . . which has the name, so here, one feels, there is no mystery.'

However, there *is* mystery, not just the mystery of meaning (the mystery that so concerns Ryle) but also the mystery of Fido-the-dog. And it is this absurd, four-legged puzzle that Derrida just cannot let go. When his mind should be on Ryle's famous argument, the Kid can think only of Ryle's exemplary dog. Professor Derrida, it must be said, is obsessed with this bloody dog – he can't stop talking about him: . . . *our enclosed friend . . . Fido* (he says) . . . *Fido Fido that's us* (he says) . . . *Fido, Fido . . . it can always bite, or bark* (he says) . . . *above all do not forget Fido.* Above all, do not forget to ask (he says), *Why did Ryle choose this name, Fido?* This question, this all-important question is finally answered by Derrida's son, Pierre, who leans across and *whispers*, as if confidentially: *'so that the example will be obedient.'*

This is, I suppose, a joke, albeit a philosophical one – the joke being that philosophers (like preachers, in fact) always want their examples to be obedient, to do only what they are supposed to do, to demonstrate a point and then lie low, play dead. Fido, though, is a disobedient example; he may be faithful by name, but he is not faithful by nature. Having always been treated by Ryle as a mere philosophical fiction, as a never-never dog, Fido is quick to follow a philosopher who finally treats him as real, as four legs and a tail that can bite and bark: *Ah yes, Fido* (he says) *I am faithful to you as a dog.*

Professor Derrida, you will have noticed, talks not only about Fido but to Fido. This is a worrying sign, I admit, but it also points up a classic Oxford philosophical conundrum or puzzle: for when one says 'Fido' is one naming the dog or calling him? *This is the problem of '"Fido"-Fido' . . . the question of knowing whether I am calling my dog or if I am mentioning the name of which he is the bearer . . . {How} I adore these theoreticians . . . {so} Oxonian.*

In Oxford, poor Fido is forever 'Fido'-Fido, forever double, forever a double-agent. Ryle may think Fido is working for him, as an obedient philosophical example, but the treacherous truth is that Fido is actually being run by the Kid. It is time, I think, to reveal that 'Fido,' as Major Ryle would have known, was the code-name for one of M15's double-agents during World War Two. By whistling up Fido, Dear Ryle has let slip a dog of war, a duplicitous dog of war. The answer to the question 'Why did Ryle choose the name Fido?' is that Ryle knew that the example would *not* be obedient.

I will add that in Ryle's little red notebook, in the first of the two cross-words which he devised, four-down (fifteen letters), was the word 'doublefacedness.' Ryle, it seems, knew he would be double-crossed. He knew that Fido would bark, would talk (talkie talkie) to the enemy.

This he does. And what Fido discloses, what Fido betrays, is not just Ryle's cryptic war but Oxford's; for the Chairman of the MI5 committee which oversaw all double-agents was another Oxford don, the historian J. C. Masterman. His committee was known as the 'Twenty Committee,' the reason being that the Roman numeral for Twenty (XX) is a double cross. The 'x' in Oxford is, you see, double. It should, I think, be 'Oxxford.' No wonder Ryle once wrote, "'When I picked up the *Oxford Mail* this morning and saw that the word "Oxford" was spelt O,X,F,O,R,D I had a sudden feeling of surprise.'" Ryle knew, I am sure, that there was one 'X' missing.

It is C. S. Lewis, the man from Narnia-by-Oxford, who lets this particular dog out of the wardrobe. This happens in 1942 when Lewis is giving one of his famous wartime radio broadcasts and, as he talks, live and over the blasted air, he invites his listeners to 'think of a country where a man felt proud of double-crossing.' This should not have been difficult; in 1942 this country is somewhere called Oxxford – the impossible home of impossible loyalties.

This impossible, wartime Oxxford was, for Derrida, perhaps a faraway country, but it was a country of which he might well have heard rumours, stories, echoes. To have done so, he simply needed to pick up *The Oxford Times* on Friday, June 10th 1977, the last day of a week-long stay in Balliol; if he did this, Derrida would have read all about Masterman's wartime double-cross work in a long article titled 'Oxford's Famous Spy Boss' – Masterman had just died, aged 86.

As you know, eighteen months later, Derrida declares that he plans *to go back to Oxford, to take the investigation to its end*. The investigation is, supposedly, into the mystery of the ancient book; I am, though, beginning to think that, in truth, it is an investigation of the mystery that was double-crossing, wartime Oxford. To speak cryptically: I think the Kid has been listening to the dog – the dog Fido.

Cue the masterful Sherlock Holmes and his famous talk of that 'curious incident of the dog in the night-time.' For Holmes, the curious incident (the curious incident that helps solve the case) is that the dog does not bark; for Jacques Derrida, however, it is that the dog *does* bark. And the dog Fido barks or talks as only a double-agent can: he talks of double-crossing. Indeed, as an Oxford dog, he talks of a double-crossing Oxford, a wartime Oxford that didn't always know whose side it was on. And this, I shall insist, is the Oxford that Derrida investigates.

It all became clear to me the moment Derrida once casually remarked that, *whenever I have misadventures at Oxford, where Austin taught, I think of him* – J. L. Austin. The Kid offered no reason as to why he always thinks of this particular Oxford philosopher, a man whom, unlike Ryle, the Kid never met. Our question, then, is: why *does* he think of Austin? Well, I shall insist (drowsily, almost drunkenly) that it is, primarily, because of Austin's role in the famous Oxford by-election in October 1938 when Quintin Hogg stood and won on a pro-Appeasement ticket. Just weeks before, Adenoid Hynkel-Hitler had tramped all the way to Austria, desperate for more *Lebensraum* (living-space, or living-room, if you will). Like most of old

Europe, Britain could not decide whether to oppose or appease the Great Dictator; then, as it happened, and when the leaves were turning angry red, a by-election was called in autumnal Oxford. Very quickly it was clear that the question of Appeasement was the one and only issue. For several weeks, the whole nation held breath and waited to see how Oxford would vote, how the leaves would fall. So too did J. L. Austin, who set aside philosophy long enough to campaign against Hogg-the-appeaser and to coin the dramatic slogan: 'A vote for Hogg is a vote for Hynkel.' Austin thus famously begged the question of Oxford's political allegiance; he rudely asked whose side was Oxford on. The dog in the autumn night was barking.

As well he might, since Tory Oxford – or, more specifically, All Souls College – had been hugely influential in choreographing the long, slow dance of Appeasement, Mr Chamberlain's final waltz with Adenoid Hynkel. Let Herr Hynkel (one, two, three) have Sudetenland and there shall be peace (one, two, three) in our time.

Particularly busy, trying to keep Hynkel and Chamberlain in step, acting as their go-between, was the immensely tall figure of Lord Halifax, former fellow of All Souls and now Foreign Secretary. . . . *to say you are right . . . becomes my only appeasement.* Long tall Lord H., by the way, was also known as 'The Holy Fox,' a tall fox that could fox-trot. *I dance . . . and I will stop only at the point of exhaustion, dead of fatigue.* The Holy Fox was so-called because he was both devoutly Catholic and considered somewhat cunning, though not by Adenoid Hynkel.

On the trail of the Fox, and the whole Appeasement set, was our friend, A. L. Rowse, himself a fellow of All Souls. Remember him? In the cellar? You know: 'Wowse, Wowse, I cannot weed my witing'? Well, almost twenty years later, Wowse Wowse finally goes 'woof-woof.' Loosely translated, this last sentence means: in 1961 Rowse publishes a controversial book called *All Souls and Appeasement*. The title says it all, for in this book the elegant Dr Rowse finally turns on certain fellow fellows and points a late but fine finger at their instinctively pro-German habits of mind. The Preface to the book, a pistol pointed at the old soul of Oxford, is dated 'Independence Day.' Rowse is another dog that has his day, his day of independence; he too turns, talks, and barks in and of the dark, the dark that hung itself from the spires of 1930s Oxford.

Let no-one forget W. H. Auden's cataclysmic couplet from 1939, the one which sings that, 'In the nightmare of the dark / All the dogs of Europe bark.'

CHAPTER FOUR

Silences

When, in 1992, my mother began to write my father's words for him, the very first two that she put down were: 'The dog!' This inaugural cry now makes me think of the time Dear Ryle sent Herr Heidegger packing, saying that Heidegger undid true philosophy by giving us 'not . . . "In the beginning was the Word" but "In the beginning was the Cry."' This is folly, implies Ryle, mere warming-pan philosophy. So, to escape the Major's censure, let us say that, in my father's case, 'In the beginning was the Dog' – God backwards, in reverse, in a lighted window after dark. 'The dog!', he cried, my poor-boy father.

One year later, in May 1993, the poor boy, as if now finally minded to complete his sentence, suddenly declared: 'The dog died.' Five months later still, and we have not just a sentence but a story as my father adds: 'They buried the dog.' Perhaps that playwright-fellow Tom Stoppard was right to insist that 'the dog it was that died.' Perhaps it was a dog, just a dog.

But if so, then to follow my father into the nightmare of the dark I must first listen to all the dogs that bark, whether that be my father's dead-and-buried dog, or Gilbert Ryle's Fido, or even the dogs of Auden's Europe, those dogs of Europe that bark in the dark of the 1930s.

These 1930s dogs barked, I have heard, most loudly at the Jews. It is, I know, difficult right now to see how this could ever help with what happened to my Christian father, but there is also the question of whatever happened to our Jewish philosopher. And, indeed, I have just begun to see that Ryle's unfaithful Fido, the dog that so haunts the Kid, has a very Jewish double, a very Jewish twin.

This other Fido, Fido before Fido, was a young German Jewish intellectual who, in 1934, tip-toed out of Adenoidal Germany only to find himself in whispering Oxford. Here, for four years, he studied for a doctorate under Ryle as an 'Advanced Student.' His real name was Theodor Adorno, but back home he was known as someone called 'Hektor Rottweiler.' In 1930s Germany a second life was sometimes needed to slip beneath the Adenoidal radar, and so young Adorno had decided to write under the name of a famously ferocious Black Forest dog. He felt the name would disguise him;

that he could be, as it were, a sheep in wolf's clothing, only the wolf was a dog. Adorno knew his place, his place as a German Jew.

It is difficult to tell what Ryle ever made of Adorno, but we do get some help from Ryle's friend and colleague A. J. (Freddie) Ayer, another Oxford philosopher who would be there to hear the Kid in 1968. Ayer once remarked that 'Adorno seemed to us a bit of a comic figure . . . with his dandified manner and anxiety.' (*There is someone in me who kills with a burst of laughter.*) But perhaps some of Adorno's comic anxiety came from the fact that in Oxford he struggled to get through, and across, to those around him; early on in his time at Oxford Adorno wrote to a friend, 'It is quite impossible to convey my real philosophical interests to the English and I have to reduce my work to a childish level.' In Oxford, thinks Adorno, the philosophers are children.

But that, says the Kid, is just as it should be: *when I was ten years old*, he remarks, *I . . . already understood nothing.* In the Kid's philosophical house there is, I see, room for the children. Not so Major Ryle; for him, philosophy is for the grown-ups; that's why he once reprimanded Heidegger for introducing to philosophy 'the language of the . . . nursery.' At such times it is hard to see Ryle as ever being too young or too childish for Adorno. Besides, Ryle was steeped, if not drowned, in German thought and language. But the stubborn fact remains, alone all alone, that Ryle never once refers to Adorno in his writings, public or private; and you will find not one of Adorno's books within Ryle's personal library, now darkly housed behind thin Oxford glass. *Together we should bring to light . . . the libraries of . . . great thinkers.*

All this, this invisibility, is despite the fact that Adorno became that strange and troublesome thing, a famous Holocaust thinker – he it was, you will know, who burdened the consciousness of the world with those three unsayable A-words, 'Art after Auschwitz.' But famous or no, it was always a long way from Adorno to Ryle. In fact, it is quite probable that Ryle was Adorno's supervisor simply because there was no-one else in Oxford who knew anything about Adorno's chosen subject of research; he was working on Emmanuel Husserl, the German-Jewish phenomenologist.

It may help (though not necessarily) if I were now to attempt the world's briefest summary of Husserl's phenomenological method. So, to reduce the Husserlian creation to just seven words (albeit seven words multiplied by three) let me say this, that: *it entails bracketing off whatever one is thinking about in order that one might think about the very act of thinking.* Though quite what happens if one was in the first place thinking about thinking, I am not sure. ('Think, think!', he said).

And so I shall, and as I carry on thinking (carry on, carry on), I think that, during the 1930s, the city of Oxford (47 Banbury Road, to be postal) was the very last place on the planet in which you would expect to find a bored and lonely Jewish Husserlian. In those days in Oxford they did not really do phenomenology, and 47 Banbury Road had been (as far as I am aware) no exception to this rule. Besides, as an institution, the University had not forgotten its Christian infancy; each and every day during term-time even Jewish students had to be present in college chapel for the roll-call. It was, mutters Adorno, 'a nightmare come true,' 'like having to return to school; in short, an extension of the Third Reich.' Adorno, it seems, found Oxford to be home from home, Reich from Reich, somewhere else he did not really want to be, somewhere else that may even had made him feel like a Jewish dog. (While in Oxford, when writing for German eyes, he still signed himself as 'Rottweiller.')

Adorno had, at first, hoped for a full academic position at Oxford, by no means a ridiculous hope, given that Adorno was now thirty-one (just three years younger than Ryle), already had a German doctorate as well as still higher qualifications, and had, before exile, held a full post at the Frankfurt Institute for Social Research. Adorno had only registered as an 'Advanced Student' because, technically, there was no other way the Oxford system could accommodate him. It should, though, be said that in Adorno's time Oxford did not always find it easy to find bed-space for Jews. These were days when, despite all the academic tramps fleeing Adenoidal Germany in cars, trains, and warming-pans, there were still hardly any Jewish dons in Oxford. Indeed, the Jewish historian Cecil Roth recalls an occasion in the early 1930s at Merton College (Adorno's college, as it happens) when he heard, or overheard that, 'College Members of the Jewish persuasion would not be welcome in the Senior Common Room.'

Dr Roth himself had to sit and wait many years at the door of the Senior Common Room; and there he waited, before the door, until one fine day he finally became one of the chosen of the Chosen. Adorno, though, was not one for waiting, and so, in 1938, he leapt high over and across the Atlantic. As soon as he was given leave to land in America, he in-breathed a freeman's breath and resumed his post with the Frankfurt Institute, now relocated in New York. All the signs, all the signs everywhere, are that Adorno and Ryle then lost touch, forever.

I am sorry, not quite forever; for in February 1968, Gilbert Ryle encountered in Oxford another anxious young Jewish dandy from the continent, and he too had begun his career by working on Husserl. On that February day, he (Dear Ryle) saw a ghost . . . *someone dead* . . . *whom I represent*. Ryle looked across the lecture room in 12 Merton Street and saw Adorno, or even Hektor Rottweiller, Fido's Jewish shadow. Is that why Ryle was silent?

After all, and after Auschwitz, what on earth could a drowned German General say to a Jewish dog? Ryle could surely not have failed to see this young man called Derrida as another Adorno. *A man came up to greet {me} . . . thinking that he recognised me, and then excused himself at the last moment*. Ryle was such a man. His silence on that day in 1968 echoed, I think, the silence that had for, thirty years, resounded between himself and Adorno.

And if this is the case then I will carry on, thinking that Ryle's silence must echo still another philosophical silence, an infant silence just six-months old, the silence that on July 25th 1967 had famously overwhelmed Martin Heidegger. Herr Heidegger it is who, three years after his own death, would manage to telephone the Kid — quite a trick, even for a German phenomenologist. However, in 1967, twelve years before this tele-phonic miracle, Heidegger received a visitor at his mountain retreat, in the Black Forest — a log cabin at a place called Todtnauberg; his visitor was a colleague of Derrida's from the École Normale Superieure, a scholar and poet who called himself Paul Celan (it was not quite his real name). The Kid, he writes, as if on Celan's behalf, *I want to stroll in the forest with you.*

This forested encounter had been long awaited by both men, Celan and Heidegger, each having been drawn, as if by gravity, to the writing of the other. But there was a problem: Celan was a Jew who had lost both parents in another forest, that blackest forest of all — the one in Herr Hynkel's head; there Celan's mother had been shot (. . . *the blood spurted from the tree.*)

Heidegger, on the other hand, had been given a dream, a philosophical dream of Being that had become fatally entangled with Herr Hynkel's dream of Germany. This is a long story, a long walk in yet another exit-less forest; but in brief, in short, in sum, in final solution it is this: that Heidegger saw in Adenoid Hynkel and friends not just a political party but a long-awaited metaphysical shock, a storm wild enough to blast open the humdrum continuum of history and trigger 'a fundamental transformation of Being.' Heidegger saw, or dreamt he saw, something altogether new in the person of Herr Hynkel; Professor Heidegger was like a man bewitched. When asked, in June 1933, how an uneducated man like Hynkel could govern Germany, the Professor replied: "'Education is quite irrelevant . . . just look at his wonderful hands!'" Prepared to kiss the palm of those wonderful hands, Heidegger became a fee-paying National Socialist in 1933 (member no. 312589) and was still paying his subscriptions in that latest of all years, 1945. Back in 1933, in his one year as the Rektor of Freiburg University, Heidegger had done the work of the wonderful hands, expelling all Jews from the teaching staff and requiring that all lectures began and ended with arms extended in Adenoidal salute. In 1935 Heidegger's own hands grew wonderful as he wrote of 'the inward truth and greatness of National Socialism'; these words he chose not to erase when he had the opportunity, in a new edition of his *Introduction to Metaphysics* published in 1953.

In 1967, as Celan travelled to Todtnauberg he had hoped that Heidegger would somehow speak about all of this, all of this history at night; but somehow Heidegger did not. *After a silence . . . another silence.* Celan came down from the mountain with nothing but a handful of silence. Less than three years later, on April 20th 1970, Celan drowned himself in the Seine; on May 1st his body was found seven miles downstream. (My father once said: 'The dog died. The dog was buried . . .'. He later added, ' . . . in the sea').

It is just possible that Celan, upon his return to Paris, once whispered to Derrida of Heidegger's silence. If so, did Derrida hear that same forested silence again at the end of his Oxford lecture only six months later? I sometimes dream this is the case and do so simply because the philosopher's book is written, in every sense, *after* the death of Celan. The philosopher wants to die like the poet: *I'd like*, he breathes, *to die . . . in a lake.* When Derrida does die in front of his Oxford audience Celan just has to be present. *Celan . . . he was between us.* I confess that Derrida here speaks of another place and time, but let us not forget that, in Oxford, the Kid *is* called to die like Celan, to be another Jewish suicide. You will remember the seductive young man on the perfected Balliol lawn. (My father said, 'Kill yourself').

And if, at the end of his Oxford lecture, Derrida does die like Celan there emerges a tableau of double drowning; a tableau in which a drowned German general sits silent before a sinking Jewish suicide. *Two drownings . . . you know what I'm talking about.*

Well, we do; the context, I confess, makes it clear that Derrida is here talking about the drownings of Paul Celan and yet another Jewish suicide (also a friend of Derrida's) called Peter Szondi. But the Kid always insisted, as a point of philosophy, that he could never fully know what, or indeed whom, he is talking about. If so, it is possible, therefore, that the Kid talks of his own drowning. And I think he does. Here, deep in Oxford silence, the Kid drowns alongside the General.

And as if these two drownings were not enough, there is, in my father's head, still another immersion – he once said: 'In the water . . . he's sinking, sinking! Don't drown.' I don't know if he did drown, whoever he was, if indeed 'he' ever were alive enough to die, or even real enough. But I will find out, and will do so by gazing again at this Oxford scene of drowning, a scene that overflows, like a flooded wardrobe, onto so many other scenes and encounters. Look long enough at Ryle facing Derrida at the end of the lecture and soon you will also see: Ryle facing Adorno, Heidegger facing

Celan, German facing Jew, reason facing madness, master facing dog, even master facing pupil. (He said and she wrote: 'the Master killed . . . ').

Right now, however, I see just Heidegger and Celan, for I have looked at Ryle and said, with Derrida, *here's Heidegger*. This is, I know, an unlikely equation, an odd coupling; but Ryle does wear, much like Heidegger, the mask of a German general, albeit a drowned one. And it is a mask that seems to become Ryle when, in November 1924, he visits Italy and sends to his mother, back in Pangbourne in Berkshire, a post-card still to be seen among Ryle's papers. The photo on the post-card reveals a uniformed Mussolini astride a magnificent but somewhat quizzical horse. I confess that, like a curious Pangbourne postman, I read Ryle's message on the back of the card; it said: 'This is a picture of the General of the Fascists . . . I am beginning to think better of Mussolini.'

You might say that beginning to think better of a Fascist general astride an ironic horse hardly makes anyone into Oxford's answer to Heidegger, but Ryle did know far more about Heidegger than any other philosopher in Oxford. Indeed, in 1929 Ryle was not only reading Heidegger but reviewing his greatest work, *Sein und Zeit*. Ryle's review is serious, very serious, at first saluting Heidegger as 'a thinker of real importance' but concluding with an astonishing anticipation of Heidegger's Adenoidal future. Ryle writes (and please note this well) that, 'It is my personal opinion that . . . Phenomenology is [here] . . . heading for bankruptcy and disaster and will end in self-ruinous Subjectivism or in windy mysticism.'

As early as 1929 Dear Ryle fore-dreams the complex disaster that would be Rektor Heidegger. *Disaster – we have dreamed of it*. And where better to day-dream of disaster than among Oxford's forest of dreaming spires? And that is why, in 1930s Oxford, you could, on a clear day, get a good view of Berlin.

Let me put this another way: in that slow and dishonest decade, Oxford was quite capable of momentary poses and postures that its enemies might just interpret as, well, let us say, Adenoidal. For example, Ralph Glasser, a Jewish undergraduate of the era, recalls a 'student at Trinity with a swastika flag in his window, and a gramophone booming out the "Horst Wessel Lied."' This mad Trinitarian gramophone boomed, no doubt, still louder on June 8th 1934 when the Oxford Union voted, by 115 votes to 29, in favour of the motion 'That this House is in favour of the rearming of Germany.' Just four dishonest summers later, in May 1938, the rearmed Germans are all but *in* the House, as a group of young Nazis make an official visit to Oxford, a visit that was duly boomed not merely by stray undergraduate gramophones but no less an organ than the *Oxford Magazine*. There you could read this: 'Among our Whitsun visitors we have welcomed to Oxford a body of Nazi students, fresh from the glories of their revolution . . . The Oxford element gained greatly in appreciation both of the fervent and unselfish enthusiasm that has been generated by the Nazi movement and of the excellent personal qualities of many of its supporters.'

You can perhaps see why Adorno could, just for a moment, mistake Oxford for an outpost of the Third Reich; there was, between the two, a strange though intermittent proximity, a proximity that Derrida also seems to see, or sense even in June 1977. This is when the philosopher is slowly returning to his guest room in Balliol after an epic voyage out to buy some stamps: . . . *coming back, going back up the stone stairs, I asked myself what we would have done in order to love each other in 1930 in Berlin when, as they say, you needed wheelbarrows full of marks just to buy a stamp.* The stone Balliol staircase takes the philosopher back, not just to an empty room but to Berlin 1930.

To be precise, though, by 1930, Berlin's shops were no longer grid-locked with the traffic of desperate wheelbarrows; that was the Berlin of the early 1920s. Time, you see, is again mistreated in the philosopher's book. *In it*, he confesses, *I abuse dates.* In this case the abused date is 1930, a year famous not for the wheelbarrow but for the philosopher – it was the year in which he was born, in the middle (as it happened) of a game of poker. However, let us not be distracted by either card-games or mere birth; for the fact remains that the Berlin of 1930 was about to see the terrible fruit of all those wheelbarrows, of all that inflation. In 1930, Berlin was just three years from being Herr Hynkel's centre of gravity, the heavy heart of his re-made Germany.

It is hard, I find, ever to resist such gravity; but especially hard to resist when one is in Oxford. For up here the mind seems to slouch so readily towards Berlin. Take the wrong turning, go up the wrong staircase, go through the wrong door, and you are there. Indeed, give the wrong lecture and you are there, or thereabouts: facing stone silence, even wooded silence, silence carved by Heidegger. In Oxford, you can easily wash up elsewhere; you can go straight through a wardrobe, clean through a look-ing-glass.

Be careful too when it comes to trains (. . . *if there were no railway . . . my child would never have left home*). So, be careful, my love, wherever you are; but be careful twice over if, like the Kid, your train passes through Gilbert Ryle's Oxford. In the 1920s, the young Ryle's daring continental reading led him to offer what he modestly calls 'an unwanted course of lectures, enti-tled "Logical Objectivism: Bolzano, Brentano, and Husserl . . . ." – he adds that 'these characters were soon known in Oxford as "Ryle's three Austrian railway-stations.'" Brandishing such unpopular names, young Ryle adopted the lost cause of putting philosophical Oxford on the modern continental railway map. But this early work was not wholly in vain. When the Kid pulls into Oxford he soon makes a connection.

This is Europe, centrale, the centre of Europe, the carte between Vienna and Prague . . . with an extension of the track or of the Orient Express . . . between Oxford and London.

It was, as I think you know, the Orient Express that brought Sigmund Freud out of Adenoidal Vienna in 1938. The train stopped in London and there Freud stayed until he went missing with a mouthful of cancer. London was, for Freud, the end of the line. For the Kid, however, the line of Jewish flight from Herr Hynkel's Europe continues to Oxford. And the Kid is right; for in the autumn of 1938, when Dr Freud was visited by Isaiah Berlin (yet another Oxonian philosopher of the Ryle generation) the father of psychoanalysis predicted a future in which he would set up a practice in Oxford. (*One day I will go to Oxford.*) Father Freud was only joking, just carrying on; but for many other Jewish exiles the train leaving Nazi Central does go all the way to Oxford. Adorno has many companions.

And the Kid, I think, is yet another, albeit a late one. Recalling the Kid's visit to Oxford in 1979, Alan Montefiore once said, 'I remember sitting in the sun with him outside the Boat Inn just beyond Kidlington and the emotion, still very much alive, with which he recounted . . . the story of his exclusion from the Lycée by the Vichy regime then still in control of Algeria.'

Derrida always arrives in Oxford on a Jewish train of thought. This train is a wandering locomotive that runs on invisible tracks, tracks which criss-cross the whole of Oxford, even the grassy quads of Balliol: *on the lawn . . . the discussion continued, {and} wandered along according to switch points as unfore-seeable as they are inevitable.* But Derrida's train is not quite the same Jewish train as brought to Oxford those great scholar-tramps of the 1930s. This is a subtly different engine of difference. For Derrida seeks not so much to celebrate the spires and their dreams but rather to investigate them: *I intend to go back to Oxford, to take the investigation to its end.*

Derrida is not the first Jew to go snooping round this famous University of Dreams. Once upon a time there was Dr Ernst Brendel, a distinguished visiting Professor of Law from the University of Vienna who came to Oxford to give a series of lectures; whilst there he was called upon to solve the murder of a don in his college rooms. It turned out that he had been shot, with a revolver, by a fellow don.

As you may have guessed, I came across Dr Brendel in a novel; it was published by Penguin, one of those green-and-white middle-brow fictions from the 1930s, a comfortable companion for anyone caught between stations on an inter-war train. This one was written by our friend Masterman-the-History-Man, the don from Worcester College who spent the war turning German spies; but who, some time before the war (in 1933 to be precise) had decided he would enlarge still further the already swollen corpus of Oxford murder mysteries. Masterman called his mystery *An Oxford Tragedy*. (By the way, that boy, lost in the lounge, once cried, 'It was a tragedy').

I should confess right now that Dr Brendel, Masterman's continental sleuth, is never actually said to be a Jew. That's left for us to detect. This, though, is not difficult since Brendel is a kind of Freud-double, a Sigmund-substitute. The symptoms are there for all to see, visible to even the less practised Freud-spotter. In the first place, Brendel is from Vienna; in the second, he smokes a pipe that (just for once) really is a pipe. But what finally betrays Brendel's secret identity is that the only German word in the whole novel is *Schadenfreude*. I think we can all spot the name 'Freud' within *Schadenfreude*, can't we? Or, at least, we would if we also note that Dr Brendel makes at least one very clear reference to psychoanalysis, as well as cite a novel by Freud's friend Stefan Zweig.

Zweig, it will be noted, is yet another Jewish suicide; he did the deed with a barbiturate and a second wife. However, our train cannot stop for the dead, there are too many; too many even for Brendel the 'new Sherlock Holmes from Vienna,' he who is so like Freud as to be the new *Shylock* Holmes. This, as the world can see, is Masterman's scrambled signal; he wants us to be warned that this 'Christian college' in Christian Oxford is being investigated by a European Jew. And even as early as 1933, the first year of the Adenoidal millennium, it was all too obvious as to what exactly the Jew would be sniffing out. Masterman's so-called novel is, I insist, not about murder at all; the killing is really an elaborate metaphor for Adenoidal sympathy.

This will, no doubt, become excruciatingly obvious when I point out that the killer, a don called Mottram, is distinguished by a single and most curious detail: namely, that, after years of brilliant research deliberately withheld from publication, he suddenly finds that 'a German in Freiburg, who had apparently been following much the same line of investigation, [had] published in a leading journal, and with a great flourish of trumpets, a paper describing his researches.' Mottram is thus ruined, overnight; and his ruin leads him to murder. To be honest, I can't really remember the psychology involved in all this; however, I shall press on regardless, for what catches the blue eye of a professional critic like myself is that our man, our killer, is a don whose research turns out be identical to work being done at

the University of Freiburg, a university that, in the same year as
Masterman's *Tragedy* is published, becomes infamous for its excessive fond-
ness for Herr Hynkel's gleaming new government.

Here (again) *is Heidegger*; for it is in April 1933, just after joining the
Adenoidal party (an event trumpeted in their press), that Heidegger is
elected as the new Rektor of Freiburg. On May 27th 1933 Rektor
Heidegger both gave and published his inaugural address; it was called,
'The Self-Assertion of the German University.' On that lost day in May both
professors and students, along with ministerial officials and civil servants,
all gathered for the ceremony, a black Adenoidal pantomime in which *Sieg
Heil* was shouted, *Horst Wessel Lied* was sung, and in the fourth verse (but
only the fourth verse) the Hynkel salute was made – right hands raised,
right and wonderful hands. The new Rektor then spoke and as he spoke he
gradually began to bark, to bark (as he said) 'into the winds.' And as Rektor
Heidegger began to bark he slowly, and before their very blue eyes, turned
into 'Hektor Rottweiller,' the Black Forest beast of which Adorno was busy
dreaming. Rektor Hektor, as we might call him, barked out that 'the
essence of the German university . . . will attain clarity, rank, and power
. . . only when . . . [its] leaders are, first and foremost . . . , themselves led
by . . . that spiritual mission which impresses onto the fate of the German
Volk the stamp of their history.' And this stamp would soon mean the stamp
of boots: 'German students,' he growled, 'are on the march . . . . [Their]
bond . . . to the German Volk . . . .will, in the future, embrace and pervade
all of student existence in the form of *military service.*'

Heidegger's bark immediately resounded across much of the pale
academic universe; in those echoic days, back in 1933, he needed no telephone to be heard, no transatlantic trunk calls. Mind you, he wasn't dead
then, just fairly famous. Whatever, his voice was certainly heard by
Freiburg's Jewish professors, many of whom were already packing their
deepest briefcases; and some, like the Latinist Eduard Frankel, took the train
that curved straight to Oxford.

So, you see, in 1933 to be associated with Freiburg was awkward enough;
still worse was to discover that exactly what you are thinking in Oxford is
being thought in Freiburg. The crime that really interests Masterman is
not, then, the shooting of a don – such death is mere trope, mere textual
trick; the real crime is a fearful intellectual symmetry, the symmetry
between Oxford and Freiburg. This, I insist, is the real Oxford tragedy; it
may even be what Masterman elsewhere calls 'the secret of Oxford.' We shall
see. What we do know is that this symmetry somehow causes our man
Mottram to murder.

So who, I now wonder, is Mottram's real-life counterpart? To put this another way: who, within Oxford, might just be capable of murder and is therefore to be suspected (just suspected) of the murder of Jacques Derrida? One answer, I fear, is the brilliant Ryle. In the 1930s Ryle was the nearest that Heidegger had to a disciple amongst Oxford's philosophers – 'most,' says Ryle, 'had never [even] seen a copy of *Sein und Zeit*.' Ryle was also, of course, alone in reading Edmund Husserl, Heidegger's predecessor both intellectually and professionally; Husserl it was who had previously sat upon the Freiburg Chair of Philosophy. Indeed, in 1928 (the year in which Heidegger returns to Freiburg) Ryle did visit Husserl – several times, in fact, on a walking tour in the Black Forest. I should add that there is, among Ryle's papers, a picture-less 1928 postcard (no Mussolini, no horse) that was once sent from Husserl to Ryle, from Freiburg to Oxford. The symmetry is there for all drunken postmen to wonder at. Between Dear Ryle and Freiburg is a correspondence that is as open as this horse-less, leader-less postcard.

But the correspondence seems, all of sudden, to be closed or fore-closed even as it comes to a climax, even as Ryle, in 1929, concludes his review of *Sein und Zeit.* You will recall how this great 'advance in the application of the Phenomenological Method' is also, for Ryle, 'an advance toward disaster.' Though seduced by Heidegger, though drawn by Heidegger, Ryle finds the strength at the very last moment to withdraw, to resist temptation. Ahead he can see disaster – disaster so sublime that he cannot, or will not, give it a name. Dearest Ryle.

This Heidegger review clearly marks the turning of Ryle. From hereon, he devotes himself to what would become the very Oxonian pursuit of 'ordinary language philosophy.' This, they say, is a method of dissolving philosophical problems by tracing them back to the abuse of ordinary terms or expressions – 'such dictions as are in breach of logical syntax.' So writes Ryle, in 1970, in a piece called 'Autobiographical.' In this confessional fragment Ryle goes on to denounce all rogue dictions as 'outcasts . . . trouble-makers and paradox generators.' According to the method of ordinary language philosophy, such trouble-makers need to be identified and then eliminated.

Ryle, you see, soon got the hell out of phenomenology, all that bloody thinking about bloody thinking. Indeed, Ryle ran so fast and so far that in later life he would dismiss his Husserlian days as a mere flirtation, a young man's infatuation: 'It is,' he says, 'sometimes suggested that in my well or ill spent youth I had been for a while a disciple of Husserl's phenomenology. There is not much truth in this.' To decode: 'I was not nor never have been a Husserlian. Above all, I was not nor ever have been Rektor Heidegger.' Ryle claims an alibi, he pleads that (when it comes to phenomenology) he simply was not there on the night in question, the broken night of Heidegger's disaster.

Instead, Ryle insists, he was busy doing purest philosophy, linguistic philosophy, the kind of philosophy that leads him to set an infinity of logical puzzles, puzzles like (to select one wholly at random): 'Does "someone telephoned" give you the same information as "John telephoned"?' (Someone called, you might say – just someone.)

Dear Ryle, I think, is keen to give the impression that he is too busy on the phone, too busy with language, to do anyone any harm.

CHAPTER FIVE

Freiburg

Let us, for the moment, accept Ryle's defence, accept that he is concerned only with language, and indeed that the only outcasts and trouble-makers he ever wished to eliminate were merely linguistic. Let us assume that he never had in his sights that ultimate generator of paradox, the outlaw Jackie (the Kid) Derrida – not even when the Kid suddenly announces (à propos absolutely nothing) that,

> I think of the bounty hunter who attaches the body of the 'wanted' man behind his horse in order to finish him off, and then brings the cadaver back to the sheriff's office stopping off at all the saloons. That's what the West is for us . . .

Let us not assume that the Kid means to say 'that's what *Oxford* is for us' – namely, the film-set for an absurd philosophical Western with Ryle as the bounty-hunter, and the Kid himself as the wanted man whose cadaver is displayed at all the colleges. It may be difficult not to assume this, particularly given that the Kid insists that his life *is* a film and, indeed, a film that both begins and ends in Oxford: *our life*, he breathes, {is} *barely a film, a snapshot . . . from Oxford to Oxford*. We must, though, assume nothing and so, for the moment, let us forget Ryle as potential killer. We must, instead, keep eyes tight shut and think, think, think if Masterman's *Oxford Tragedy* does not point us toward another suspect, another Mottram.

So, who else in real-life, real-time Oxford might correspond with Freiburg? I hesitate as soon as I inhale the answer – for it is, I fear, the Kid himself. Forgive me, I am simply following, dog-like, my line of enquiry; and this one dictates that I investigate (if only for the flicker of an eye) the man who I had hoped would solve my father's case. Thus far, I do realise, I have suggested that the Kid is, most obviously, a kind of Dr Brendel, the Jewish scholar busily investigating murderous Oxford; indeed, at one point, this Brendel figure even sounds alarmingly like the young Jacques Derrida, with his mind still hedged around by Structuralist scaffolding: 'I have learned,' says Brendel, 'the grammar and the syntax of murder.' However (and on this I must drunkenly insist), Derrida is also a kind of Mottram, the scholar who sees his work fatally reflected in Freiburg's high and yet breakable windows. You see, this book of Derrida's, this book of Oxford, doubles as a Freiburg book; the Kid's flickering fascination with post-cards, post-boxes, post-offices and so on and on is, in truth, a deliriously postal reply to something that Rektor Heidegger had famously posted in *Sein und Zeit*. 'Being,' he had scribbled, 'is what is sent.'

As you will know, the German for 'there is' is *es gibt*. To speak literally, this means (they say) 'it gives,' and what is given, of course, is (usually) sent. It may help, though not necessarily, if I add that Heidegger once muttered something about 'a giving which gives only its gift, but in the giving holds itself back and withdraws, such a giving we call *sending*.' To put all this together – both that being is giving and that giving is sending – you might then say that: to be is to be sent. Forget Bishop Berkeley (to be is to be seen); forget Descartes (to be is to think). Instead, hold on to this: to be is to be sent.

I like this; though confess that I am not entirely sure as to what it actually means. For example, does it mean (or include) being sent away? sent out? sent back? or even sent for? I'm not sure, but it has just hit me, like a mail-train, that my father might just have known. This is not because he had ever read the work of Professor Heidegger – 'I'm waiting for the film,' he would have said. No, it is rather because, as a boy, first my father was sent away, sent away to school ('Mother don't make me stay'), then he was sent back again ('Mother, don't make me go back'), and then (one day) he was sent for – he once said: 'I don't know why she sent for me.' It seems that someone had called for my father, someone who terrified him. But who? Who's there? I don't yet know, but the important thing, for now, is that my father knew well that Being is, as it were, postal.

But what, you ask, if Being were to be lost in the post? to not arrive? to be intercepted? to be read by someone other than the intended? Indeed, what if Being is not so much a sealed letter but a post-card? These are questions to be fast-forwarded to the Kid; he forever writes, you see, on *the post card of Being*. This metaphor is sort of comic, almost a kind of verbal slapstick, but we get (I think) the message; the message being that – well, that . . . Being is a message. Does that help? I hope so, but the trouble is that, as the Kid says, there is, for Being, always *the possibility, and therefore the fatal necessity, of going astray*. (He said, and she wrote, 'He ran away'). In other words, it is possible, even inevitable, that Being goes the wrong way, takes a wrong turning; I am destined, as it were, to go astray, go astray from myself, to lose myself. (He said, and she wrote, 'Oh my body'). And if this is true of everything that *is* then each and every thing must, in some way or other, be split or divided. *As soon as there is, there is différance.* Perhaps that's why my father once said, 'Her heart . . . it burst!'

I am sorry. I have allowed things to get out of hand, to go astray. Faithfully following the spell-binding Heidegger has led both the Kid and myself back to that boy in the living room, a boy in a storm; but perhaps that's bound to happen if, like the Kid, you follow Heidegger to the letter. In 1929 Ryle could already see the Heideggerian storm-to-come, and so was quick to wash his shaking hands of all phenomenology. Perhaps, then, Ryle really does have an alibi. The Kid, though, certainly does not. He is, to quote the title of one of his very last books, *Without Alibi*. You see, before retuning to Oxford, the Kid does quite literally follow Heidegger, all the way to Freiburg. Once there, he comes across *a photograph of Heidegger (young, in military uniform)*. The uniform does not, though, alarm the Kid; having met Major Ryle our Kid is accustomed to militarised philosophers and so, while in Freiburg, will happily walk where Heidegger walked, lecture where Heidegger lectured, be wherever Heidegger was.

9th May 1979: . . . You can imagine the extent to which I am haunted by Heidegger's ghost in this city. I came for him. I am trying to reconstitute all his paths, the places where he spoke . . . to interrogate him, as if he were there . . . to sniff out, to imagine, etc. To respond to his objections, to explain to him what he does not yet understand (this morning I walked with him for two hours, and then I went into a bookstore . . . and I fell upon two books of photographs that cost me a great deal, one on Freud . . . the other on Heidegger, at home, with Madame and the journalists from the Spiegel in 1968).

The men from *Der Spiegel* ('The Mirror') had come, one September day, to interview Heidegger about all those lost Adenoidal days. However, the mirror-men made their visit not in 1968 but in 1966; that's when they went in with their huge looking-glass and sat down with the master-thinker and his wife. For some reason, however, the Kid gives 1968 as the year. Once again, a date is being abused and the clock stops still. On this occasion it comes to a halt at 1968, the probable year of the Kid's long-ago lecture at 12 Merton Street, Oxford. In the film in his head, the Kid has (I think) crossed the moment of Heidegger's trial-by-mirror with the hour of his own trial-by-Ryle. Although he is in Freiburg the Kid is still thinking of Oxford – *this morning, in Freibourg,* he says, *the secret of the post card burns.*

This is, I think, just like *Oxford Tragedy*, for in both books the universities of Freiburg and Oxford endure a kind of correspondence, a correspondence of guilt. I say 'guilt' because of the way the Kid (as you know) so carefully remarks that *in Freibourg . . . the secret of the post card burns* – and (as you also know) only *guilty* secrets burn. Is this to suggest that the Kid is guilty by his association with Heidegger? Or is Oxford the long-lost source of Derrida's guilt? Well, the secret *burns*, he says, and I think that *is* the guilty secret. I think, in fact, that the guilty secret of the Oxford post-card is the secret that it has the capacity to burn. And this, I insist, is the secret of not only the Oxford post-card but of the city itself – it is, in

Masterman's phrase, 'the secret of Oxford.' It has to be said (but never let it be written): Oxford burns.

Some may protest and say, 'But, we have always known that Oxford burns, or at least is in constant danger of burning, what with all those dry, un-drowned books. After all, that is why we had to swear, when first we stormed the Bodleian, "not to kindle therein any fire or flame."'

That Oxford should burn is, they say, an open secret. This I accept; but what *is* so very secret is that in certain quarters of Oxford it is not just books that live in fear of burning, it has also been people. And our nocturnal philosopher, he knows this; when he calls from that Oxford phone-booth he is watched by a local drunk for whom the philosopher fears – that night, he says, *I . . . dreamed . . . of the Englishman staggering around the telephone: he was rubbing a new pencil against a box of matches and I was trying to stop him. He was in danger of burning.*

In Derrida's Oxford there is, in fact, danger not just of a small fire but a great fire; he says: *I intend to go back to Oxford. . . . Upon my return, this summer, the great act of faith, the great burning of us.*

Somewhere there is a word for 'great burning,' or at least 'total burning' – that word, I have gathered, is 'holocaust,' a once-ordinary word. All this begs, then, one solitary question – namely: is the *real* secret that Oxford (dare I say it) burns Jews? Is that why the secret of the Oxford post-card burns in Freiburg, the city of Heidegger?

I am not yet sure, but I do think that Freiburg, with its pale memory of the Adenoidal Rektor, is one clue as to the nature of the fire with which Oxford burns. And we are given another clue: for the drunken Englishman so in danger of burning beside the phone-booth turns out to be a Jew. Or at least, our night-philosopher dreams him Jewish: *I had surnamed him Elijah, you know the secret.*

The secret that we know (you and I) is that 'Elijah' is the philosopher's Jewish name, the one that was given to him a world ago, on the day of circumcision. The drunk in danger of burning down Oxford is, then, (in a way, in a world) the philosopher himself, or at least the Kid's closeted Jewish self. I accept that the Kid is only dreaming of his burning Jewish drunk; but it is, I dream, a true dream. You see, the philosopher's phone-booth seems to be on Broad Street (in fact the booth is still there – just waltz out of Balliol, turn left, dance for a 100 yards, then leap across the road), and Broad Street would make sense of the burning because it is there that, in 1555–6, the 'Oxford Martyrs' (Ridley, Cranmer and Latimer) were burnt at the stake for being Protestant. Again, just stumble out of Balliol, turn right, march twenty yards and there, in the middle of the road, you will find, if you kneel upon the asphalt, a cross that marks the site of the burning. To this day, you can see (if you ask the right porter) the old Balliol doors, still blackened by the demented flames.

Some might say that these flames enveloped peculiarly Protestant bodies, but the truth is that they are tongues with a memory of hot Jewish flesh. One scholar who could see all this was Cecil Roth who, in January 1946, reminded the University's Jewish Society that long before, on April 17th 1222, at Osney Abbey, one Robert of Reading, also known as Haggai of Oxford, was fired alive for having converted to Judaism. 'This,' said Dr Roth, 'was the precedent in Common Law for the burning of heretics in England,' the very law that did for the Protestant Bishops three hundred years later; in fact, the flaming case of Haggai was cited as a precedent in their trials. The Bishops burnt, you might say, like Jews.

There are some historians who say there was no Haggai of Oxford, that this is a memory without an event but, in June 1931, the memory was strong enough for Osney Abbey (at the end of Mill Street) to be thought worthy of a plaque, worthy of being 'a site of Jewish interest in Oxford.' You can still see this plaque on the only surviving wall of the now back-broken abbey – perhaps the Kid saw it. He may well have seen the flames on Balliol's blackened doors, and would certainly have seen the Jewish names on so many of Balliol's *un*-blackened doors; then, as now, Balliol had an exceptionally high number of Jewish dons including, you will recall, the Kid's host, Alan Montefiore.

All this makes me wonder sometimes, wonder if the Kid, a boy lost in the Oxford forest, ever felt the last remaining flames of the Holocaust. For, as the Kid himself insists, he goes back to Oxford precisely in order to seek out a huge conflagration . . . *this summer, the great act of faith, the great burning of us.*

To be exact, however, there is no great burning of *us*, only a burning of *you*. By this I mean that, in the philosopher's dream, when Oxford's very own drunken Elijah was in danger of burning he called out not my name but yours – kindly note that . . . *he screamed your name.* As well he might, for *You were right nearby {and} you were burning.* My father, the beggar-boy in our living room, he saw this too; he also felt the fire at your throat. He said: 'The fire! . . . Burned . . . Oh, you can't burn.' So you, *whoever you are*, look out, be warned; it is you who are at risk of being burned, not us.

Here follows an interjection from the Oxford University Jewish Society

'We are sorry, we have moved too fast, talked too fast and thus may have left you, perhaps, confused. What you must understand is that we, the Jews of modern Oxford, are never burnt, never Holocausted; there was no great burning of us. We did once write to you, brothers and sisters, to you who did not escape the fire; but we ourselves were always safe, terribly safe.

Take, for example, our dear friend Theodor Adorno, or Teddy, as we knew him; back in the thirties he enjoyed the security of a room (with piano) in Banbury Road. Throughout his time up in Oxford dear Teddy was busy writing letters back home to another now-famous German Jew called Walter Benjamin; but even as Teddy played his piano (he liked, by the way, to play four-hand) Herr Benjamin was trying desperately to emulate Teddy and make his escape, to limp away as fast as he could. In 1933 Herr Benjamin finally boarded a train that limped from Berlin to Paris; and in 1940, when the boots marched into France, he seized a brief-case full of manuscript and walked all the way up the Pyrenees, hoping there to jump the border into Spain. In the end, at the border, Herr Benjamin did not get to jump. He did not make it across. He was told (wrongly, it turned out) that the door before him was closed; and so Herr Benjamin did what German Jews at the time had learnt to do best: he committed suicide, swallowing a surfeit of morphine. (By the way, the brief-case has never been found, nor the manuscript).

So, you see, we whose letters are postmarked 'Oxford,' we *did* write to you who passed into the flames. In fact, we felt just like Professor Jacques Derrida when he says, in his famous Oxford book, *I write for dead addressees.*

We should perhaps explain that Professor Derrida here imagines he is none other than Franz Kafka crouching in Prague and writing to a woman called Milena, a woman who would die in Ravensbruck. Professor Derrida, you might say, imagines he is writing not only from Oxford with love, but from Franz Kafka with love, from Prague with love. The Professor, he says, *I am writing to you between Oxford and London*, a once-local line that is now *an extension of the track {that runs} between Vienna and Prague.*

To summarise: Professor Derrida's Milena-dreaming postcards take the mail-train from Oxford to London, from London to Vienna, from Vienna to Prague, and from Prague to Ravensbruck. In short: the cards are sent from Oxford to Ravensbruck with love. The moral of all this is that when you, the Jews of Europe, were burning, we the Jews of Oxford were thinking of you.

Let us put this another way: we the few but faithful members of the Oxford University Jewish Society, a largely undergraduate group, did from time to time debate the situation on main-land Europe. For instance, on May 22nd 1938 our minute-book sets down what Dr Roth told us that day: he said that, 'after a short period of enlightenment and emancipation, we are retuning to an era of darkness.' Again, on October 29th 1939, another popular speaker declared that 'this is a black hour for all Jews.' It is there, in our minutes. Yet again, in January 1943, we organised a public meeting on the plight of European Jewry, and persuaded the Union to debate the matter too. Six million minutes later, on June 19th 1946, we welcomed as our speaker one Dr Leo Baeck, a survivor of Theresienstadt. Not quite so many minutes passed before, in November 1946, we agreed to welcome to Oxford a whole group of survivors; this time, though, the survivors came not to speak. In fact, they were largely silent, being children from Belsen; and silent they remained even for the duration of the party we organised for them (. . . *four corners and blind man's bluff.*) As we record in our minutes: 'It was decided to hold a party for the Belsen children on the Sunday after Michaelmas Term,' just before Christmas (. . . *you know what this represents for us, for us Jews, finally*).

So, you see, we did correspond with you our brothers and sisters of ash, we did get the postcards you sent, and we did write back. For instance, anyone who goes to the Bodleian can see for himself, in the minutes of a meeting we held on January 26th 1946, that we accepted our President's proposal to adopt Prague University under an international Jewish 'correspondence scheme.' At the time, some of us remarked upon how the proposal reminded us of an earlier correspondence; we had in mind a letter of solidarity that our university sent to the Catholic University of Prague following the Munich Agreement in September 1938. The letter was signed by most of our famous dons, including Dr Ryle and Dr Ayer; they wrote (and we quote): 'You, in your moment of isolation should feel that from us you are not quite isolated.' As Professor Derrida-Kafka will write (or so nearly write) some forty years later: 'Dear Prague, Love Oxford.'

But, we wonder, do letters sent from Oxford to Prague ever arrive? The Professor himself famously warns that *the letter can always not arrive.* And in our case, the case of Oxford University's Jewish Society, it certainly did not arrive; primarily because, alas, the letter was never actually sent. This unfortunate fact was established in the meeting we held on April 26th 1947; as our minutes record: 'The President commented adversely on the Society's notepaper policy and demanded some for himself. It was, though, pointed out that if he

was so interested in notepaper he should be reminded that, over a
year ago, the Society had adopted the Prague University Jewish
Society and, yet, had not written to it.' . . .

```
Dear Prague,
We are so sorry we did not actually write.
Love,
Oxford University Jewish Society
```

P.S. You may not, perhaps, be so surprised that Oxford
should, as it were, let you down like this. After all, we
did, as a city, vote for the pro-Munich candidate in our
by-election. The Munich Agreement was, of course, part of
that policy of appeasement which some, like Dr Rowse, blamed
upon the grand old men of All Souls College – men like
Geoffrey Dawson, editor of The Times, and Lord Halifax,
Foreign Secretary. He it was, the Secretary, who went to
see the Great Dictator in Berchtesgaden, to talk about the
living-room (ha,ha). They had their photograph taken
together, with the tall Secretary towering absurdly over
the little Dictator.

P.P.S. You may find some consolation in the fact that the
OUJS continues to be very active. We still hold our well-
supported Annual Dinners and Purim Socials; the latter
usually featuring a running buffet, and sometimes a raffle.
Indeed, notwithstanding events in Europe, we retain a sense
of humour. Take, for instance, the visit of a certain Mr
Shaw Desmond whose talk to the Society on June 7th 1946 (as
summarised in our minute-book) covered the following topics:
'Mr Shaw Desmond, the Catholic Church, cricket, Mr Shaw
Desmond, reincarnation, gladiators in Rome, Pierpont
Morgan, Karl Marx, Ireland, Julius Goldstein, and . . . Mr
Shaw Desmond.' No less witty (we think you will agree) is
our record of Mr Desmond's second visit on May 7th 1949
which simply reads: 'Mr Desmond, who complained of a surfeit
of chicken, ice-cream, and cider, stated that he was not
sure where he was.'
Not quite so amusing, perhaps, is the written response
to a meeting held in November 1944 when we had the privi-
lege of having as our speaker the well-known publisher Mr
Victor Gollancz. Our minute-book records that, 'after
enlarging upon the suffering endured by millions of Jewish
people on the continent, Mr Gollancz enlarged upon the solution to the Jewish Problem – namely: Zionism.' To this solemn
minute is added, in the margin and in quite another hand:
'He must have been quite a size by the end.'

End of interjection.
Professor Schad now resumes his investigation

By the end, you know, he was *no* size at all — my father, that is; his beggar's body was so wasted and thin that when the nurses lifted him up he almost folded in two, like drapery in a Renaissance painting.

CHAPTER SIX

Esther

I am so sorry. Like Mr Shaw Desmond, I am not sure where I am. Part of me is with Victor Gollancz, his body enlarging and, by the end, visibly swollen with Jewish ash. But another part of me is with the beggar-boy, his frame, by the end, so very shrunken with . . . well, shrunken with what? I still don't know. As I say, they never did quite decide what was wrong with him, what he was wrong with. So, could he (just possibly) have been somehow and somewhere sick or afflicted with . . . with the afflictions of the Jews? (The beggar-boy himself once said: 'Burn, burn . . . hell fire . . . tattoo').

My father certainly used to preach that each one of us is called to share in the suffering of one particular Jew, the Jew that was Jesus. My father would also preach that He (Jesus) had suffered, or foresuffered everything and anything that would ever be suffered, and I don't see why this should not include what happened to the six million. Thus, would it not be fair to say (please bear with me) that to share in the suffering of one Jesus is also to share in the sufferings of six million Jesuses?

I am sorry, I heard too many sermons when young and I reason very badly. But please, just for the while, allow me to suggest that there is at least a fearful mystery within suffering – it is, if you like, the mystery of every-thing, everyone, everywhere, and everytime. It is, I would say, that absurd feeling that as soon as you suffer in that instant the whole world of pain is in your head. (The philosopher, he says, *our memory {is} so much vaster than the entire history of the world*.) It is, you might say, a tragic version of Mr Shaw Desmond's infamous address on 'Mr Shaw Desmond and Anything and Everything Else I Can Possibly Think Of, Or, Indeed, Has Ever Happened.'

Mr Desmond, it would seem, was never sure where he was – even, or especially, when he was in Oxford. He clearly had no need to indulge in a surfeit of chicken, ice-cream, and cider to achieve such uncertainty; the talent for mental diaspora was there, all along, in his sheer Shaw Desmond-ish everywhere-ness. Indeed, it was there, all along, in his Jewishness. So, am I saying the same of my father? Day after day he too had absolutely no idea where he was; was that, therefore, because . . . because of, well, some hidden strain, however faint, of Jewishness?

I ask because, of late, since my father's death, my mother has suddenly (all out of the blue) begun to wonder if my father's father was Jewish. This father to my father, a kind and gentle man, was Swiss, from near Basel. (*I am writing you now from Basel . . . near the bridge*). In July 1905 he came, as an alien, to England via Paris, altogether alone, aged 24. The young alien soon moved to London where he entered a rubber company in the City. In 1926, twenty-one years later, the alien, now in his forties, was finally naturalised (. . . *this is your demon, someone from your family . . . from middle Europe*). We know very little about the alien's continental past; he didn't really speak about it, or at least not according to my father. But then my father never said much about his alien-father; as a young man, if ever asked about his father, he used simply to declare, with due comic seriousness, 'My father is in rubber.'

Our man-in-rubber, being Swiss, had more than one language, and thus more than one name. When feeling Swiss-French, he would call himself 'Jean Jacques Frederic' – as it says in his naturalisation papers; however, when feeling Swiss-German (and his accent was certainly Swiss-German) he turned into 'Johannes Jakobus Frederick.' My father's birth, though, seems to have precipitated a certain Englishness since the birth certificate, dated March 5th 1930 (that's over a month after the event), does itself give birth to someone called 'John James Frederick,' someone who may only have existed for as long as it took to complete the certificate. I don't think he had ever used that version of his name before or that he ever used it again. Strange that, just one day of being English, the lifetime of a may-fly.

It should be noted that JJFS (to initialise) had arrived in England at a time when many of those entering the country were Jews; so many, in fact, that in August 1905, just one month after JJFS had ghosted in, the Government passed the infamously anti-Semitic Aliens Act. After this, 'leave to land' was no longer granted to 'undesirable immigrants.' It is, I admit, unlikely that JJFS was himself a Jew, if only because the Jewish community in Switzerland has always been small; and still smaller (if not minute) was the Jewish community in 1920s Cheam, a suburban paradise lost somewhere in Surrey, the paradise in which JJFS eventually lived and was married. Nevertheless, that JJFS was in some measure Jewish is an idea, or fantasy that grips me, takes my hand. If I were to diagnose this fantasy, I would call it (and here I glance at George Eliot) a 'Deronda Complex,' or in my case a 'Deronda–Derrida Complex.'

Yesterday . . . Jonathan and Cynthia guided me through the city . . . . While we walk, she tells me about her work projects (18th C correspondence and libertine literature, Sade, a whole plot of writing that I cannot summarize, and then Daniel

Deronda, by G. Eliot, a story of circumcision and of double-reading) and we turn into the labyrinth between the colleges.

The philosopher, I see, disappears into Oxford's collegial forest while thinking of Daniel Deronda, a man who gradually discovers he is of Jewish descent. I am doing much the same, vanishing into my father's labyrinth while dreaming of myself as someone who slowly realises that he is descended from the one and only Swiss Jew in Cheam, and (indeed) in rubber.

And, as the labyrinth slowly envelopes me, I grow to expect a Minotaur; the philosopher, he remarks, *'One day we shall go to Minos.'* I do not want to go, do not want to meet the monster that is there, or indeed the monster that is not there; but the fact that the philosopher enters while thinking of Daniel Deronda is my Jewish clue, my thread, my way back – something given me by Ariadne.

She (my Ariadne) once said, 'Look, look at the photo. Don't you think Grandpa Schad looks Jewish?' I did, and I do. In fact, I recently saw, standing nonchalantly on a family sideboard, an old photo of JJFS that I had never seen before and that, for a second or two, I thought was a photo of Woody Allen. It was just like the day *I burst out laughing when I found that Martin {Heidegger} has the face of an old Jew.*

I now remember that my father did have, in his comedy cupboard, one Jewish joke. My mother says that it came from JJFS who used to tell, she says, many a Jewish joke. The joke my father inherited (and there really was only one) would make a special guest-appearance whenever my father had any excess money; on these red-letter days his voice would be masked by a stagey Jewish accent as he cried:

'Hymie, Hymie, now that we have won the lottery what shall we do about the begging letters?'

Hymie (once called 'Hyman') would then answer: 'Keep sending them, keep sending them!'

I am now embarrassed by this fragment of music hall that now seems like a joke *against* Jews; but back then my father somehow told it as if it were a joke *among* Jews. For the duration of his performance he was completely at home as lucky Hymie Schad, the only Cheam-born son-of-a-crypto-Jew in Watford. Looking back, I see a man momentarily blessed by a comic line of Jewish blood – a line finally thinned to one frail joke.

This is, I know, an improbable flight of thought, this Semitic flight of mine. It is, no doubt, the thrashing-around of a drowning man; but I am still clinging, I guess, to the straw that is my surname – for I am told that about one in five-hundred 'Schads' is a Jew. Consider, for example, a woman called Charlotte Sara Schad who, it is recorded, fled Mainz in 1939 and ended up as a domestic servant, at 17 Marsh Lane, Stanmore, Middlesex –

back in Mainz this Jewess had worked in a shoe shop. Stanmore is not that far from Cheam, but Charlotte was no relation of JJFS. Or at least we presume not; for, as I say, we know very little about his Swiss relations, except that he had a sister called Esther, and 'Esther,' of course, is a Jewish name. As is 'Jakobus,' though not perhaps when it is 'Jacques,' or 'James.'

But I am wandering, losing my thread, which is that JJFS had come to England in order, we think, to escape a marriage that was still-born, a liaison that had never been consummated. Allow me to say all this again: JJFS and his English bride were married at a town hall in Paris on July 4th 1905 – their marriage was not, however, consummated. In a warm hotel room in Paris, lost in a corner of the French-kissed night, their lonely bodies somehow missed each other. And, in the morning, the maid could tell. Sometimes it isn't difficult to tell. As she served the married strangers at breakfast, waiting at their empty table, she could see what had not happened the night before, the still sadness of it all.

JJFS

And this sadness now (or now and then) makes me think of the biblical text that was hung on the modest, modern pulpit from which my father preached for seventeen years in Watford; I wondered at this inscription every week, always not quite reading it. Suspended, just a few inches beneath my father's head and shoulders, the words glared like the sub-titles of a film, only this sub-title was in Latin. It read: *nec tamen consumebatur* which, being translated, means 'not however consumed.' This orphaned text refers, as you know, to a miracle burning in the wilderness, a bush which, one day, Moses came across; the bush was burning but it was not, however, consumed.

The B-movie star in the pulpit once explained that Moses came across this flame or fire when he was on the run; Moses, he said, had recently killed a man but that when he saw the bush he removed his bloody shoes. My celluloid father went on to say that we could read about all this in the book of Exodus; 'It is,' he said, 'a history of flight.' And now, as I read through another story of flight, the story told by my grandfather's naturalisation papers, I read something like 'it was not however consummated.'

These words, or (as I say) something very like them, come from a letter that is dated April 16th 1924 and written by the gynaecological surgeon at St Mary's Hospital, Paddington. The letter details his investigation of my grandfather's first wife, his un-wife from Paris. The surgeon writes that, 'after hearing the history of her married life, I found that she had infantile sexual organs'; this historian of tears then solemnly adds: 'Mrs Schad states that she has not menstruated since November 1904.' That was in Paris, eight months before she was married. Her clock had stopped; but perhaps she was still hoping it would start again, perhaps she had been waiting twenty years for another tick of the clock that bleeds.

JJFS, though, had known there was no point in waiting; astonished to find that he had married a child, he slowly walked away, backwards, still with his broken face toward her and saying sorry all the while. 'I'm sorry, I'm sorry, I'm sorry.' The apologetic man then carried on walking backwards right across the Channel, all the time looking for England. His abandoned bride, his Ariadne, was left to love alone, somewhere in Paris . . . *the virgin who traverses everything with a love song.*

I sometimes feel I should condemn the virgin's disappearing husband; he was perhaps wrong to go. But then, who am I (drunk with lack of sleep) to condemn anyone? Besides, had he not abandoned her, I would not be here, or at least not here in England. And the boy in our living-room once cried: 'It was a girl who was bruised. . . . You can't leave her! . . . He ran away.'

✠

The runaway, having made it to England, fell silent upon his past, a past that I now picture as not just a Paris of frozen lovers but, before and beyond that, a Switzerland of Esthers and Jakobs, a mythical Jewish grand-father-land, on the far side of the Alps, just over the border, not far from Watford. No, not far from Watford; for my sister has always said that when, as a family, we went to the cinema to see *The Sound of Music* she could spy, out of the corner of an eye, that our father was crying as the film reached the end, when the Von Trapps, escaping Adenoidal Austria, finally make it across the Alpine border to neutral Switzerland. My sister had never before seen our father cry, and I don't think any of us ever saw him cry again, not until the final, living-room years.

It is possible, I suppose, that he had cried when, in the summer of 1954, he himself jumped the border to Switzerland for the first time in his life. He crossed over on a 125 Bantam motorbike, with a tiny side-car attached. Not so attached were the spokes on the wheels, which kept falling off. And, did he cry? Was he moved? I doubt it, but he certainly wasn't laughing since (as the girl in the side-car recalls) they crossed the border six hours late. The side-girl (my mother) also recalls that, despite this spectacular tardiness, they found my father's Aunt Esther still there to greet them. As they drove into the town of Müttenz there she was, standing at the side of the road, patiently waiting to greet a young man she had only ever seen in a photograph. She was, the girl says, dressed in national costume and just waiting, waiting as if all the Swiss clocks in the world had stopped; a woman waiting by a road, just standing there, in national costume, a woman called Esther, as if standing for her nation, her people.

I'm sorry, my mind has wandered again, this time toward a woman who fascinates the philosopher,

 . . . *the one*, he says, *I call Esther. . . . Éster is the Queen . . . she saves her people from . . . a holocaust without fire or flame.*

Esther, you will know, is a biblical heroine, the Jewish Queen of the Persian King Xerxes, the man with a double cross in his name. Despite, or because, of this double cross, Esther famously risks her life by daring to protest when King Xerxes accepts Haman's plan to exterminate the people of Israel; she dares to stand before Xerxes and speak, and thus her people are reprieved. The Jews are not (or at least not yet) to be consumed.

Esther stands and resists; in the instant of absolute danger (when even clocks hold breath) stands a queen called Esther. She is a woman who, at one hour, turns into my father's far-away Swiss aunt. At another hour, Queen Esther turns, and turns, into the philosopher's mother – *Esther,* he whispers, *{was} her sacred name, the one not to be used.* At still another hour, biblical Esther pirouettes into a young woman called 'Hadasseh,' her Persian name;

and, as Hadasseh, she becomes 'you,' the philosopher's beloved: *you*, he insists, *are Hadasseh*.

More and more, I begin to suspect that there is a young woman, perhaps even a girl, who waits, abandoned, at the still centre of my turning mystery, this turning Oxford mystery of pastor and philosopher. My father once said: 'It was a girl who was bruised . . . Hear her, hear her, hear her . . . A female.'

So, what is she saying? What is her story, her history, this girl whom my father insists we must hear? I am afraid it is difficult to tell, if only because he also said, 'She is gagged.' If gagged, if unable to speak, she is compelled to write, and so she did. Like a tongue-less Philomela, my mother took a pen and wrote in the gathering dust, setting down everything her disappearing husband said. But the doctors could not hear her, or would not hear her. They said the poor man's words did not signify, revealing little about his condition and even less about anything that might ever have happened in his past. My father was right to say, 'She is gagged.'

And so she kept on writing, kept on transcribing; and, as she did, it is (I admit) just possible that she changed my father's words, that she was not so much setting things down as setting things up, editing my father's crazy sermon. I do doubt this; but if it were the case it is only what Queen Esther did. As our philosopher tells the story: *Haman {it is who at first} . . . wields the king's signature, gives the order of extermination . . . dictates the horror;* however, when Esther changes the King's mind she it is who wields his signature, re-writes the order of extermination: *Esther suspends the carnage by detouring a letter . . . she substitutes another one for it . . . {a} counter-order . . . .Finally, she sets things up . . . to have Haman, the minister, hanged, yes hanged.* So, Esther never writes, she only ever re-writes – detours the letters, counters the orders; above all, she counters the order of extermination, reverses a holocaust. This is, let us dream, a case of counter-holocaust.

But could we ever counter holocaust? The philosopher insists we can: let us (he says) *light counter-fires . . . in order to avoid a holocaust.* This is mad, a pipe-dream, and yet I sometimes think it's what I am trying to do; for the philosopher says that *to investigate {is} . . . to burn,* to fight fire with fire. And this I do, or imagine I do, in the name of Esther, she who counter-signs and counter-orders. Hers is a counter-intelligence, an intelligence that rights the wrong, saves the condemned, and returns to life the as-good-as-dead. It's like those nights when I dream that my father is still and somehow alive, that he never quite died, that he has had some impossible reprieve, or remission. And the philosopher says this: *I . . . hope for a new 'remission' . . . of an illness that I will not get out of alive.* Such hope is the hope that Esther can inflict; Esther is the opposite of history, she sets it down in reverse, writes it backwards. She is, thank God, a *perverse copyist,* a writer not to be trusted.

So, where was Esther when, in January 1942 at the Wannsee Conference, the order once again was given that the people of Israel should evaporate? Why wasn't Esther taking the minutes as Herr Hynkel's men dictated the horror to-come? If only she had been there to revise, rewrite, get the minutes wrong, switch the names of the killers and the killed, ignite a second and counter-holocaust. *I am dreaming*, says the philosopher, *of a second holocaust that would not come too late.* But in 1942 Esther must wait at the side of the road, wait until it is too late, until six million have limped past. Then, and only then, does she get to pick up her heavy pencil and begin to set things right.

And this she does at the beginning of Michaelmas Term 1946, when one Miss Esther Unger (an undergraduate of Somerville College) becomes Secretary to the Oxford University Jewish Society. At long last, Esther is ready for a counter-holocaust – and so too is a world: on October 16th 1946 the Nuremberg Trials climax with the hanging bodies of eleven Nazi war-criminals, each one turning on the end of a rope. Eleven, exactly a football team; though it would have been twelve (enough for a substitute) had not Herman Goering poisoned himself at the last.

Three days later, on October 19th, the Jewish Society meets at Corpus Christi, and Esther Unger has her heavy pencil sharpened. She records that there was a solemn reading aloud of a fragment from her very own book, the Book of Esther. To be precise, it was an apocryphal version of her book, a textual corpse, something 'unearthed from the Bodleian . . . and trans-lated by G. Wigoder of Oriel College.' This is what they read out, for all Oxford to hear:

'To Xerxes, King of Persia . . . greetings from Peep-bo the hangman. As thou hast commanded, O King, the sentence of death by hanging has been carried out on the eleven men whom thou has convicted of crimes against humanity. They were hanged early this morning . . . . The leader (Haman or Hermann) attempted to stab himself but was foiled by the vigilance of a guard. . . . Before his death their leader spoke, saying: "Verily I am inno-cent. All that I did was done on the advice of my superiors. Hail Ahasaerus. Long live Persia."'

Just in case the sharpened point of all this should not break our skin, Esther adds, in parenthesis, 'On October 16th the eleven Nazi criminals met their death by hanging and shooting. Hermann Goering poisoned himself at the last minute.'

This, as it happens, is Esther's own last minute, or rather her last minute for this particular meeting. In the academic year that followed, so brilliant and quick, it would be Esther's task to minute several Shaw Desmonds, so monstrous and slow. She had also to put into pencilled words all the routine busyness of the Society, above all their plans for the annual Purim Social. I should perhaps enlarge here, and explain that Purim is a festival to celebrate not only the killing of Haman and his allies but, in all, around 75,000 other Persians. At the last moment, Xerxes had dictated that the Jews should not be killed but rather that they should kill, and kill as they wish. Purim, we might say, is a festival of inverted massacre, a wonderful-terrible memory of Queen Esther's bloody miracle. Sometimes this takes the form of murdering a likeness-in-rags of the evil Haman, sometimes it's simply the shooting of real-life Hamans. On the day of Purim in the year of 1994 (February 25th, I am told) one Dr. Baruch Goldstein is said to have shot dead twenty-nine Palestinians in Hebron, at the Cave of Machpela, the Tomb of the Patriarchs.

We must, though, return, quick and un-shot, to Oxford, to a place where Purim is marked not with a massacre or even a riot but rather an annual social, with running buffet and raffle. This is a very English Purim; as if this ancient carnival of far-away butchery had been somehow taken up by the Church of England and re-staged as a lost cause in a dreary church hall. It all feels familiar, comfortingly dull. And so too do the pale records of the Central Council for Jewish Religious Education; these reveal that, in 1973, Purim is marked, for the children attending the Oxford Synagogue's weekly Hebrew Classes, by the showing of a film-strip or two: one on Purim and one on Moses. The Visiting Inspector reports that, 'the Moses film-strip was voted interesting and instructive.' A bush was burning, frame by bloody frame. As regards the Purim blockbuster there is silence; the less said the better, it seems.

I sometimes wonder if the children would have preferred to make plas- ticine models for Purim – as they had done at an earlier class on David and Goliath. Of this the Inspector (then in jovial mood) remarked that 'the Goliaths were particularly fearsome and convincing.' Perhaps, though, models of Haman and the team, or, indeed, their Jewish hangmen, would have been all too fearsome and convincing. When it comes to Purim, Oxford might stretch to a buffet or raffle, but the line is drawn at plasticine.

I'm sorry, that's not quite true. The fact is that, after dark, Oxford can manage a pretty terrible Purim fire, as it did on May 8th 1945, V-E Day. War in Europe was over, the Great Dictator's epic home-movie was finally finished, and most of Oxford joined in a torchlight procession along The Broad to St Giles where, at the site of the Martyrs' Memorial, a ragged effigy of the Great Dictator was burned. Here Christian Oxford burnt as if it were pure Purim. One Oxford Jew who was there, Ralph Glasser, could see the Purim in the air: 'there were,' he writes, 'sudden orgiastic couplings on the pavements . . . as a huge crowd seethed in mindless release along the length of the Giler, the contents of the apocalyptic crucible, a boiling mass of lost, directionless bodies.' . . . *the end of the world by fire.*

This time, then, no running buffet, not even a raffle. Still more remarkable is that Glasser, though a Jew, does not mention the ragged Dictator, the tramp in flames. It is as if that wasn't the point of the fire, as if (like all those lost bodies) the Oxonian fire was itself directionless, its sparks barely knowing to fly upwards. And perhaps it *was* such a fire, all perverse and paradoxical; for, by burning the evil Hynkel at the Martyrs' Memorial, at the very place that remembers the burning of Protestant saints, Oxford superimposes good fire upon bad fire; Oxford burns against burning. And this can be done. We can, says the philosopher, *light counter-fires*. It is possible.

Yes it is possible, but a terrible risk is born. Our counter-fire may get out of control, be turned against us, become a counter-counter fire. There is always reason to fear that Esther may not succeed in reversing holocaust; her counter-intelligence may itself be countered; she may not, necessarily, be safe.

And I do, now and then, fear for the safety of Oxford's Esther – Esther Unger, the Jewish Society's Somerville secretary. I fear whenever I nod and dream, that, thirty years later, she is following the philosopher through the directionless streets of Oxford exactly as Eurydice followed Orpheus along the endless pavements of the underworld. Orpheus was attempting to lead Eurydice out of the flames but knew he would fail should he ever, even for a moment, look back at his wife. (He said and she wrote: 'He's turning, he's looking'). Just like Orpheus, the philosopher is certainly tempted to turn, tempted to look back at his Oxford Eurydice. And the philosopher confesses to this, even as he walks through the collegial maze, a maze in which he only ever names two colleges – Balliol and Somerville: *I walked for more than an hour {and} I entered Somerville College on my last legs . . . everywhere I felt myself followed by a girl and from end to end, along the entire itinerary, I was dying to turn around.* I dream (forgive me) that Esther Unger is this girl.

As for whether the philosopher did, in the end, turn round, I am not sure. I guess we are led (if we follow) to say that he did not turn; but, like a child at a pantomime, I find myself echoing the blind-boy in our lounge, the one who cried: 'You have turned!' It is difficult to forget that Orpheus himself did turn his head and that Eurydice died among fires for ever. (*You are dead, like the dead woman*). I do, though, find comfort in the fact that Esther Unger survived. Esther, the Somerville girl whom I dream to be the philosopher's Eurydice, did, in the end, escape; she did get out of Oxford, running away to London for a doctorate before sailing slowly to the Caribbean to be an Assistant Lecturer in French at the University College of West Indies. It is possible that she thought there was no place further away from Oxford than the West Indies – except, perhaps, Watford.

This westward Esther (we must note) somehow managed to rewrite even the fate of Eurydice. But that is what Esthers do best. Consider, please, another Jewess called Esther Unger, one from Hungary. This Esther Unger was also eighteen in 1945, also of an age to go to university. However, in April of that year she was not preparing for lectures and lovers but for a death-march to Sachsenhausen, at the end of which she was somehow still marching or, at least, shuffling. Her point of departure was a camp in Reinickendorf; before that she had been held at other Adenoidal theme-parks including Ravensbruck and Auschwitz – the theme was death.

I have sometimes wondered if, at Ravensbruck, she ever met Franz Kafka's beloved Milena. Did she, I wonder, see Milena die? Did she even write about Milena in the postcard that we know she sent to her father from Auschwitz? If so, her postcard would have been read with bleeding eyes by Kafka, had he been the postman, and had he still been alive. But we need not write the history of un-fallen tears.

The postcard in question was not, I think, that official postcard from Camp Auschwitz which so many of its early guests were made to send back upon their arrival. This is the one that read: 'I am well. I work and am in good health.'

These dictated postcards make me think of the day my father looked down at the carpet and whispered, as if in confidence: 'They said, "You'll have a lovely time."' I don't think he did; and he made sure, in the end, that we knew this. Esther Unger was the same. She too would not write home as commanded; her postcard was bound to be different. Or at least, I think so. In her memoir she doesn't really say what she wrote, only that it did arrive, that 'Papa did get the card,' and that it reached him via the 'care of neighbours,' such is the half-kindness of half-strangers.

So, Papa did get the message, he did hear her. But Papa still died; 'he died alone,' writes Esther, 'with no one at his bedside.' She does not say why he died; perhaps he died *because* he heard her, thus died of hearing. The letter, it killeth, you know. And, did something similar happen to *my* Papa? Is it just possible that he could have died from hearing an after-cry from after-Auschwitz? My demented question is overheard by Dr Freud who looks concerned; he then caresses the beard on his cancerous chin and scribbles: 'History is precisely the way we are implicated in each other's traumas.' Emboldened by this, I whisper to myself that my father's dream of a hell experienced at school was somehow caught in the barbed-wire fact of the hell lived at Auschwitz.

These two hells (one is never enough) certainly bleed together in the wounded head of the philosopher; but then he was in a French-Algerian school run by Vichy bureaucrats – he was, as it were, within ear-shot of the camps, or at least could be reached by phone. In contrast, my father was in an English public school run by Anglican bureaucrats; nevertheless, by the middle of the war, the school was not so Anglican, not so English. With the arrival of boys blasted out of Europe there was a sudden coming of unpopular names. As the school historian writes, 'By 1943, besides ninety-four confirmed Anglicans, there were nine Jews, not to mention five Roman Catholics, and four Nonconformists.' My father (a Methodist originally) would have been one of the four Nonconformists – so, not Anglican, not quite or fully English. He was to be numbered, instead, with the others, with the five Roman Catholics and the nine Jews; numbered and perhaps even named; for, alongside these nine Jewish names from Europe, the name 'Schad' suddenly looked less strange, less alien – less German, less like the Enemy. Alongside these faraway Jewish names (names already scarred by rumour of massacre) he was suddenly given a second false identity: not that of enemy, or Nazi but that of refugee, or victim.

There was, you see, no avoiding the stench of the concentration camp, not even in an English public school and not even (though hard to believe) back in 1936. That was the year in which the Headmaster's wife remarks on the school's 'overpowering smell of gas.' Ten years later, in March 1946, the School Magazine reports that the Debating Society had taken as its topic 'Palestine and the Jews' and that a certain 'Mr Heller gave a harrowing picture of the condition of Jews in Europe.' I cannot be sure that my father was there to see this moving picture, but his best friend certainly was, since the magazine records that he 'spoke in defence of the Arab cause'; surprising, perhaps, for this best friend went on to be a professional Shakespearean actor noted for his performances of Shylock.

I digress. My point is that picture postcards from the death-campers of Europe did reach the school. In fact, the school had already seen, or imagined a little holocaust, and one that took place in, of all places, the chapel. According to the boy-editors of the school magazine, the chapel was normally a kind of theatre or stage for 'the sermons of unhappy preachers'; but, on this occasion, the unhappiness performed was still more dramatic. As forever, I am thinking of that in-house mystery, *Which Way Came Death?* Here there is a funeral, at the end of which, as the coffin is being borne out, one of the school matrons is overcome with grief; to be precise: 'Miss Hale, with a pitiful gesture of outstretched hands, uttered a little moan and fell amid a holocaust of hymnals and prayer-books to the floor of her pew.' I would suggest that 'holocaust' is an unlikely and alien word in a thirties' murder-mystery. A word with such a terrible future should clearly not be boarding at an English public school, not even at the time of a funeral. Mind you, the murderer (or at least the supposed murderer) is that master with the Nazi manner. And I now recall how Paul Celan will sing, of the camps, that 'Death is a master from Germany.'

I shall confide that, until now, I had been imagining that, in my father's case, death was purely and simply a master. As you know, my father once said, very simply: 'the Master killed.' But perhaps I should be thinking specifically of a master from Germany. ('Last thing he said . . . German,' whispered the living-room boy). It is true that, by 1945, some of the masters had come *back* from Germany, having been there to fight; so, is it possible that they brought death with them in, say, their very breath?

Question: Which Way Came Death?
Answer: It came back from Germany.

This is, perhaps, a pirouette of an answer. We shall see. But, first, what of those masters who served on the home-front, those for whom the scream of war was, like poetry, something not heard but overheard? Did they also breathe death into the life of the school? There is certainly the case of the young master who arrived in 1943 (the same year as my father) but who, as the school historian records, 'soon left after having a fit in the chapel.' Thus, just seven years after the Headmaster's wife had *imagined* a holocaust in the chapel (outstretched hands, crumpled body, tumbling books) the whole school witnessed *for real* another falling down in the chapel. This time the holocaust was no fiction. Faith Wolseley's novel turns out to have told the future, to have foreseen the master's fit.

And if this murder-mystery can see, ahead of time, someone actually crumpling to the polished chapel floor, can it also see ahead, down the line, someone actually being murdered? In short: was there a murder in 1943 that was as real as the new master's epileptic fit? I don't know, not as yet; but the fit itself was perhaps a snap-shot of death, with the fitting master immediately leaving the school. He never retuned. In the eyes of a thirteen year-old, still in his very first term, this falling, jerking, and foaming body may well have looked like someone dying. I now wonder if it was this fitful master that my father, sixty years later, could see in the corner of the lounge.

CHAPTER SEVEN

'They Weren't Really, You Know'

The master's fit, and what survived of it, six-foot deep in my father's brain, may well yet signify; but certainly significant is the master who followed the master. This new master, he too fixes my eye, as I squint down the long, narrow barrel of sixty years. Still squinting, I read in the school history that in September 1943 the new man 'founded . . . a rhythm club which ran into controversy, being denounced in the magazine as a group of "devil worshippers."' This damning judgement appeared, in March 1944, as part of a letter to the Editor from someone who signed himself 'Sufferer'; it reads:

> Dear Editor,
>
> On Sundays (of all days) the Rhythm Club troop to their shrine (Classroom A) to worship the Gods of Discord and partake . . . in orgies which drug the intellect . . . . That such a cult of devil-worshippers should exist is an insult to the school.
> Yours,
>
> 'Sufferer.'

Some might say that we have already heard enough from young 'Sufferer,' or perhaps that his talk of the devil is purely humorous. But I am not sure I get the joke. You see, the boy in the lounge, the one with darkness in his mouth, once said: 'Satan . . . horrible, horrible services . . . book, incantation . . . occult game . . . 666.' In this poor boy's head there was a hell that tends, I find, to bedevil all devil-jokes, gag all Satan-gags. The philosopher knowingly sighs: . . . *infernal noise.*

Like my father, the philosopher had a nodding acquaintance with a world where devils really mean something. *When I was a child*, he says, *my mother used to pass salt over my head . . . to ward off the evil eye.* And thank God she did, for when the child reaches Oxford he looks into the pupil of more than one evil eye. Even as he stares into the picture of Plato and Socrates his handsome face turns white; he says, *I . . . feel them both diabolical . . . The devil is them.*

It is true, I accept, that the Kid can still smile, even laugh, but he does not do so until, in the end, he saunters out of hell. Celebrating his exodus, he cries:

You were walking on my arm bursting with laughter, we had left hell with all its maledictions only two or three clock hours behind us.

This is all very well for the philosopher, but my father could not so easily make such escape. In my father's hell the clock is stopped, still; still as an un-ravished bride.

The clock began to stop the day my father started at boarding school, in late-September 1943. The clock on the cricket pavilion had not been working since before the war, its arrested hands both pointing up in frozen, ecstatic appeal. And now, as if in deepest sympathy, the church clock in the village had also given up its ghost. Exactly one hundred years before, in September 1843, the Bishop had set down the founding stone; now, at the turn of its very own century, the church clock would tell no more time – as if dumb-founded by the very thought of all those years. (*Stop time itself*). The local newspaper is itself completely at a loss, asking 'What's the time?' before answering, 'We have no time; the church clock has stopped.'

For the suddenly timeless folk of the suddenly timeless village there is only one possible response to this hour of vanished time – namely: a jumble-sale, with tombola. Even when there is no time at all there is, in England, still time for a jumble sale. And so money is raised and soon (or at least they think it is soon) the church clock is persuaded to work again. Tick. As for the pavilion clock, that duly melted and moved again in the warm summer of 1947. Tick. It is not, though, so simple for the boy that was my father; for him, somewhere or other a clock was hesitating forever.

When, fifty years later, he sat on the edge of his half-made bed and talked to himself about the devil, the little-old boy kept a still eye on a clock that no-one else could see, or hear. He said, 'Ding ding, the clock . . . . Purple, singing, the clock . . . Bells ringing, the clock.' I had always thought that hell could have no room for a clock, that a clock was too orderly for an ever-lasting inferno, too much the icy work of cool reason. But I was wrong; at my father's school, when he and his peers have reached the sixth-form their most wild and hellish dreams are dreams about clocks. I am here thinking of two particular peers, one of whom, as it happens, was Honorary Secretary of the School's Devil-Worship Society (cunningly masked as the 'Rhythm Club'); together, the two sixth-formers write a stunning surrealist fantasy called 'They Weren't Really You Know.' It is an account of a party, 'one of those really happy parties' – the kind of party where 'you pour drink on the carpet, insert the cat in the fire, quietly vomit upon the sofa, and walk on the ceiling.' What, though, made the party particularly splendid was, apparently, that 'John was teaching his watch to swim in a glass of port while George injected the electric clock with custard.' I have no idea who John is, nor George, but had they ever been let loose near the church clock in the village it is no wonder it stopped.

I once read somewhere that in nineteenth-century Paris at times of revolution (in other words, most of the time) they were inclined to shoot at the clocks. In post-war England it seems that we simply injected them with custard. How very English. But bullet or custard, the effect is the same: the time machine is arrested and so too the pale laws that make us behave, make us move like dutiful dolls. As long as the clock has stopped, as long as history is on holiday, we can do whatever we dream. It doesn't count, it can't be dated, it will not have happened. Whether I draw my breath in revolutionary Paris or a very particular timeless Sussex village, I am free to do whatever I wish – however appalling, however terrible, however exquisite. And here, in the village, in the school, whilst wrist-watches drown in port and clocks are surfeited with custard, someone is busy exquisitely killing. The two sixth-formers write all about it, and do so with astonishing candour:

'They carried me upstairs to the bathroom where I was dropped on the floor and subjected to a quantity of falling water. This stimulated me to great efforts and I managed to shoot two seagulls as they flew across the bathroom frieze; but as I was plucking the second I realised, to my horror, that the birds were legally protected; cringing with fear, I hid the carcasses behind the bath, and burnt the feathers in a pile on the floor. With all traces of my atrocity thus concealed, I sedately walked down the banisters, and rejoined the party.'

This is a strange heap of words, shocking in their way. But then, it is March 1947, just two years after a war in which so many clocks were stopped and so many laws suspended that home-front atrocities could easily be overlooked, easily concealed. In London during the Blitz it was well known that a murderer could hide the carcass of his victim in the ruins of a bombed-out house – behind the bath, in a pile on the floor. (He said and she wrote: 'Pull it in the bath . . . the basins.') A body beaten for, say, ten minutes with, say, a lead pipe could easily be mistaken for a body smashed by masonry.

And besides, a closed eye was being slowly turned to the indiscretions and misdemeanours of soldiers, particularly those from our Allies, those being lovingly rounded up for D-Day. These boys were waiting to walk on water, waiting leave to land, to hit the beaches – a doomed tide, waves that would break and kneel already condemned. These brave boys, waiting to die, drunk with boredom and fear, can surely be forgiven for stopping the occasional clock, suspending a few laws, shooting the odd seagull. 'They threw the bird,' cried the boy in the lounge.

On December 1st 1941 at the local Assizes court, just a few miles from my father's school, one particular judge, fading with anger, sighed and said that, 'with the exception of about five cases, every one in this calendar year involves a soldier – bigamy, housebreaking, rape – and I shall be told in every case that he is an excellent soldier and that the Army cannot afford to lose him.' It was in the national interest that certain victims be ushered quietly away, and some even concealed, behind the bath, in a pile on the floor.

To twist this another way: if you were to sit in a library and turn every thin and giant page of the local paper, from September 1943 to the end of hostilities, you would find not a single murder, not one. You would, though, find a hatful of suicides and a clutch of 'accidental deaths.' Like the local man who was 'knocked down by an army vehicle which was said to have swerved' – they all swore blindly it was an accident. Or again, like the sailor who died from a bullet to his handsome head, a bullet that had come from another sailor's revolver; the former had seen the gun and had asked if it was the latter's – 'he said "Yes," and went to "break" the revolver when it went off.' This too was purest mischance, they said, under oath.

With all traces of atrocity thus concealed (I steal these words), the guilty can walk sedately down the banister (more stolen words) and rejoin the party, the party thrown for the D-Day boys – a knees-up held right across the South of England. It was, though, a largely silent raising of knees in a very silent England, silent-movie England, where no-one dared to talk lest the walls should hear. This England had become a nation of mutes all unable to say whatever it is they see. The boy once said: 'Not to tell . . . don't tell.'

I saw the look on his face when he said this. His wide-open eyes were tightened not with fear but earnestness, even loyalty; after fifty years he still felt under oath not to tell, as if nothing had changed, as if the clock were still stuck. And that is why he sometimes told us 'not to tell' and told himself 'not to tell' – not to tell of those 'horrible, horrible, horrible serv-ices . . . book . . . incantation . . . occult game . . . 666.'

A child, even a child, can see what this is all about; that's why he said 'they would not listen to me . . . they would not listen.' *Listen to me, listen to us.* But should someone, anyone, listen? Indeed, why should *you* (of all people) listen? It is all, I know, so hard to believe. In recent years, many have claimed to have been victims of The Friends of Satan but few have listened. Some, though, have listened and believed – some psychiatrists, indeed some courts of law; there have, in fact, been cases carried to convic-tion and to prison. But even today such cases are rare birds, and back in the 1940s there were none. He said: 'they would not listen to me.' And so he soon gave up, seeing that there was a war on, and in wartime you are forever told 'not to tell.'

Perhaps that's why the boy from Vichy-run Algeria grew up to be the philosopher who kept on saying, whatever the question, *It is . . . difficult to tell*. The deconstruction-Kid was always slow to speak. Like Jackie Coogan, Jackie Derrida was never really happy in the era of the Talkies, the age of the Voice. That is why when he looks at the picture of those comedians Plato and Socrates, in the middle of their medieval routine, each one wearing the other one's hat, Jackie D. lovingly mouths two slow words: *Silent movie*. Like wartime children, these ancient silver-screen philosophers know well, it seems, that 'Careless Talk Costs Lives.' Perhaps, I think, they have seen this caption as part of that most famous Fougasse cartoon, the one with the man in the telephone booth surrounded by fourteen eves-dropping Adenoid Hynkels. Well, perhaps not – but what the Kid seems most to love about the thirteenth-century funny-men is that they refuse to talk, that they seem to know so well that 'Mum's the word.'

He said and she wrote, 'His poor Mum.' And *his* Mum, his own Mum is poor, I think, because she too is silenced; even Mum may have had to keep Mum. That is why, I think, her gentle nerves finally broke in 1952, once it was all over, once she had left hell five or six clock-years behind her.

The Kid, he sympathises, and talks to me again of his mother in Algiers warding off the evil eye with salt. My father's mother was not, alas, so adept at warding off evil eyes; she was a Methodist and that's not the kind of thing Methodists do, or least not in Cheam. Mind you, I could believe it of Anglicans, particularly those who ran my father's school. There, desperate boys pray extravagantly against the dark. Like when, for no apparent reason, in July 1944 the editors of the school magazine sign off with: 'From Witches, Warlocks and Wurricoes / From Ghoulies and Ghosties and Long-leggity Beasties / From Editors that cry out in the night – Good Lord deliver us!'

I do think this is a strange thing to write, but then I spot, out of the corner of your eye, those devil-worshippers from the so-called Rhythm Club, and I too begin to pray, to pray with salt. And I juggle yet more salt when I encounter the schoolmaster called Mr Stoner, or at least that's what the Headmaster's wife calls him in *Which Way Came Death?* . . .

"'This afternoon," said Miss Hale, "I'd just had my tea after reading to little Jacks, who's in the sick-room with a throat . . . when with hardly a knock my door was flung open, and Mr Stoner came in." Remembrance proving too much, she stopped again.

"Yes," said the headmaster's wife.

"Oh Mrs Carey, I can't tell you how he looked," Miss Hale pressed her hands, with the dishevelled handkerchief between them, closely together; "he looked like – Satan . . . .Really, I was terrified, and the things he said . . . I couldn't repeat them.'"

This scene worries me more than it should. Perhaps, it's because it is all too much for a middle-brow murder mystery; Satan just shouldn't be here, he's wandered into quite the wrong book. But I suspect there is another reason why I don't like the scene; it is that my father's mother was once a Miss Haile – it was her maiden name. In fact, if I narrow my eyes and squint I can see her sitting in the sick-room. And that makes sense, because this Miss Haile, 'my' Miss Haile (if you will), must have suspected something, must have sensed something strange at the school. 'Mother,' he said, 'don't make me stay.' 'Mother,' he said, 'don't make me go back.' But she did. So, why? Was it because someone silenced or frightened her? I now think so, and I think it was a master like Stoner, one whom to remember 'proves too much,' proves far too much. This real-life Stoner could well have spoken like Satan, thus freezing the woman's tongue. 'She was gagged.'

But Miss Haile is not quite alone in the room with the master. We must not overlook that boy in the background, the boy called 'little Jacks,' the boy with whom the woman is reading in the sick room. This bookish boy never appears again, not once; and we know nothing about him except that he reads, which is why it now occurs to me that 'little Jacks' is 'little Jacques' – little Jacques Derrida, the bookish, Jewish boy who is told by the master at his school that he must leave . . . *to the devil with the child . . . .* This cursed and bedevilled child, little Jacques, must surely be the boy almost lost in the background, the boy who saw what happened, who saw the terrifying master. It would explain why the philosopher knows so much about my father: his life, his death, his illness, and . . . even his name.

The philosopher, he writes that *I will never seek you any harm, take this word at its most literal, it is my name.* I will indeed take this word, this word 'harm,' at its most literal and, as I do, the word turns (like a spy) into my father's name: the German word 'Schade' means 'harm.'

In Oxford, just outside the phone-booth, the half-cut Englishman once *screamed your name*; here, and now, the half-cut philosopher whispers my name, my father's name – 'harm,' or 'Schade.' I remember now the day my father cried: 'He's naming me !'

Once, when my father was writing to my mother in 1951, that faraway year in America, he set about teasing her over any American pronunciation she might pick up; to conclude his mock-serious tirade he reminds her that, 'The "c" in "schedule" is silent, as in "Schad."' This 'c' he would, one day, make not only silent but invisible. That day was April 6th 1965 when, by legal deed, he made an oath; this was whilst we still lived in Swindon, the railway town. They swore a lot there. And my father, he swore, before the law, to 'absolutely renounce and abandon the use of the surname SCHAD and in lieu thereof to assume, as from the date hereof, the surname of SHAD.'

A strange affair this, perhaps, this changing of names, as if trains. Looking back, it seems to have been rather late in the day to anglicize the Germanic-sounding 'Schad,' particularly since JJFS had lived in England (albeit cocooned in rubber) for two world wars without feeling the need to cut the silent 'c.' Perhaps, though, my father got the idea from the Atlantic where he met a deck steward who was, as my father once wrote, 'a Jew, a nice fellow called Sam Collins who changed his name from Sam Cohen.' This Jew, so full of sea, had given his ancestral name the slip; presumably, he felt it was a noose.

In contrast, my father changed his name simply because he felt it was unfair to have two un-spellable words on one church notice-board: 'Presbyterian' was bad enough, but 'Schad' was a word too far. I am sure this was the case, but in these fitful days I sometimes wonder. After all, my father had been a Presbyterian minister for over ten years, so why did he wait so long to change his name?

I now day-dream there may have been another reason for all this renouncing and abandoning – namely, that my father wanted, though quite without knowing it, to separate himself from a past that was at last beginning to come back to him, to come back to him as *Schade*, as harm. The trick is an old one: you will recall that Paul was once 'Saul'; new person, new name – a scar of conversion.

My father's own conversion had happened (if conversion ever 'happens') around twenty years before, so it is not perhaps important here; but, still, by abandoning 'Schad' for 'Shad' my father might well have felt, if only for the while, safe from harm, safe and separated from that boy at school and young man at Oxford, separated by the nearest of all possible distances, the distance of a silent 'c.' A tiny Atlantic.

Turning round, looking back, I fear I was wrong to restore this Atlantic, to return to 'Schad.' This I did at university and, within just a few months the dementia, or whatever it was, had begun. The clock had started not to tick. My father was running down, unwinding fast and, all the while, standing in front of him was someone called 'Schad,' a young man he had not seen for over thirty years. *I have taken your name.* My father was now staring at a past reflection, an old mirror. He said, 'Hanging, the mirror . . . In a mirror, 666.'

All this is not to say, that, in the final sickening years, he ever really looked at me, ever really saw me. If I ever tried to address the stranger in the living room, face to face, his wild-boy eyes would dart to either side of me, as if studying a crossword: first left, then right, then three down and four across – watchful, vigilant. It was as if this revenant 'Schad' had alerted him to some very present danger, or harm.

You may say, in your schoolmasterly way, that 'Sticks and stones may break our bones, but names will never harm us.' What, though, if one's name is 'harm'? What then? *Harm, take this word at its most literal, it is my name* – my name, I say; and, above all, *his* name, my father's. He was the boy called 'Harm' to whom harm was somehow done. But that was bound to happen, if name is destiny; which it must be, since I read so in a book I found in Gilbert Ryle's private glass-bound library, in Linacre College. The book, which he had scarred throughout with pencil, was another strange book from the thirteenth of centuries, a Latin edition of an ancient Arabic work called *Secretum Secretorum*. The pages that Ryle had once turned so learnedly I now merely flicked, transforming ancient mystical lore into an absurd and animated cartoon; I still managed to discover, however, that many secrets are to be revealed through scrutiny of all sorts of phenomena – some natural, such as the stars and the planets, and some slightly-less-than-natural such as 'the finger-nails of bewitched virgin youths.'

These finger-nails caught my eye, as they did Ryle's – he had under-scarred this line. But still more eye-catching was the secret and magical life of names. So I flicked on, and as I did the blurred, textual cartoon gave quickened and Disney-esque life to what became, before my very eyes, the mad-mad world of thirteenth-century onomancy; at frantic, loony-tune speed all sorts of mad-cap capers of prediction chased across the paper screen. I must have seen a thousand, maybe more, but my favourite, my most dearly beloved, was the one about foretelling the outcome of a disease by using an arithmetical combination of the age of the moon, the numerical equivalents of the letters of the sick man's name, and (finally) the name of the planet that ruled on the day the sick man fell sick.

I did in fact try this, right there in Linacre College library. I began with considerable enthusiasm, even though to be honest it would be very difficult to say what day the man (my father) fell sick, let alone the age of the moon; however, in my eagerness, I felt these numbers could probably be approximated well enough – if necessary, guessed at and simply rounded up. So, armed with a pocket calculator, I set to work. *I have a small sheet on my table, I am accumulating figures on it and several very simple operations.* From the edge of my eye I caught the bewildered expression of a young librarian; but what, thought I, could she possibly know of the arcane science of medieval onomancy? I did, though, just begin to doubt how much I knew myself when realising that I had become confused as to whether one was supposed to be turning letters into numbers or vice-versa. And my confusion was complete when I finally arrived at eleven consonants without a single vowel for company. I did then thump my head on the mahogany desk before me, but I don't think the librarian noticed the emergent bruise on my forehead as I swept out of the college library exuding scorn for every possible form of medieval divination.

'It is all,' I cried, 'complete stuff and utter nonsense!'

This view, I now suspect, was eventually shared by Professor Ryle himself, notwithstanding all his pencilled marginalia. I say this because, just the other day, when reading an essay of Ryle's, I noticed how, in the middle of an extended logical analysis of the difference between names and epithets, he suddenly declares:

'I know that there is a day of the week on which I shall die, but I do not know what it is.'

I was tempted to think that Ryle, with his MI5 background, should have been able to pick the lock to his own death-day; indeed (I thought) could he not have drawn on his extensive, medieval knowledge of the predictive magic of names? Clearly not – he clearly understood that names knew no more about his death than he himself did.

Names, though, do speak to Ryle, including his own – in the very same essay he observes (please note) that 'my name . . . rhymes with smile.' Ironic this, given that Dear Ryle was hardly famous for smiling. It is true that, as his Oxford friends would say, children were 'never frightened' of him; but they would also say that he was usually slow to express emotion – in particular, affection.

Freddie Ayer tells a story of travelling in a car with Ryle all the way to Vienna for the World Congress of Philosophy, and of how, when conversation flagged and finally crashed on a road somewhere in France, Ayer turned to Ryle and asked if he was a virgin. Ryle, apparently, replied tersely that he was.

'And if you were to sleep with someone, would it be more likely to be a boy or a girl?'

'Boy, I suppose.'

They drove on, says Ayer, in silence.

It is funny the things we will say in a car to the person beside us; presumably because, as in a confessional, we are not actually having to look them in the eye. But dear Ryle, I guess, was not smiling. And I don't think he often smiled at Adorno, or Derrida, or indeed (come to think of him) my father. I confess that I can't be sure Ryle ever had the opportunity to smile at my father; but I do feel that he would have been reluctant to smile at anyone called Schad – for Ryle was well aware of the harm of this name. I know this because when, one fine Oxford day, he was philosophising on how badly we ever know ourselves, he suddenly declared: 'I may, for example, fail to find "Schadenfreude" in my "serves him right" attitude, though it is there.'

And indeed *he* is there, Schad-en himself; he is a boy, I fancy, in the background of Ryle's life and work. I can see him there, my father; in fact, I can see him as a clumsy undergraduate poised to bump, quite literally, into the great Professor Ryle. Please read, just for me, the following philosophical scenario from Ryle, and I shall rest my heavy case. Here it is, in Ryle's own words:

'You cross The High on the way to college where you have to take down the oral examination of a few candidates, and a young chap in a gown swerves out rather wildly on his bicycle and bumps into you. Much to your surprise, the very same chap presents himself some fifteen minutes later for his exams. Your shin is still pretty sore and you would like to take it out on him . . . .'

Some may say this is merely a homely philosophical exemplum, an ethical hypothesis or parable, but I know better, even as my weary blue eye slides off the page. For I have come across this 'young chap' before, in the pages of the school magazine; he appears in a letter sent from Oxford describing the Oxonian fortunes of various old boys. The letter reveals that someone called 'Richard ('Dick') Schad . . . is to be seen at times in The High and its adjuncts, stalking along with a somewhat glazed eye and, usually, an umbrella.' I admit that Richard ('Dick') Schad, this boy in the background, is not, at this moment, in a gown or on a bicycle; however, he is a young chap, he does stalk the High, and he does have a glazed eye, just the kind of eye that makes for an Oxford accident.

Don't get me wrong, I would not wish to argue that Ryle ever sought to 'take it out' on my father, to take terrible revenge on the careless owner of the glazed eye. Ryle would not hurt an undergraduate, a mere child as it were – not even when taking down an oral examination. I acknowledge that Ryle never had children of his own and that, at death, was survived only by his disabled twin sister – *that twin sister that you do not have*; but despite Ryle's childlessness, or perhaps even because of it, he does seem to have felt for the child who is lost, and in a strange place. This thought comes to me when Ryle writes, as if from nowhere (nowhere near Oxford), that,

'The child is not so much baffled by a strange house if, wherever they may actually lead him, its banisters feel to his hand like those he knew at home.'

CHAPTER EIGHT

The House

One house that, for my father, was always a strange house was Christ Church, which is, to this day, also known to its inmates as simply 'the House.' I don't quite know how the banisters in the House felt to my father's hand, to his touch; or how that compared to the feel of the well-polished banisters at home, or indeed the well-trodden banisters at school. (There, if you recall, its surrealist sixth-formers were forever trying to walk down the banisters). I did, though, make a point of running my hand along these same banisters on the one occasion that I have ever visited the school.

It was a long, hot day late in June, late in Sussex; and the teachers were full of kindness to this stranger, but the banisters still felt cold to my touch. In fact, everything I touched on that day felt cold, as I walked around without ever the courage to say quite why I was there: cloister, chapel, dining-hall, library, dormitory (now partitioned). I wanted to explain myself away but could not. I felt guilty, clumsy, and alien. But I did want to stand where my father might have stood, sit where he might have sat, pray where he must have prayed. And, as I say, I wanted to clasp any banister I could find; it was a way, I had thought, of holding the boy's hand, of holding it still. But as I did, the hand turned, turned over and ever so slowly into the condemned hand of a condemned girl. He said: 'Her hand! anyone! her hand. . . . I saw it sinking, her hand! her hand!'

I am sorry, I am getting lost again, somewhere in our lounge, and am afraid. But being lost and afraid in this house, our house, means you find your way back to *the* House, the one by the water-meadow in Oxford. This House was, I think, a place in which my father grew, now and then, both lost and afraid. It is true that Professor Ryle (for twenty years a man of the House) knew enough moral philosophy not to take revenge for his sore shin on the glazed undergraduate; however, other men of the House were perhaps not so morally advanced. I shall say this because the College kindly let me see the young chap's termly reports. In one report his college tutor declares that 'Schad remains a muddle-headed man,' in another that 'what is not obvious eludes him,' and in still another that 'he started lazily but has improved under the whip.' I recall now that my father, his head framed by the pillow beneath, once whispered: 'They were whipping him.' He was, of course, wrong; the muddle-headed man was, characteristically, missing the bloody obvious: namely, that 'the whip' was a Christ Church figure of speech, just a sharp turn of phrase in a place full of sharp turns.

My father, I guess, was in some ways a literalist. Someone in his congregation once told him that this was his problem when interpreting the Bible, particularly its rumours of a devil. He said, this man in the pew, that my father was a fool to believe such medieval myth. Others, I know, would say the same; I shall, though, pass over them, blindly.

The only exception to this rule will be my father's most famous Christ Church tutor, an historian called Hugh Trevor-Roper, a double-barrelled killer of myth. Just three years before my father went up to Oxford, HTR had been sent to Berlin by MI5 to shoot down the bird that said Herr Hynkel still breathed. During the first part of the war HTR had worked in MI5's Radio Security Service, reading and analysing intercepted German messages; later he was moved to 'the War Room' to prepare for the occupation of a defeated Germany; however, as soon as the war was over he set about proving that the Great Dictator was also over, and out, forever. As HTR records in his diary, 'the Germans are saying that the old boy's alive.' Indeed, they were saying that the old boy now lived, albeit disguised, as a shepherd in the Swiss Alps, or a hermit in a cave beside Lake Garda, or a fisherman in the Baltic, or (just possibly) a master at an English public school.

All such rumours of old Hynkel's survival were, though, lined up and shot on November 1st 1945, when HTR addressed the press of the world in the Hotel-am-Zoo in Berlin. Here 'The Sleuth of Oxford' (as he was hailed) accounted for every last detail of Hynkel's last day, last hour and even last minute. By the time HTR had finished, Hynkel was irretrievably dead (except in Russia where they did not accept the findings) and HTR himself was irretrievably famous – often to be heard on the radio, the Third Programme, an unseeable star of the wireless post-war air.

Soon he was also irretrievably rich, with his book, *The Last Days of Hynkel*, selling so well that HTR could buy a grey Bentley from the royalties and, for a while, was reputed to hold the record for driving from Oxford to London in under an hour. Going at such a speed, HTR had little time for the slow motions of rumour, and this included not just rumour of Herr Hynkel's resurrection but rumour of the occult – HTR later composed a book on the folly of those who, lost in the seventeenth century, had believed in the magic of witches and the existence of their master, Satan.

I don't know whether HTR detected, in 1949, that every week he was tutoring, in Christ Church, an undergraduate so muddle-headed that he too believed in the existence of Satan; but I think our Sleuth-in-the-House may have had an inkling. In his report at the end of the Hilary Term, he writes this: 'Schad is a weak scholar who wanders through the subject without any obvious purpose, or viaticum. But he will arrive somewhere at length.'

I shall say that I find this a strange thing to write. The sustained and elaborate metaphor of purposeless travel seems more than should be merited by a first-year undergraduate, even one whose eye was glazed and head muddled. In fact, like me, HTR seems to have somehow mistaken the weak scholar from Cheam for a wandering Jew; this chap, thinks HTR, not only wanders but has 'no viaticum' – he lacks, that is, the sacrament usually handed to a dying man, the pale Christian food needed to sustain us on our final journey along the way, the *via*, to death. Young Schad, thinks HTR, has no food or provision for his end; he is to be likened to someone dying without Christian comfort.

I am, no doubt, overreacting, but this report is now beginning to shake me; it is, I fancy, almost a prediction, even (dare I say it) a curse – erudite and unintended, I admit, but (as the philosopher whispers) *this did not prevent me from cursing you.* And if HTR's report were indeed a kind of cursing it certainly worked, my father being a man whose way to death was comfortless, quite the hardest way. Let me add that, although born twenty-six years after HTR, the weak scholar died seven years before the strong scholar. By the end of his life the strong one was both Lord and Master: Lord Dacre of Glanton and Master of Peterhouse College in Cambridge.

This is why I shuddered when I first grasped the force of the word 'viaticum'; and even as I shuddered I felt like the philosopher, for he too knows what it is like to seize this very particular thorn. Listen as he cries, all and sudden, as if not for a reason: *I truly understood the word 'viaticum.'* This word comes, like an elegant thief, all out of the grey; it is so rarely glimpsed and yet here it is, under the philosopher's gaze, thirty years after it is used in Oxford in relation to my father. The philosopher must be getting my father's calls not only from school but also from Oxford. The weak scholar of Christ Church may have waltzed without purpose but he does arrive somewhere at length; he arrives somewhere called Derrida.

This is why I think that my father did, in the end, escape the House. One day, I recall, he stared at the living-room door and said: 'Oh someone take me out.' And I think someone did, someone I must still call 'someone.' (*I hear you open the door*). But whether it was wise to leave, to get out, I am not so sure. Even now the philosopher, sitting still in the Bodleian, is turning another page of medieval future and, from all its hundreds of riddles, selects just one more burning question, or half-question. The first, you may recall, was *Si puer vivet*; the second is this: *An erit bonum ire extra domum vel non.* It translates as: 'Whether or not it is good to go out of the house.'

So: is it? Is it good to leave the house? My father certainly dreamt so; looking away from the door, he said: 'Best thing is to get out and stay out.' But what does the fortune-telling book say? What answer does it give? I need to know; and so must chase the Kid through the flickering pages of his book. But he is quicker than I and limps ahead, clutching his riddle to his broken heart. Finally, the riddler declares that I must work out the answer – he calls: *Guess what it says.* Desperate and without breath, I call back:

'I will – but only for as long as it takes me to return to Oxford to see what the bloody book actually says. Like you, *I will go back to Oxford to take my investigation to its end.*'

The Kid looks alarmed at the thought that I should continue to stalk him, but I don't care. I must determine, finally, for myself, whether it is good or not to get out of the house. It all depends, I presume, on the house, or House in question.

Some might, I suppose, think that *the* House (the Oxford one) is a safe house but I'm not so sure, if only because HTR is not so sure. I say this because I once read (albeit very hastily) the book he wrote about witches; a ridiculous book, by the way, that compares the pursuit of witches in the seventeenth century to the pursuit of Jews in the twentieth. However, as the book begins to fade and HTR charts the declining and falling of witches, he says, just in passing and over his shoulder: Oh, by the way, 'the old beliefs still linger in school and cloister.' So speaks (I think) a man who knows only too well what or, indeed who, tends to linger in cold school and dull cloister.

And one who haunts the same dull cloister as HTR, the same Christ Church cloister, was that weak scholar Schad, the one HTR saw loitering without purpose. Young Schad's glazed eye may also have been weak, but I think he too saw some of the old beliefs that lingered, dark beliefs, beyond beliefs. I say this because, hundreds of years ago, long before he slowly disappeared, my father used often to remark that Oxford had been full of what he would call 'clever devils.'

Looking back, I think this conviction was borrowed from that famously Christian man of Oxford and all-round clever angel, C. S. Lewis (also known as 'Jack,' though never 'Jackie). As Angel Jack sat at his fog-bound desk in wartime Oxford, where not a bomb had dreamt of falling, he set about writing as if, instead, he himself had fallen, as if the angel had fallen. The book he was writing involved a 'Training College' for young devils, a college devoted to a higher education in the finer arts of Hell. I have recklessly called it a book but in truth it is yet another collection of letters; they are, it is whispered, an 'infernal correspondence,' letters from a senior devil in college to a junior in the field, as it were, both desperately trying to tempt dull mortals into eternal damnation. From Hell, you might say, with Love. And this love, this terrible love of Hell, soon reaches my father's school, or at least the letters do. The school magazine records that they were added to the library in 1943, the very same year that my father also arrived in the post; they were delivered together, the letters from Hell and the boy from Cheam.

Five years later the boy is parcelled up and forwarded to Oxford. Angel Jack was still there, still thinking about his now-famous college for devils. Within Oxford's tangle of colleges this was a parallel, virtual college that no-one could quite see; or rather it was a place that no-one could see save the weak scholar with the glazed eye. No-one but our muddle-headed man could see infernal Oxford, and he only just saw it, out of the corner of the corner of his eye. In June 1949, at the very end of Hilary Term, he faces what is, supposedly, a mere Latin exam, but he somehow knows that it is, in truth, something far worse – note with me, the muddle-headed critic, how my father writes that, 'the horror takes place this Saturday.' The horror . . . no more, I think, need be said. Again in February 1951, with Schools only weeks away, he is working for seven hours-a-day with just one hour for hockey or what he so tellingly calls (and I quote), 'similar sinister pursuits.' At this, our philosopher, who has again drifted off while watching daytime TV, suddenly awakes and asks (rhetorically):

Sinister, no?

To this I respond with a knowing and confirmatory nod; I then solemnly add, 'Sinister indeed.'

My point (muddled, I know) is this: that the college they call the House is the most haunted house in Oxford. The most famous old boy to live and die there, Lewis Carroll, he certainly knew the House to be haunted; he knew that, within the House, just the other side of its looking-glass, there are innumerable other houses, other spaces. To begin with, there is the house that once, back in our thirteenth century, belonged to a Jew, a house on which site was built Tom Tower. And then again there is the room in which, one day in a seventeenth century, they found dead a man called Robert Burton, a college librarian and author of the famous *Anatomy of Melancholy.*

Think, pleads the echoic philosopher, *of the Anatomy of Melancholy.* I will, and it makes me think of this death, this death in the House that was perhaps suicide, for some say that they found the librarian hanging in his room, forwarding his theoretical discourse, as it were.

I will bear this in mind, this reference the philosopher makes to *The Anatomy*; it is (I am sure) another clue, another crumb, from the philosopher's turning table. But, for now, I must run on, pointing out, as I go, that within the House is yet another house – namely, Peckwater Quad, the quad in which my father lived among, he claimed, a host of 'ennobled lunatics.' He used, once upon a time, to talk about these wonderful figures. One was a duke, a keen huntsman, who came up to Oxford with a whole pack of beagles; another was a lord who had nothing better to do than open church jumble sales in Swindon; and yet another was a baronet who, after serving at sea in the war, felt compelled each morning to take to the river and row himself unconscious. Curious grows the House.

And the House has no choice in this, this becoming so curious. For, as my father writes, 'the House is just opposite the city Post Office.' Many, I know, overlook this wan and late-Victorian dream when they visit the House, but our philosopher will not let me do that: *the post office,* he says, *is the site of the great affair . . . a church in which . . . everything is possible.* And in Oxford's central post office the everything that is possible is that, with every collection, words gleefully depart the city of scholars, libraries, and dictionaries; here, at the post office, words finally go on holiday, play truant, pleased to mean what the hell they like. And, over the years, this wonderful leave-taking must, I think, have charmed the House across the road. Indeed, it may just explain the invention of Wonderland, or even why my muddle-headed father so relished word-play, the more inane the better. Like when he would ask, 'Why put up with a shampoo if you can have a real poo?' Or, 'What is the point of a seminar if you can have a full nar?' These, we felt, were lines learnt as an undergraduate, evidence that in the House many a word was on vacation, or at least packing its case. The House is indeed curious.

And in the curious house is a curious undergraduate room where the weak scholar sits, taking a break from his purposeless wandering. It is May 1949 and he writes,

'My room is very grand now because the fellow I share it with has purchased a most peculiar picture during the vac. It is a vast canvas in a gilt frame and it fills one wall. The scene is full of oddments that ought not to be there such as a church with a dome, a spire and tower all in one, and a cliff suddenly appearing on a green hill.'

He is right, a cliff really ought not to be there; a green hill should not, without asking, give way to a sudden cliff, sudden fall, or sudden anything. But the weak scholar should not be surprised, for he is up in Oxford, a vertical place, the city of 'The High,' a city of nothing but precipice. Here there are staircases, spires, and everywhere towers.

'Last Sunday,' he writes, 'May morning, I got up at five o'clock in the morning to watch the traditional ceremony in which the choir of Magdalene College sing a hymn from the top of their tower.'

And from there they may fall as well as sing. That's what towers are like;

and my father knows this well, for Christ Church boasts that most terrible joke, a tower called 'Fell Tower.' 'Down the stairs,' the poor boy said, 'down, down, down.'

He's right; up here, in Oxford, both things and people can fall, get broken and smash. Even here we have our riots and our breaking glass. In Eights Week, June 1950, my father writes that 'the Bump Supper culminated in one exuberant rioter hurling a loaf of bread through the Junior Censor's window. It was, unfortunately, not open at the time.' A few months later, in early November, my father declares: 'Guy Fawkes Night was relatively quiet . . . though a policeman lost his helmet, the odd van was tipped over, and an Indian Restaurant lost its windows' (. . . *one of the numerous Indian restaurants in the city*, whispers the philosopher).

As I say, things get broken; but that was always the way in never-never, Oxford, with its all-male colleges and bachelor dons, a hide-out for lost boys of every age. One such boy, Freddie Ayer, once recalled how, as a young don, he and HTR attended a lengthy undergraduate drinks party that finally ends with HTR finding a college servant's bike in a Merton garden and 'disporting on it until it broke.' For this breaking of a servant's wheels after dark, HTR is made to surrender his key to Merton College, where he was at the time a Research Fellow.

He is, though, never made to surrender the American-made revolver he used to keep, a 1930s Smith and Wesson. I don't know when or how HTR came into possession of this gun and how he managed to keep it; but when he died, in January 2003, the House was asked to hand the pistol over to the Thames Valley Police. As I say, in Oxford things and people could get hurt, really hurt; there pistols and revolvers are for real, not just the furniture of detective fiction. Oxford is a precarious place, a place from which to fall, jump, or simply be shot and then pushed. 'They threw me to the floor,' he said.

And this, all this, is, I think, in part, why one fine day my father saw four children on a cliff in Oxford, standing at the very edge of a precipice. Writing to my mother in May 1951 he describes how, one afternoon, he had volunteered to entertain the children of the Minister at his Oxford church, St Columba's. Unable to think of a safer place, the weak scholar took them to the river, by the College boathouse; here he found that these children of the Manse, three girls and one boy, were 'as wild as they make them,' so wild that they 'completely took over the roof of the boathouse, walking along parapets thirty feet above the ground, not to mention the river.'

My father, I think, is seeing again that picture, hanging in his room; a cliff, a precipice, a parapet has suddenly appeared where there ought not to be one, and he sees what no one else seems to see – that is to say: four wild children on an Oxford precipice, silhouetted against the sun, as vigilant as angels.

And has he seen these parapeted angels before? It is, I think, just possible that he had seen them on a war-time cliff, on the Sussex coast – the coast not far from his school. Throughout the war, these cliffs were turned into parapets, parapets manned by angels made of khaki. But, could my father have seen these mobilised cliffs from Oxford? Perhaps, for they can be seen from across the Atlantic, by our philosopher, as late as 1993. Even though in America there is peace and it is forever daytime, he leans across the waves and sighs: *It is still evening, it is always nightfall along the 'ramparts,' on the battlements of an old Europe at war*. Or let him say, 'old England at war,' for it is, above all, England's ramparts that draw the dark philosopher: *I don't know how to describe the narrow . . . stormy passage (the Channel at night) from which I perceive the shores, the cliffs. . . .*

And these, as it happens, are the self-same cliffs that, from his rooms in Oxford, Professor Ryle can see, or tries to see. 'We can,' he says, '*describe* the danger of the cliffs in Sussex, but we cannot *observe* the danger.' I am struck by this, by the fact that, of all the cliffs and all the edges in all the world, the cliffs that Ryle can describe from Oxford are the cliffs of Sussex. This is, I think, because he too went to a Sussex boarding school, a different one; for Ryle, the cliffs of Sussex are, above all, a danger to the schoolboy far from home. Cue my father; for these are surely the very cliffs, the very coast that he was trying, in the lounge, to describe, even observe. He said: 'the sea . . . the gun . . . the sand . . . legs . . . hands . . . trunk buried in the sand.'

Ryle is right; on these Sussex cliffs there are dangers that cannot be seen. If we were to see them we would ourselves become the wild children on the cliffs, as wild and mad as the boy on the cliff in our lounge. And what or who, if anything or anyone, did this boy really see on the mined and barbed-wired coast? The legs, the hands, the trunk buried in the sand – it is as if he is seeing someone merely playing at burial, a purely mock-internment, as always happened on summer holidays. In fact, it was usually my father to whom we gave the low-tide burial. (He said: 'they buried the dog'). So: should we say that he is simply misremembering, misinterpreting an old, white-framed, holiday snap?

I cannot tell, not yet; but there is a clue in the four loose children of the Manse. And there is another clue when, exactly a year later, on another sun-crashed day in May, RMS *Samaria* has taken him as far as possible from old Europe, exhausted by war, and he has landed in Quebec, exhausted by peace. The ship is in dock, and so too is time, and he is free to walk the cliffs; he writes, 'It is Sunday evening, it has been a beautiful day and Quebec is very lovely in the sunlight with gorgeous views from the cliffs over the St

Lawrence.' The light, just like the light, soon goes West; and my father carries back to the ship, folded in his hand, a photo of this view from the cliff. And wherever he went, for the rest of life, he took the view with him, under his hat and balanced on his head, just like a postcard that is too precious, in the end, to send, to let fall from your hand into the postal abyss. This view, those cliffs, he told himself, he would never let go.

I suppose that is why on summer holidays, when all of us were young and invariably damp, he would get us climbing to the top of hills; up there he too was a child, safe on the giant shoulders of another father. But all this changed the day when we, the children, were following him along a cliff-top in North Devon, just above Linton, the Valley of the Rocks. They also call it Little Switzerland. At a bend in the path our great leader, for some reason, turned round to see one of my sisters move towards the alpine edge, close her eyes, shorten her steps, and stretch out her arms as if feeling her way after dark. (*It is always nightfall along the ramparts*). This sister was, though, still yards from the edge of the cliff, so we the children laughed wildly; but the man who only watched had a suddenly lost and elsewhere face, as if he had glimpsed what ought not to be there, a far more sudden cliff. For a moment he just stood there, wordless – a *silent movie*, without the movie.

After that he began to tread in fear of heights and edges, both seen and unseen. *I . . . fall*, sings the Kid, *all the time.* My father's greatest fear was that his children would go too near an edge, particularly if it was the edge of a cliff. Something about children overlooking water, especially the sea, profoundly troubled him; and even when we were no longer children, he remained uneasy. Please allow me to tell you about a single moment in a single summer. It was 1981, about the time when my father was beginning to remember, and to forget. That summer he was forgetting what is so often forgotten – the usual: names, keys (*I had forgotten the keys*), children, where he had left the car, which side of the road to drive on, etc.; all forgotten, quite forgotten. (*It's you who are losing my memory*). And in this forgetful summer of ours, he and I helped to man a church-camp for boys on the Isle of Wight. One afternoon, during a war-game along the beach, I saw my father emerge from behind a sand dune. *You were there,* says the Kid, *in the sun.* And, just as my father reached the crest of the dune, looking (for all the world) like a hero of the desert, one particularly wild boy ran clean into him. For ever the first and last time, I heard my father swear – just one word, just one moment; for that endless moment, he was a picture that could not move, a statue in the sand and thinking of something else.

Perhaps, just perhaps, he was thinking of that famous painting called, *And when did you last see your father?* Or was I the one thinking about it? I'm not sure, but I do know that within this painting it is the seventeenth-century, England is at war with herself, and there is a boy in the foreground, the son of a Cavalier; the boy is being interrogated by Roundheads and they are after his royalist father, their enemy. I know this will sound all too neat but, believe me, this painting was a favourite of my father's. Or, at least, it was a painting he would quote.

And he loved to quote. He always had quotations tucked in his otherwise empty pockets, some picked from the pockets of Shakespeare and some the King James Bible; but the best thing about these quotations was that, in my father's head, a blatant head for blatant comedy, they all went wonderfully wrong. He used particularly to like, 'Look where sadly the poor wretch comes reading' (*Hamlet*), which always became 'Look where sadly the poor wretch come *weeding*' – this one he usually saved for me. Another favourite was 'Even the stars in their courses fought against Sisera' (King James), this would invariably turn into 'Even the stars in their *corsets* fought against Sisera.' As children we didn't actually get the 'corsets' for 'courses' substitution; but such was our extensive biblical education that we did know that Sisera had a tent-peg driven through his head – which, my father said, was enough to put anyone off a camping holiday.

Fortunately, my father's head was not driven through with a tent-peg but merely stuffed with cultural litter, most of it picked up from the pavements of Oxford, and this included, as I say, the Parliamentarians' question, 'And when did you last see your father?' In my case the answer to this question is 1981, as my father hesitated on a tower of sand; that was the last time I saw him, or the first time I did not see him; a mock-heroic statue in shorts, an effigy already toppling, in the sun.

The philosopher saw him too. At the time, in his notebook, he wrote:

What has entered my life this year, from May '80 to August '81, irreversibly I fear, is the sinister, not the disaster which still has something of the sublime about it . . . but the sinister . . . disaster losing even its height . . . while I was walking in the sun.

Our philosopher-in-the-sun is again speaking as if he is my father; for I am now more than ever persuaded that, in 1981, my father's flickering mind was the work, or after-work, of something 'sinister.' This is the word on which our philosopher-in-the-sun insists, and which beckons me back to the Oxford of April 1951, and to an undergraduate tempted by 'sinister pursuits.' In my father's house, 'sinister' has many meanings but among them is Oxford. I am, therefore, by no means surprised that the sinister enters the philosopher's life in May 1980, for this is just nine months after he revisited Oxford. Indeed, the Kid had returned in order to turn, one by one, the pages of a sinister medieval book:

all of a sudden . . . the small volume was there, on the table, I didn't dare touch it. I think that this lasted a rather long time, to the point of intriguing my neighbour. I felt watched just at the moment when I would have liked to be alone . . . Finally . . . I hold the book open with both hands.

Sitting in the same reading room, over twenty-five years later, I can still spy upon the hesitant philosopher; and, as he finally spreads wide the long-awaited book, I overhear him say, as if to himself: *everything seems open, offered, prepared for who knows what obscene dispensation of occult knowledge.* Afraid for his soul, I feel compelled to smash the library's glassy silence, a silence that has lasted for five hundred years; I shout: 'Don't look!' and then my sick-father joins in, crying (as he did): 'Don't read!' But it is too late, a quarter of a century too late; the philosopher has already looked, already read; the occult knowledge is his, and within a year the sinister has come his way – in 1981, when in Prague, he is falsely accused of smuggling drugs in his suit-case and is put in prison. He is cursed and knows it; he has discovered it is folly to open the occult Oxford book.

I have dreamt that he tried to warn me, the first time we met, just three years before his death, though I am not sure how many years before mine. We shared an evening meal, in a hotel near Loughborough; there were, for some lost reason, candles on the table, and around it we were six in all. I tentatively asked the world's most famous living philosopher several questions, each one more inane than the next, beginning (badly enough) with 'Do you like Bob Dylan?' before swiftly descending still further to 'Do you still enjoy football?' (To this, by the way, he said that he didn't play any more but that he still could not walk by a ball without kicking it). Terrified that I was hurtling helplessly towards 'What's your favourite book?', I attempted to arrest my descent by affecting a nonchalant air and making casual mention of Oxford; not quite in the form of a question but my pitiful words were begging, I guess, the Oxford question. He paused for a moment, and as he did so he looked (as someone said) like a painting; it was, I think, a trick of the light conjured by the candles, light seduced by the philosopher's Mediterranean skin.

This is a moment that I now tend to confuse with another man's memory of the painterly philosopher; this man, who knew the philosopher far better than I, tells me that in 2003, after a whole day of lectures, the Kid sat down for another meal. He was, by now, a condemned philosopher, the city of Athens having sentenced him to die of pancreatic cancer; but still he spoke and still he listened until, finally, as the meal was drawing to a close, he began ever so slowly to fall asleep, his head on the shoulder of his friend. No one knew quite what to say to a philosopher who was dreaming.

I don't quite know how this story ended, so I shall return to the meal we had three years before when I stupidly spoke to a painting about Oxford. The painting responded with just three words, a kind of telegram; he said (and I quote): 'Oxford – don't read.'

But how to read this 'don't read'? It is possible, I suppose, that it was a kind of calumny, a slur suggesting that at Oxford they do not read well, or closely, or even at all; *one must take into account*, he mutters, *the fact that they do not read.* Our philosopher had perhaps been listening to HTR; back in May 1951 this man-about-the-House declared, in a letter, that 'reading, at Oxford, is the last desperate resort of those who have, for the time being, no opportunity of talking, electioneering, dining out, or intriguing.' Wonderful.

There is, though, another way of decoding the philosopher's telegram, and that is as a warning; in other words as: 'Oxford – don't read! Don't read the Oxford book, the only Oxford book, that sinister, occult book!'

I can't, as yet, say what makes this book so sinister, but I think it may have something to do with its being written in Latin. It must be understood, and quickly, that Latin is a kind of curse. Just ask the weak scholar about Latin and he will cry 'Horror!'; so too the echo-Kid, who is branded with Latin like a tattoo, like a mark of Adenoidal ownership – looking back to the occupied days, he remarks that *the little Latin I know . . . {I} begun to learn . . . when Vichy had made it, I believe, obligatory in the first form.* When, thirty-six years later, the philosopher sits alone in the Bodleian it is not just the book before him that is sinister but the non-simple fact that he can decipher its Latin. He reads (he suspects) exactly as the Adenoids, via Vichy, had taught him to do.

And he is, as it happens, on to something; for within just nine years he will be all but accused of reading like a Fascist, as if blinded by a flick of Adenoidal light. This was in 1987, in the wake of a terrible storm that blew around and about the Kid's late friend and intellectual ally, Professor Paul de Man, of Yale. (By the way, I often think that the name 'Paul' must have always hit hard the Kid's ear, it being the name of the Kid's unfathomably dead brother: *Paul . . . dead I know not how or from what . . .*). Sorry, I have lost my way among names, and must turn back to the de Man storm. This dramatic change in the weather followed a revelation made just three years after de Man's death; the revelation was that de Man had not always been on the side of the intellectual angels, and that in fact he had once belonged, so to speak, to the devil's school of thought.

This had been in Brussels during the war when, in 1940, the Adenoid Hynkel Show high-kicked its way into town. At the time Paul was still a student, just twenty; but the boy was already old with war. As soon as the Show arrived he had, like two million others, run west, through France, hoping to cross a border to neutral Spain; but there was no crossing. After a summer hesitating in the Pyrenees he crawled back to Brussels, with his partner. There was, by now, a child on the way. There always is. Then, in November 1940, the Gestapo interrogated young Paul in his apartment; they wanted to know whose side he was on. So, what could or should Paul have done? Indeed, what would *you* have done – resisted, collaborated or merely co-operated?

Please don't ask me. My orders are simply to career on, tell my story, and say that Paul was soon writing for Belgium's biggest daily newspaper, *Le Soir*, then under new, Adenoidal management. The Great Dictator was busy dictating, and most of the newly-appointed journalists were busy setting it down. To be fair to a dead man, Paul was writing as a freelance cultural correspondent, and most of his one hundred-and-seventy articles, usually on literary topics, are uncontroversial, even banal. Mind you, Paul does seem to have had Adenoidal moments; as when he describes the German invader as 'dignified . . . just and . . . humane.' Indeed, so dignified is the Great Invader, so profound the movement He embodies, that He is, for Paul, not only the Great Dictator but also the Great Prognosticator. In October 1941, looking forward (over his shoulder), Paul hastily writes that, 'the future of Europe can be envisioned only in the framework of the possibilities and needs of the German spirit.'

These needs (they go without saying) included the moving on of the Jews. And so it is that, in March 1941, Paul speculates upon how little difference it might make to European culture if there were created 'a Jewish colony isolated from Europe.' Some say he was thinking of the Madagascar Plan, a scheme to put to sea thousands of displaced German Jews and giving them leave to land on a beautiful African island, an Adenoidal dream earnestly discussed with Herr Hynkel by both British and French governments. Others say Paul was thinking of something worse. Still others, however, point to the witness of Esther, Esther Sluszny, a Jewish acquaintance of Paul's who would, in the end, recall how he had once sheltered both her and her husband when, one thin Adenoidal night, they were beached on the streets of Brussels long after the high-tidal hour of curfew.

Paul, I see, did at least one good thing in the occupied dark, but it is clear, like air, that he also thought at least one bad thing in the dark, in the evening, in *Le Soir*, or what embittered Belgians called *Le Soir volé* – 'the stolen evening.'

Stolen it may be, but the evening does not simply go away, is not dismantled at once. Even fifty years later, even in night-less America, a memory of evening lingers. In 1993, in California, the philosopher murmurs, *It is still evening . . . on the battlements of an old Europe at war.*

CHAPTER NINE

Stolen Evening

Over here, in America, where Paul, our friend, had lived and worked since 1948, we had thought that the shadows of European evening could not fall on us, could not arch right across the Atlantic. The day we discovered that they did, that the man called Man had hidden these shadows in his eyes, was a hideous day, all swollen with world and fact. All of a sudden, something had actually happened in our universe, in the still, slow and eventless universe of literary criticism. The silent movie of artful reading was, at last, a Talkie; it suddenly had something to say, or rather scream as the 'Paul de Man Affair' was now the film showing everywhere. Very soon big-selling newspapers such as *The New York Times*, the *Nation* and *Newsweek* were running articles on the sheer shock of it all.

And the iron screw of scandal was given another and final turn when they said that Paul's widow (also our friend) was not his first wife, nor indeed his only wife, that he had still been married to his first and Belgian wife when he married again, this time in America, within three years of his landing. Paul, it seems, had mistaken the Atlantic for a divorce, an ocean for an annulment. Paul, our friend, had misread the sea.

Once this was also revealed, de Man the dead man was posthumously tried, judged and damned; and so too was our 'school of deconstruction,' as they called it. They, the Enemy, were swift to say that deconstruction was, with or without knowing it, an elaborate way of getting the hell out of history. And they had a point: after all, and after Paul, deconstruction does announce that every utterance shifts and cracks, that meanings can never be nailed, histories never tracked down, pasts never properly known. So, yes, if during the war, way back in castle Europe, we had painted upon the battlement words that we now regret, it might well make sense, once safe across the widowing water, to question the possibility of ever finally catching the breath of what we say, or of what we have ever said, to anyone, even to those closest to us. Perhaps, just perhaps, that was, all along, why we said that our words will always mean something other than we intended . . . the poor and abandoned Intended. It was, some might say, a way of erasing the past, of questioning it out of existence, reading and rereading it until nothing is (quite) left standing, standing alone. If this was deconstruction, then it was (we confess) like a defeated army of occupation that retreats backwards, always ensuring that no evidence of atrocities is left in its wake – no facts, nothing substantive.

I am sorry, this last extended simile is more stolen evening. I stole it from a newly-dead man, a Jew; I rifled his pockets. His name was Emmanuel Levinas, a thinker who had long been drawn to the work of our Kid. Then, one day, as if looking straight into the sun, Monsieur Levinas somehow mistook the Kid for an army, saying:

'When I read him, I always recall the exodus of 1940. A retreating military unit in an as yet unsuspecting locality, where cafés are open, where the ladies visit the "ladies' fashion store," where the hairdressers dress hair and bakers bake; where viscounts meet other viscounts and tell each other stories of viscounts, and where, an hour later, everything is deconstructed and devastated.'

In 1996 this astonishing passage was brought to the attention of the philosopher, and they said to him something like,

'Doesn't it bother you? Look at what they are accusing you of now. You are like the enemy army!'

He paused, but not for long; he knew the passage well. He then turned and said to them: *But when you see what he says, I mean, that when I passed through it was as if the German army had hit town . . . it makes you wonder.*

So it does, but the Kid, of all people, has somehow misread the passage – he's got the wrong bloody army; the only army that marched backwards in 1940 was the French army, not the German. Monsieur Levinas means to say (whatever that means) that, although the Kid devastates our everyday lives (our hairdressing, our baking, our storytelling) he does this not as foe but as friend – he may do violence but it is necessary violence. For Monsieur L., all this hairdressing, all this baking, all this peace, it needs to be devastated; he wants us to know that the terrible army passing through is on our side. But the philosopher does not get Levinas's message; he thinks it is a bullet. After the Paul de Man affair the Kid is so used to being accused, so used to being framed, that he immediately sits in the place of the guilty, takes a seat at Nuremberg.

It is, though, the case that the Kid was, in general, quick to accuse himself: *I always feel guilty*, he sings. This he would sing, again and again, to the damned and damning music of endless duty; *responsibility*, he would sing, *is infinite, or it is not*. This singing philosopher thinks that we are responsible for everything and everyone, or that we are responsible for nothing and no-one. I am smashed by this, as good as devastated. And I accept that it does help to explain why, when faced with Monsieur L.'s peculiar wartime analogy, our philosopher should so readily mistake himself for a terrible invading army. But I cannot help thinking that this mistake also has something to do with Paul de Man, something to do with our philosopher having somehow dreamt Paul's secret history long before Paul's death, and even longer before that history had been floodlit with ten-thousand headlights.

The philosopher himself insists that he had never suspected Paul, never had even an intimation of Paul's part in the stealing of evening. And I do, you know, believe him. But had the philosopher never dreamt his way to suspicion? I ask, merely ask, because, well, for a start, everyone knew that Paul's famous uncle, Hendrik de Man, had been a kind of collaborator, and that he was convicted in absentia after the war, before dying in exile, in Switzerland. It is true that most of Paul's colleagues believed, or assumed, that Paul, in contrast, had run with the angels. But our philosopher may have had reason to dream otherwise; if only because he did know that a fragment of Paul's life had been buried. The philosopher made this clear very late in the day, around about 2000. It was then that he wrote this:

'Toward the end of the 70s, at Yale, Paul . . . said to me one day something like this . . . "If you want to know a part of my life, read . . . 'Hölderlin en Amérique.' Henri Thomas, whom I knew here, in America after the war, published this text in *Mercure de France*, and it was reprinted [in 1964] . . . as a novel [called] . . . *Le parjure*. I confess that I did not rush out looking for the book . . . .Years later, at a bookseller's in Nice, where I was on vacation, I came upon *Le parjure*. I read it very quickly, but very quickly understood that the principal character . . . Stéphane Chalier, resembled in certain features the real person of Paul de Man; [the novel told] . . . the story of a second marriage, in the United States, whilst a first marriage in Europe had not ended in legal divorce. Hence the accusation of bigamy and perjury . . . .After my reading I remember that I wrote to Paul de Man, a few words, as discreetly as possible, in conformity with the customary tone of our exchanges, saying that I had been 'bouleversé,' bowled over. We never spoke about it again; just as I never spoke about it with Henri Thomas whom I didn't know at the time and whom I nevertheless telephoned, years later, in 1987 . . . to hear his response to what . . . had just [been] discovered about the past . . . of Paul de Man.'

I sometimes think it odd that the Kid had known for so long that there was something silent about the film of Paul de Man, that this was a secret European film hidden, for all to see, in a novel. And as I fall, again, asleep from a tower of postcards, I fall to wondering if the Kid might also have known that Paul had once been a wartime journalist. To work this out all the Kid had to do was to ask a mutual friend, a Yale colleague called Geoffrey Hartman.

Hartman is also a famous figure from the school of deconstruction; and he too, like Paul, had arrived in America with a bagful of European evening. In March 1939 Hartman was a Jew on a train leaving Frankfurt; it was a kindertransport train, an exodus train for Jewish children. The boy himself was in a carriage crammed with boys; but his closest companion on the long iron road was an elegant violin. By the time, however, the train had reached London (Waterloo, to be precise) the battered violin was barely a violin and, within months, it was something else altogether; its body had cracked and, for the first time ever, the boy could see inside. There he saw a label and a signature which, together, revealed the secret that his companion had once been a priceless Stradivarius. It was now a priceless post-card.

On another train, at another time and in another country, there was a girl that the boy from Frankfurt had never met; her train was going not to London Waterloo but to Bergen-Belsen. There she stayed, until the Liberation. One day, in America, their trains collided, and there and then they were married, man and woman.

I am sorry, I have been distracted yet again; it is just that this man from Yale spoke about these trains the day we met, a couple of years ago, just before Christmas. As we sat in a university restaurant, and even as he spoke of kindertransport and Belsen, his words moved barefoot in and out of the yuletide musak that insisted on playing for ever: 'I Believe in Angels,' 'When a Child is Born,' 'Simply Having a Lovely Christmas Time' and back again to 'I Believe in Angels.' Our Jewish guest, a man full of books, was not derailed by this eternal circle of Christian banality, the man's shoeless progress all the while taking us to the far, far side of banality of any kind. And so he spoke of the girl from Belsen (she who was not, by the way, one of those treated to a party in Oxford). And so he spoke of his dead friend Paul.

What the man said of the friend he had lost was this: that he had always wondered why Paul's list of publications only dated back to 1948, the year in which Paul had been storm-blown backwards across the Atlantic. The man added that he had, one day, back in the seventies, put this question to Paul himself, who simply looked around from behind a book and replied: 'Mere journalism.' The man did not question his friend Paul any further, and never thought again of Paul the journalist, or at least not until 1987.

However (and here's the sting) I once dreamt that the Kid also knew something of Paul's journalistic pre-history, and that he left a coded sign to that effect in this strange book of his, this whole book of cryptograms. Try this one, for example:

. . . EGEK HUM XSR STR . . .

When you know what it means give me a ring. But don't worry, the de Manian clue is far easier to grasp. It is to be found in three words that were first jotted down in 1979 and, like most clues, comes hot-foot from nowhere. You already know the clue; it is, quite simply, *Dupont and Dupond*, Hergé's pair of bowler-hatted detectives. And what makes them a clue as to the wartime journalism of Paul de Man is that the two detectives made their very first appearance in a story of their own as a daily feature in *Le Soir*. This was in September 1943, just one year after Paul was writing for the same paper. Two detectives in hats are, it turns out, on the amazing case of Paul de Man no less than eight years before anyone else.

And it is a case that leads, in the end, to the case of Jacques Derrida; for when, in 1987, they find out that Paul had helped purloin the Belgian evening it is the Kid who is left to answer for this thief of the night. I do think, however, that the Kid had almost foreseen this moment, and had most nearly foreseen it when he was in Oxford; there being something about this famous home to impossible loyalty which somehow, in the mind of the Kid, already connects with Paul de Man.

In 1979, when Derrida visits Brussels, the city of Paul's un-fought war, the Kid sends a postcard to his friend back in Yale; it is not, though, a post-card of Brussels but yet another of those Oxford cards: *I just sent one to Paul de Man*, he says. And he writes, I imagine, something like this:

```
Dear Paul,

Wish you were here (wherever 'here' is . . . but I
think it's probably Oxford, as you can tell from the
card).
Yours,
Jacques

PS They said I would have a lovely time.
```

But he didn't have a lovely time; not in Oxford, not when they openly denounced his work, nor when he endured a silent trial at the end of his lecture, nor (indeed) when they tempted him with suicide. *At Oxford,* he says, *I have misadventures*. And it is, in part, these misadventures that, for the Kid, connect Oxford with de Man; they are, you see, de Manic misadventures:

— first, the **denunciation** – in 1943 Paul was one of forty-four *Le Soir* contributors who were publicly condemned by the Belgian Resistance;

— second, the **trial** – in 1945, suspected of collaboration, Paul was interrogated by a military tribunal in Antwerp;

— third (and finally), **suicide** – an option taken by others in Paul's position, including, some say, his uncle, on June 20th 1953; his car hit that train, the one in Switzerland.

Like the train no doubt, the uncle was bang on time, for exactly sixteen years before, to the very day, Paul's mother had also hit a train, an invisible one as, on June 20th 1937, she sentenced herself to dance by hanging. It was, perhaps, a way of remembering the death of her son Hendrik, who had died in 1936 – also (so it happens) on June 20th. Hers was an anniversary hanging, and it was Paul, her sixteen-year-old son, who found her, and had the task of taking down the slowly revolving dancer. (The living-room boy once said: 'Get her down! . . . My mother, I saw her . . . Hanging, I saw her').

Denunciation, trial, and the slow ghost of suicide – Paul's wartime epic is rerun, frame by frame, in the Kid's Oxford movie. That, as I say, is one reason the Kid's mind wanders back to Oxford whenever he thinks about his friend. Like when, in 1984, just months after Paul's death, the Kid tries to remember a letter he once wrote to Paul; the Kid struggles, however, and eventually fails to recall what he wrote – so simply says: *the only thing that I today remember is that I wrote it to him from Oxford.*

```
Dear Paul,

I am writing to you from Oxford.

Love,
Jacques
```

Memory may have a mind of its own, but it is still strange that the philosopher remembers only Oxford. It is even stranger that he bothers to *mention* that he remembers only Oxford. It's more than we need to know. It's like writing again from Oxford, like going back yet again to Oxford, to yet again write to Paul from Oxford. The philosopher does not yet know about his friend's unspoken war; however, it is almost as if he does, for what connects Paul to Oxford is, above all, I now see, an unusual talent for a certain kind of closeted war.

Consider, for instance, our Oxonian dramatis personae: Ayer, Austin, Masterman, Ryle, and Hugh Trevor-Roper – they all fought secretive wars; indeed, HTR contrived to fight a war that, like that of de Man, was not only secret but graced by a certain ambiguity. When, in 1968, HTR is asked to write about Kim Philby, his wartime colleague and infamous traitor, the BBC's favourite radio don, our historian of the air, decides he will climb to the top of Tom Tower and broadcast to the world a revelation concerning his own hour of infamy. He announces, through a crackling megaphone, that one night in 1941, he was 'summoned to be dismissed' on the grounds that his superior, known as 'C', suspected him, 'with' (he crackles) 'some justice,' of 'irreverent thoughts and dangerous contacts'; 'I was,' he bellows, 'secretly denounced as being probably in touch with the Germans.' At the trial, in camera, HTR was acquitted but 'it was,' he shouts, 'a tight squeak.'

Like Paul de Man, HTR had a war that begs questions but, again like de Man, the boy can't help it; HTR is intellectually predisposed to fight a questionable war, a war in which he demonstrates the sheer impossibility of loyalty, of any simple sense of who is friend and who is foe. Whether in his grey Bentley, or on his hunting horse, HTR moves so fast that such distinctions are blurred; this Cavalier is all too busy with 'the zigzag progress' of his life, buffeted as he is from day to day by 'enraged husbands, enraged papists, exacting editors, and inebriated Bolsheviks.' It is no wonder he should insist that most of history is 'pure farce,' for HTR is, at times, himself the great farceur, a zig-zag man who could not help but have irreverent thoughts and dangerous contacts. To turn all this another way: HTR was, if you will, the Paul de Man of his day, Oxford's answer to the infinite ironist of Yale.

By the way, in this connection, I should mention that the two men shared the same secret soubriquet, the name of that elusive god of writing and thieves – the one the Romans called Mercury and the Greeks called Hermès. In 1948, when Paul set up, in Brussels, his own printing press it went by the name of Hermes; meanwhile, back in Oxford, HTR was busy assuming the *nom-de-plume* of Mercury. As you may have detected, *The Spectator*'s special Oxford correspondent, 'Mercurius Oxoniensis,' was none other than HTR.

Hermes and Mercury, hermetic and mercurial, irreverent and dangerous, our friends HTR and PdM are (I think) the Thomson and Thompson or *Dupont et Dupond* of our story. And, as you know, this comedy duo, 'they resemble twins who are constantly lost, running to catch up, beside the question, always on the wrong trail' – so wrong, in fact, that they end up running, helter-skelter, straight into those oncoming and sombre twins, Good and Evil, aka Innocence and Guilt. If you don't believe me, listen to what Paul de Man had to say in 1979.

'It is always possible,' he said, 'to face up to any experience (to excuse any guilt), because the experience always exists simultaneously as fictional discourse and as empirical event and it is never possible to decide which one of the two possibilities is the right one. The indecision makes it possible to excuse the bleakest of crimes because, as a fiction, it escapes from the constraints of guilt and innocence.'

It is possible, you see, 'to excuse any guilt.' Every crime, even the bleakest, is some kind of fiction, an account, a form of words that, inevitably, are frail, alterable, mercurial, hermetic. So, don't go there, don't go back there, back to the scene of the crime.

But HTR did. He had to; simply because, as an historian of the last days of Adenoid Hynkel, it was his task to meet, interview, and listen to the stories of those people who had breathed and sweated closest to Herr Hynkel. At the very same time as he was supposed to be tutoring young Schad, HTR was busy meeting such as Hynkel's photographer, Hynkel's personal pilot, Hynkel's executor, Hynkel's valet, Hynkel's chief body-guard, and (still worse) Herr Himmler's masseur. For HTR, one day it was a tutorial in Oxford with my father, the next day a meeting in Berlin with a man who had flown Herr Hynkel, or taken his photo, or guarded his body, or brushed down his jacket or (still worse) massaged the pink marsh-mallow flesh of Reichsführer-SS.

In 1952, HTR wrote that, 'these are the people among whom my life must now and then be spent.' HTR had to get as close as possible to the humdrum life of the bleakest of all possible crimes and bleakest of all possible criminals; as close as the lens of a camera, the next seat in a car, or even the jacket he wears. HTR got as close to the event as was allowed by its bodyguard of sublimely ordinary people – people who iron shirts, fly planes and take photos; people who smile, shake your hand, and sit down with you, or call you on the phone, even sit beside you in a car. Like when, in 1955, HTR hired a car in Munich and drove all the way to Pilsensee with Herr Hynkel's pilot, Hans Baur. 'He was,' writes HTR, 'a well-spoken man . . . and we talked all the way and got on very well with each other.' As they continued to talk, the former-pilot explained that he had once been inter-rogated very closely by the damnable Russians.

'Why?,' asked HTR.

'Because,' replied Baur, 'I happened to watch the shooting, in Simferopol, of 20,000 Jews.' Herr Baur went on to explain that he had not taken part himself but that he had had 'the good fortune' (his words) to have a friend in the SS who took him there as 'a *Zuschauer* (a spectator).'

As a pilot Herr Baur, I suppose, is accustomed to seeing the world from a distance, from, let us say, twenty-thousand feet – one foot for each and every Jewish body that jerked, swayed, and then toppled. One damned foot after another, and so on and on, twenty-thousand times; for each foot there was one shot, one report. Thus speaks the pilot to the don, in the tutorial, in the car.

So: are they still getting on well? I don't know, but HTR did once happen to say, 'I dislike shooting parties: I can't hit the birds.' He was explaining why he could not accept an invitation to the Astors.

I remember now that my father once said: 'Went in a car . . . guns . . . kill kill . . . don't shoot.' I don't suppose he ever said this in a tutorial, to HTR, in one of their car-less, Christ Church tutorials; but had he done so, HTR might well have understood – since HTR knew what it meant to have someone tell you all about the last shooting-party they had witnessed. Mind you, HTR may not have actually believed my wide-eyed father, not after HTR's experience in the car with Herr Baur; not after the discovery that it was only ten thousand Jews that were murdered at Simferopol, that there may have been twenty-thousand shoes but there were, in fact, only ten-thousand corpses. That's all; the numbers had been enlarged. The lesson is clear: we must count bodies with care, must distinguish them from shoes.

I should here mention that my father once suddenly began counting; he said: '6, 7, 8, 9, 10, 11, 12, 13' Why, I now wonder, did he start at six? If he too were counting the Jewish dead, and doing so in millions, then he too was exaggerating and is clearly not to be trusted. We must be careful; it is possible for a figure to be horribly swollen. This is what that history man called David Irving infamously said. He is the one they eventually put in an Austrian prison for saying that there were no gas chambers, or at least that it was not six million that had died. I should add that HTR (it is claimed) once wrote that Dr Irving was 'one of the few guides I would entirely trust . . . indefatigable in pursuit of evidence [and] fearless in the face of it.'

HTR would soon change his mind about Irving; this early praise was penned long before Irving had (you might say) holocausted the Holocaust. At this point Irving was merely arguing that, until late 1943, Herr Hynkel had no idea that the Final Solution was happening; that what killing there was had not been scripted by the Great Dictator. But, nevertheless, Irving is right, we must not believe every story of killing we come across; that man in the hire-car was exaggerating, so too perhaps the boy in our lounge. I must, therefore, hold lightly to my father's words; a memory may kill many more than a pistol ever could. The weak scholar Schad (John Schad) must understand this. He needs to recognise (like the strong scholar Irving) that we must go through the ash with care, must be prepared to find fewer dead than we had expected: fewer, not that many, hardly any . . . none, in fact. We must, as HTR is said to have said, be 'fearless in the face if it' – fearless in the face of it, and fearless in the face of not-it, of nothing. Nothing, its face (the face of nothing) may even now be pressed up against the memory-glass, its nose squashed, its lips open and swollen, its cheeks grotesquely inflated like a drowned man. The true sleuth is prepared to go face-to-face with monstrous nothing, perhaps even kiss it, the obscene corpse that never was, the never-never dead boy.

There is, I think, an irony hereabouts, the irony that, in 1945, Oxford's famous sleuth had gone to Berlin to say, before the world, something like:

'Yes there *is* a copse, the old boy is dead, he did die, we didn't just imagine it; we may not have the body but we do know there was one, we just do, the evidence is overwhelming. Some, like those inebriated Bolsheviks, say that we in the West are imagining it all, but we're not — there was a boy and he is dead, most certainly dead. It is no fantasy.'

I will cling to this verdict. The Sleuth of Oxford is, I find, my kind of detective, the kind I shall employ to solve my father's case, the case that I clutch with stiffening fingers. I have always needed a sleuth who is prepared to believe that something in the way of death really did happen.

It is true that, on one famous occasion, HTR famously mistook a fake past for a real one, but this could happen to anyone, even you. It happened to HTR in April 1983, when he was taken down into a darkened Zurich bank-vault to gaze upon almost sixty beautifully hand-written notebooks. Having gazed, eyes wide at the sight of a wonderful hand, he paused and then said 'Yes.' Re-emerging from the Swiss cave, and still blinded by flash-bulbs, he declared, again before the world, that these notebooks were the lost and secret diaries of Adenoid Hynkel. For forty years, they said, the diaries had been hidden in an East German hayloft, just like a poor fallen airman way behind enemy lines. Within days, however, of HTR's authenticating 'yes,' it was discovered that the diaries had been composed by a pseudo-Hynkel. Hynkel himself had not written them, he was not the author, it was not his hand, not his writing, not his paper — the master mind of the bleakest of crimes, the man swollen with the ashes of six million, had not lent over these pages, not breathed over them, the shadow of his lowered head had not crashed upon the once sheet-white, virgin paper.

HTR had been wrong, wrong about the author, and said so, to anyone that would listen to him. The man from The Home for Lost Causes and Unpopular Names was himself now lost and unpopular; meanwhile, in the press (said a friend), *Schadenfreude* was everywhere.

Just a few months later, in Yale, Paul de Man would die; and even as he died he would say, as always, that (when it comes to writing) there never is, was or will be someone there, purely and simply there — or at least not the someone you thought would be there. (Tell this to HTR). The very last entry in Paul's notebook, made in the Fall of 1983, when he knew his body was fatally inscribed with cancer, is this: 'the referential function is a trap.'

Before finally going, Paul de Man wanted us to know that it is folly to insist there is something to which language really points, however wildly it waves its wonderful arms. To insist that there is anything purely and simply outside, or beyond the four padded walls of language is a snare. As long as you are possessed by such a ridiculous fantasy you are caught like a fox in a trap – like a fox that is slowly dehydrating, incontinent with fear. Paul would not be seen dead in such a trap. But he was, and he knew he would be; in the entry in his notebook he writes that, though a trap, the referential function is 'inevitable,' unavoidable. He knew that, once dead, he would be ensnared in the referential trap, the history trap. And so too, in 1983, was HTR – caught in the trap of authentication, there for all to see.

CHAPTER TEN

High Places

In the end, the end that came in 1983, Hermes and Mercurius, Yale and Oxford, dead man and derided man are both caught cold and in the same ironic trap. And as I stare at the two, for the very last time, they seem as if to throw around each other unwanted arms and legs. I continue to stare as Hermes and Mercurius meet, entangle, and become one flesh; and as this happens they together spell out an ancient name barely recalled – that name is: Hermes Mercurius Trismegistus, the philosopher of ancient Egypt.

It is said that Trismegistus (it means, 'the Triple Master') was a master of paradox and yet servant of truth who, from time to time, would say something to prove it – something like: 'Providence is a circle, the centre of which is everywhere and the circumference is nowhere.'

I do realise that, right now, dear Dr Watson might interject, saying, 'But, this hardly looks like a clue toward the eventual resolving of the damnably difficult case of your father.'

To this I would respond by effortlessly remarking that, 'Hermes Mercurius Trismegistus is, to this day, the source of much that passes for esoteric wisdom behind the slow doors of that world-wide secret society known as Freemasonry.'

In reply, Dr Watson might well cry, 'But, in heaven's name, man, what on earth have the Masons got to do with our case?'

I would, though, conclude our pleasant Socratic dialogue with this: that very early on in my father's illness, late in 1983 (I think), my father received a telephone call; and someone at the far end of the line (I forget who) happened to mention, just in passing, that one of the leading members of the church at which my father was then helping was also a Freemason. At once, I am told, my father fell upon the chair by the phone and, handing the receiver to my mother, he simply wept; he had not wanted to weep down the phone. *Never . . . have I cried so much. On the telephone, you understand nothing.*

This is a thread, a line I must follow. The Kid is certainly thinking along this line, along the line of what he calls (under my breath) *a very powerful secret society in the open air.* The Kid might almost be referring to the strange society that is philosophy, a society within which you will find (whispers Gilbert Ryle) 'an almost Masonic reserve.' The truth, however, is that the society which the Kid has in mind is (wait for it) . . . the international community of collectors of post-cards.

Such people are, perhaps, rather alarming in their way, but they are not quite the secret society I had in mind as the final solution to my mystery; there is not, I think, quite enough ceremony, dressing-up, and ritual sacrifice among the collectors of post-cards. If they ever were a society dedicated to occult practices they would, you feel, go about their infernal father's business in a very decent way (tombola, bring-and-buy, cake-stalls etc.). And I suppose much the same could be said of the Freemasons, especially of those at my father's school, which then (like most public schools at the time) had a Masonic Lodge for its old boys.

There was no secrecy about this; a quick glance at the school calendar makes clear that the Lodge used to meet regularly in London and that, once a year, it would come down to the school, on the third Saturday in May. This latter arrangement in itself inspires confidence; anyone who spends time counting Saturdays is, I feel, bound to be a decent sort. On a third Saturday in May there were, I suggest, very few bohemian ties or homburg hats, and certainly no Nazi manners, the Freemasons being (please note) high on Adenoid Hynkel's list of undesirables. I also take heart from the fact that these annual gatherings included taking tea with the Head and listening to a talk on a topic of general interest, such as the fascinating and well-received address (with accompanying slide-show) given by H. G. Davis Esq. on Saturday May 17th 1947. His topic was 'The History of British Railways' – an unlikely code for arcane ritual, I think you will agree. After all, our national rail network tends not to lend itself to the rolling up of trouser legs, the wearing of aprons, the swearing of oaths, and pledging (should you ever break those oaths) to have your throat cut, your tongue torn out and your body buried in the sands at low watermark. Equally reassuring is the fact that the Master of the Lodge has no less than three Christian names, whilst the Secretary gives as his postal address a particularly leafy road in the better part of Beckenham, just by the cricket ground and well above the watermark.

The Secretary at this time is particularly keen to attract new members; throughout the war the lodge has held no meetings, or at least no official meetings, none that appear on the calendar. Hence the Secretary's enthusiasm 'to bring to the notice of old boys the existence of the Lodge.' It should, though, be added that being an old boy does not in itself entitle you to membership of the Lodge – it simply makes you 'eligible' for membership. I have no idea what other criteria might be evoked, but moral and even spiritual standards would seem to have been very high. I am here thinking of Charles, the Headmaster in *Which Way Came Death?*, who is described both as 'a complete Freemason' and also as one who 'really minded about Christianity.'

His wife, I would admit, was not quite such a good egg. Blackmailing a bounder may be forgivable, but it is hard to overlook her tendency, as Charles himself complains, to go about 'saying appalling things.' Among the favourite topics of the Headmaster's wife are, I am afraid, the following:

1. 'the Sterilization of the Unfit';

2. her willingness to hang a murderer, or in her own words, 'to stand on the scaffold and work the drop myself';

3. the 'incredibly voluptuous' nature of marsh-mallows, especially the pink ones;

4. the fact that 'sometimes it is our duty to forget, especially if remembering means distress for others.'

So speaks the Headmaster's wife before the world, and before the war; indeed, if we were to glance at the real-life Headmaster's wife, the author herself, we would add that it was also before her son was killed at Dunkirk. The boy did not come back, he was trapped on the killing beach, on the coast, in Hitler's snare; this fox did not grow old.

His sister, she did; or at least his sister-in-fiction, the fictional daughter of the fictional Head. An elegant and much-desired figure she, like her mother, speaks with a loosened tongue, saying things like (and I quote): 'Half the rows in a place like this are due to repressed sex,' and 'It's a wonder there are not more murders in public schools when you come to think of it.'

So, let us not think of it (murder, that is), and instead recall that Charles, the Headmaster, seems to be a fine man; perhaps a little open to blackmail, given the women on the loose in his house, but he is surely not the sort to tolerate secret societies – apart, I suppose, from his own Masonic Lodge, with whom he breaks biscuits, every May.

Mind you, during the war, the school keeps under its hat and up its sleeve a thousand secrets, codes, and ciphers. In July 1943, in the school magazine, the word is that 'the School's very own Home Guard now flashes out messages in Morse Code across the North Field.' At this, the philosopher knowingly whispers: *an emitting-receiving device . . . secret society in the open air*; for a moment, I think the Kid has been reading the school magazine, perhaps while at Oxford, in the Bodleian, where old issues can be found. I would love to think so. I would not, however, like to think that old-boy

Hynkel ever leafed through the magazine – a possibility that its editors do entertain, albeit with a smile. But they can't be too careful since what the school platoon flashed north across the playing field, through the summer's softest air, was the whereabouts of anti-aircraft units, each one being moved, like a chess piece, at night, every night.

But during war, time (some of the time) moves as quick as fear, and so too the technology of secrecy. Keenly aware of the limitations of Morse, the platoon has, by December 1943, 'turned from the simplicities and naivety of the signalling lamps to the intricacies of the No. 18 Wireless Set.' Their training is not yet complete but the boys now live among days when, as they say,

'With awe we study cryptic messages on the board announcing to the fortunate initiate that "netting time" is at 15.00 hrs – frequency 7,500 kilo-cycles. We hear the initiate mutter vaguely to himself such mysterious injunctions as "Wilco" or "Roger" and transmit vital messages that would shock the tender ears of the unsuspecting instructor.'

Quite what these shocking messages were, I may never know. I will suspect, though, that they had most to do with what, in 1941, the boy-editors of the magazine call 'the idiosyncrasies and *sub-rosa* activities of the staff.' These include, we are told, the operations of 'the science master' who is (by the way) 'suspected of having mined the school, with the intention of blowing it up when it was next visited by some high official from the War Office.' Perhaps this was one of the myriad secrets that ghosted in and out of the No. 18 Wireless set, electrified postmen peddling through the night on the ethereal wheels of 7,500 kilo-cycles. If so, HTR and the Radio Security Service would have been very interested. And perhaps they were, perhaps they did listen-out for the explosive master prepared to blow his own school to kingdom-come just in order to take out the man from the War Office; perhaps this master was the real-life bounder with the Nazi manner – if so, we have on our trembling hands a suicide-bomber with a homburg on his head.

Secrets, secrets, secrets. It is no wonder the boys were so adept at code; it was an art they perfected, and no text was more coded than the school magazine. Its seraphic editors openly confess to this, whispering that 'the more numerous and juicier the titbits of local scandal that the Editor can get pass the censor the "better."' So, dear boys, read carefully; read the whole magazine with an analytical mind: the editorial, the notices, and the poems too. Consider, in particular, a poem published in October 1940 called 'Very Queer.' I have selected, or isolated just the fourth stanza which goes like this (the blanking of names is there in the original):

When the changes and the chances of this fleeting world have fled,
  And you change your sense of joy for pious fear;
Into Chapel comes a small brown dog, with waving tail and head –
  It is queer, O Mr C——t, — very queer!
And when the service finishes, the organ starts to blow;
  As its pond'rous rumblings take you in the rear;
There will creep into the volunt'ry a tune you think you know, —
  It is queer, O Mr D——s, — very queer!

To summarise: there is a dog in the chapel and an organ takes you in the rear. (The boy in our lounge, he said: 'Young men turn to do it.') Yes it is queer, I fear, a queer kind of code, but not one I would dare to break.

Besides, the boys are the real code-breakers, they are the ones who can identify the truly cryptic word. Take, for instance, the 1943 Higher School Certificate in Mathematics; for most candidates this was just another exam paper, but to one anonymous boy at my father's school it was a cunningly concealed cryptogram. This nameless pupil records his act of decoding in the school magazine, in December 1943; it is a spell-binding work of quite insane intelligence called 'A Case from an Amateur Detective's Casebook.' Here our boy-Sherlock reveals in astonishing detail how, when first confronted with the seemingly innocent exam, he did nothing so naïve as simply answer any of the questions. Instead, ever alert to the possibility of cipher, he descends on one particular question, Question 4; having read it through just once, our hero 'immediately realised its sinister implications.' This so-called Question 4 was not really a question at all, being without either answer or echo anywhere in the known mathematical universe. (He said, in our lovely lounge, 'so many numbers'). The un-question was long and complex, all to do with calculating the increased profit to be made by a certain unidentified 'man' who sold certain unidentified 'goods' and who, at the outbreak of war, had advanced his selling price by 250 per cent. Our nameless examinee soon sees that this is a 'thrilling story of the Black market'; indeed, he sees that the blackness of the Black market is but the beginning of its 'sinister implications.' This he knows because below the question was what he calls a 'sinister phrase'– namely: **Turn over.**

Sinister, no? Let's face it, really face it, there is no more sinister command than 'Turn over.' Listen to the philosopher as, staring at the Oxford post-card, he says to himself, *Turn it over*. And once he does turn it over, the Kid is faced by an image of Plato and Socrates that he mistakes for an algebraic equation; he says: *But who are they? S is p, my equation with two unknowns.* I find this sinister because when our boy-sleuth turns over the cold paper before him he too is faced with an equation, this one:

$$e = \sqrt{\frac{t-e}{e(1 + et)}}$$

This might seem a regular equation, not that different from *S is P*; but what the boy alone knows – alone among all the other boys – is that it is, in reality, 'a phonetic message.' Having made this lunatic leap, the boy-analyst interprets the so-called equation as follows:

'. . . the top-line, (t–e). Obviously, tea. And the bottom line, (e (1 + et)). Quite simple; in fact, elementary; e (he) and I eat. So, he and I had tea at the bottom of a tree with square roots, leaving e (him)!'

The boy now pauses, his powers of decryption reaching heights matched only at Bletchley; this child-Ryle then concludes with this astonishing claim:

'A poor School Certificate Examiner has been poisoned or kidnapped – tragedy!'

Tragedy, indeed. As the beggar in our lounge would one-day confirm, 'It was a tragedy'; and the philosopher he adds, *the tragedy of myself*. In the case of the boy-sleuth this self-tragedy is that, strangely enough, no-one will believe him, no one will listen. In fact, this particular case from the amateur detective's casebook ends not with the higher certification of the exam board but the lower certification of the psychiatric hospital. The detective concludes his case-notes thus: 'The hospital I was in was very comfortable; even the walls were padded.'

There is no way out of a padded room or indeed (as my father would find) a cushioned room; and I do, now and then, wonder if this arithmetical boy was actually my father. It's something about the particular way this boy sees the words 'Turn over' as sinister, as (I presume) a direction to turn himself over. This is exactly how my father, back when he was well, would some-times choose, just for the heck of it, to misread the universe; should there be a lull in any kitchen conversation, he would pick up a bottle, a carton, or a jar, stare at its 'Directions for Use,' and then ask us why on earth he should 'Twist Slowly,' 'Tear Off' or (indeed) 'Remove Cap'? Indignant, he would announce to the world, as assembled in our kitchen, that he would do nothing of the sort. Besides (he would insist) he never wore a cap – or at least, not since he was a boy at school; otherwise (he would continue) he had remained resolutely bare-headed, apart perhaps from the occasional and reckless fling with crash-helmet or mortar-board.

This last, however, was not strictly correct; for, in stray or idle moments at the ends of meals it was his custom to place upon his fine head an impro-vised hat. Or rather 'hat' – for anything would do: a sweet-wrapper, crisp bag, paper-cup or even (in priestly moments) a cornflakes box – *unbelievable hats,* cries the Kid, unbelievingly. Once a meal was finished we knew it was only ever a matter of empty time, a few minutes of digestion, before the mad-hatter (once of Christ Church, now of Watford) would be at his unbelievable work. It was a habit so strong as to be, I now dream, the precious vestige of a long-forgotten religious practice; something to do with the arcane rituals of the lost Jewry of South Cheam. It was only because he had no skull-cap to bless his head that my father would reach for a sacerdotal cornflakes box. (*I had put on a hat*).

But what, I wonder, would have happened if we had not been there to witness this? Did he ever cover his head in solitude, without an audience, with no-one there to see except his God? Perhaps he did, at times, just sit there, in our council-house kitchen, balancing a favourite paper-cup on his muddled head; never happier, quite contented, quite blessed, pausing, a very happy man – a still and holy fool, he might have said, openly.

And open he was, like a door; for my father had no idea that he had so many secrets, that he kept so much under his hat. But then, the Kid says that we all keep something there, even if it is only philosophy; the Kid whispers: *under her hat (which she had whipped up with her own little hands), she had conceived dialectically.* Thinking (I have learnt) takes place under hats; and we can't help but *keep* our thinking under our hats – for there is always something secret about thinking, and thinkers. It is, in fact, quite astonishing what thinkers keep under their hats; apparently, Plato had a small *pocket tape-recorder . . . under his pointed hat.*

So says the philosopher, who seems to suspect every hat of a secret. In particular, he has in mind (absurd though it is) the secret of whoever it is that makes your hats. He is, it turns out, strangely obsessed with *the secret of your milliner.* You may say that you have no idea who this mystery milliner is, let alone her secret; but the clue to both is that she is, as the philosopher keeps saying, *your 1930 milliner.* Your milliner, it seems, is above all defined by the year 1930; she is, says the Kid, *that . . . elegant woman of 1930.* This skirted enigma, she seems to follow the Kid, appearing time and again in this book of his, and yet all the while we know precious little about her, except that she is *coiffed with a little hat . . . {a} little (unisex) hat from 1930.*

There it is again, that year 1930; and I need no reminding that it is the birth-year for both philosopher and pastor. It seems to me that I must suspect this woman of being some kind of mother. The philosopher certainly does, sighing and saying that *this elegant woman of 1930 is a small maternal spectre.*

But, this ghost of a mother, who is she? And what does she mean? Indeed, is she seen by anyone else? I think so; in fact, I think she is seen by my father, who once said: 'My mother . . . I saw her.' But when? When did he see her? When did he last see his mother? At school? In the vacation? Or later, in June 1951, when, finally down from Oxford, he went (as he writes in a letter) 'to bring Mother home from hospital'? . . . No, not quite 1951; reflecting, I think it was one year later when, mid-Atlantic, he received a letter from his father informing his sea-borne son that 'Mother has had a nervous breakdown.'

These last two words must have hit the boy-in-the-boat like bitter waves, cold but familiar – for he had (as you know) first been struck by these very particular waves when on dry land, back in 1945, on the day that his school sought to explain the Headmaster's sudden resignation. So: is it, in some way, the same nervous breakdown? Is it the same neural Hiroshima? The same 'Little Boy'? If so, if true, the fall-out that will eventually destroy my father, the hard mental rain of which he will finally die, reached him via his mother. And the philosopher almost sees this; he does seem to say that devastation comes through the woman of 1930:

I still have the impression, he murmurs, *that the final blow is coming to me from . . . {that} small maternal spectre, . . . {that} elegant woman of 1930 coiffed with little hat.*

The philosopher is certainly right about his own end; twenty-three years later, in December 1991, the very last blow will indeed be the death of his mother, one Georgette (Esther) Derrida, a death from which he will never recover – thereafter forever *burying her under the word . . . weeping her in literature*. But the philosopher may also be right about my father's end, his 1930 twin, a man who may, in part, have died of a breakdown that his unknowing mother had once passed on. You might say that one cannot die of an inherited breakdown, but the words 'nervous breakdown' were (you will recall) only ever a screen, a code for the something even more serious that really caused the Headmaster to pack up and go. My father had learnt very early that 'nervous breakdown' means code, means secrecy, the murderous gift of secrecy. And this gift is the blow that comes via the woman of 1930; it can be seen in her little hat, the hat she wears not in order to seduce but rather so that she might hide things – things like thoughts. *The secret of the milliner*, your 1930 milliner, is secrecy itself.

It is, though, a second-hand secrecy, a secrecy that comes to the coiffed and elegant woman directly from my father's school, from the master with the look of Satan, the master who so terrified Miss Haile that she could not repeat whatever it was he had said. He drove her to silence; so unrepeatable were his chosen words that she had no choice but secrecy. 'She was gagged,' said my father.

And so she was; she was gagged by a school deep and in love with secrecy.

It was a romance, or affair, that had much to do with the war, a time when secrets seduced as never before; but some at the school were already seduced – those loving brothers of the Lodge, the Freemasons. Should anyone doubt me, let them take a look at an anonymous letter sent to the school magazine in June 1941. It first begs the question of why the school is so full of secrets, and then answers that question:

'Why is it,' asks Anon., 'that the date of the publication of the School Magazine, along with Certain Other Events, has always to be cloaked with a veil of secrecy, shrouded with an air of mystery, veiled with a cloak of – or what, in other phraseology, a frustrated journalist may deprecate as the practice of the Ministry of Information? . . . Sir, the fault lies with the cryptogogues, the Freemasons in high places, just as the Führer (or was it one of the History Sixth?) has remarked.'

I admit that when the boy says 'Freemasons' he may well be speaking metaphorically; but if so, this is only *just* metaphor, metaphor only by the smallest of all possible margins, for Freemasonry is so famously secret, so famously in 'high places,' and so literal a presence within the school. Should I, therefore, echo the letter and say that, regarding my father, the fault lies with the Freemasons?

This verdict would be good enough for the Führer, and perhaps for my mother, she being the one who had to pick up that abandoned telephone and explain why my father was no longer able to speak and why his face was now raining. He was suddenly sad and he hardly knew why, his only clue being that someone had said the word 'Freemason' and it had hit him like a stray bullet.

I do not yet know if my mother (or indeed the Führer) is right about the Masons, but I did watch as, hour after hour, the boy in the room tried in vain to pull up one leg of his trousers, in would-be Masonic salute. He once said: 'You had to pull them up.'

And so he tried, and the leg that was half-revealed, the leg of half-untrousered skin, was strangely hairless. In fact it was so smooth as to appear almost polished, as was the other leg, it too was quite innocent of hair. I should explain that this was nothing new, my father had always had this particular pair of legs, and I had often thought them odd. I used to think that he had somehow been given the wrong legs, the legs of a boy who had not lived, not lived to be a man. But I have recently learnt that one of the late-effects of trauma can be loss of hair. The experts do not usually have in mind a man's legs, but I do. Legs are important, they sometimes know what that the rest of us have long forgotten.

The philosopher taught me this; he thinks a lot about legs: *It is*, he breathes, *the legs that I love.* And he loves them precisely because he thinks they remember. Several times the Kid pens a hasty note to the effect that, in French, the word for legacy is *legs*. That is why he keeps reciting this absurd four-word refrain: *the . . . Legs de Freud*; he means 'the legacy of Freud,' but he also wants to say that legs are themselves a legacy, a memory, a trace. He wants somehow to say that legs bear witness. (*This*, he says, *is my body*).

And perhaps that is why my father tugged so often at the bottom of his well-worn trouser-leg; perhaps he was trying to show in pantomime what he could not quite say. *This is my body.* And what he displayed, to the world, was a leg to be compared with the leg of an elegant woman, hot from 1930.

Whenever this distracted thought comes to me I feel like the philosopher reassembling (brick by brick) that dream he had, when in Oxford, of his father:

. . . all around someone sick and visibly in danger of death, several doctors. . . . The death sentence won't be long now. . . . The disease is visibly at chest level (my father) . . . Something in the sheet is raising itself up, like a theatre curtain . . . and there is a woman's leg, beautiful enough to drive me crazy.

Here, right here, is another father with the wrong legs, a woman's legs. Like demented me, the philosopher thinks he is dreaming of a father only to find that he is dreaming of an elegant woman, or at least the beautiful leg of an elegant woman. These are legs to be investigated, followed up – if necessary, removed, put in a bag, and examined. These legs will surely tell me something about my father.

I must, then, rush back to the philosopher's Oxford dream to determine to whom these legs belong, to which elegant woman. This task does not last long, for when it comes down to legs (as it so often does) the philosopher makes quite clear of which woman he is thinking: her name is *Josephine Baker*.

As you will know, Josephine Baker is, or rather was (they said) 'a demon of immorality,' a Black-American dancer who once shimmied right across an astonished Atlantic. One day in the 1930s her ship sailed from New York, one day in the 1930s her train pulled into Paris; and there she grew ever more demonic the more she danced – so black and so nearly naked. She was, some said, 'a savage dressed only in a postage stamp'; this postage stamp (once famously made of bananas) barely covered her breasts, it certainly did not cover her legs. That's why, when the philosopher dreams of *Josephine Baker . . . stretched out at the back of the room* he finds that, *on awakening . . . the desire of her legs . . . {was} everything.* These legs mean almost everything to the philosopher, who later begs this one and overwhelming question:

Should I, he asks, *keep the dream of Josephine Baker because of the legs?*

You can see why I think that the dreamt leg is hers, the leg that is attached to the dying father in the philosopher's Oxford dream.

And as I stand and think on this leg, this black and beautiful leg, once again there comes into view a woman who is as good as gagged, a woman made madly mute. Just look at her:

I entered into the house, Josephine Baker was stretched out at the back of the room. Everything was gathered around her mouth, apparently a cancer that swelled her lips and paralysed her in a kind of frightful muteness.

Josephine really had died, just three years before, but not with a mouthful of cancer; no, she had bled her way to death – a brain haemorrhage it was. All this muteness, all this silence, is just the philosopher's dream. Josephine could speak if she wanted; and this the philosopher soon discovers, whispering that, *as soon as I arrived, after my first steps toward her, everything changed, she began speaking.* Her silence turns out to be temporary, something she had willed, something (I think) like the studied silence she had learnt during the war, through her work for the Resistance.

She had found that Herr Hynkel's idiot-boys could always be fooled by a woman wearing only a postage stamp; and so, for four years, this human envelope had zig-zagged across the barbed-wire borders of Adenoidal Europe from one ambassador's party to another, all the while collecting the rumours of war. Afterwards, back in her room, sitting on a perfectly-made hotel bed, she would set it all down in invisible ink on perfectly-made sheet music, sheet upon sheet (*only the sheets, movements of a white sheet*).

I finally understand; our lady of the beautiful leg, the dark lady of the philosopher's dream is silent with the silence of the Resistance, the silence of invisible music. (. . . *like a member of the Resistance under torture*). And all the time her ebony leg is outstretched, her toes pointed like a knife as even now she slowly draws on a long, silk stocking. I pause, desperately hoping to be seduced; but her sharpened leg, it points me, directs me, right back to the drab house of wartime secrets. And that way lies my father's school.

I had hoped that my father's beautiful leg would take me elsewhere, anywhere else; and this hope had grown when, in the philosopher's dream, the dying father's exquisite leg turned into the leg of Josephine Baker – for a moment I had thought my investigation was about to lead me far away from my father's damp and draughty school. But there is no getting away, the holidays never really come, and I should not have been surprised at this. I should have known that my father's leg would point in the direction of Sussex, it being a leg half-bared in pathetic Masonic salute, a salute he could only have learnt at school.

And the rolled-up trouser-leg was not the only Masonic signal, or symbol to be tattooed upon his days and nights in the living room, each day and each night stretched like tightened skin. He said, and she wrote:

'Who held this bowl? . . . knives . . . You must come up and sip it . . . A sword . . . He was grand – very . . . He came to me with a knife . . . he had a mask . . . He had a sword.'

This sword, the one my father sees before him, might well be a Masonic sword, but it returns me (I admit) to another sword altogether, one he was given in 1944. It was not a sword of the usual, material kind. Indeed, you or I might have easily mistaken it for a Bible; my boy-father, however, knew better, he knew it was, as St Paul breathes, 'the sword of the Spirit.' This spirit-blade had been given to him by an organisation that, like Freemasonry, still swallowed the medieval air of the Knights Templar; they were called 'The Crusaders,' a Christian youth movement that first drew its sword in 1904, principally to seek and to save all the lost boys of England's finest public schools.

My father used to say that he had joined the all-male Crusaders in order to get away from the soft-fleshed, clean-smelling girls that seemed to emerge from every cupboard and drawer at Sunday School; he would then go on to say that this early burst of misogyny was a prejudice that in time he heroically overcame. Nevertheless, he remained with the Crusaders, in Sutton (near Cheam), and it was through them that my father was (all at once) converted, born again, saved, surprised by joy, and led to Jesus; he had, in other words, passed from darkness into light, enlisted in the King's army, commenced his walk with the Lord, begun to look to Jesus, made a decision for Christ, and asked Him into his heart. There are, I think, a head-full of ways of saying he was never the same again, that something had really happened, something hilariously different and wildly good, something more wonderful to him than anything else, something never understood. I don't know exactly how this happened; perhaps not even to whom. Right now, as I write this, I can hear the philosopher's holy rumour:

Conversion, he murmurs, *ought to be the surprise of an event happening to 'myself,' who am therefore no longer myself.*

So, be warned: avoid conversion; it will erase your past, you will not have one, you will not be the person you once were, the child you were; you simply will not have been there, it will have been someone else, someone who merely looks like you, an effigy. No wonder my father had so little to say about all those un-days and non-days that someone else had lived before he joined the great Crusade. As soon, though, as he becomes a Crusader he begins to record his days; in particular, he sets down the days he spent at two Crusader camps with which he helped in August 1950. To judge from the photos and the letters, these camps would seem to be primarily occasions for rising at 6.30 a.m., going on 15-mile walks, eating nothing but bread, jam and cheese, and (above all) wearing voluminous canvas shorts beneath blazing school blazers.

The first camp is spent at Studland Bay, a 'deserted and rocky stretch of Dorset coast,' writes my father; 'our tents,' he adds, 'are pitched on the edge of the cliffs down to the sea.' The week seems to have climaxed in what he grandiosely calls an 'aquatic display,' which proves to feature just one boat that is constructed out of an upturned table, the tops of two smaller tables, and a tent tarpaulin – 'a serviceable craft,' he remarks, 'heavily ballasted with half the rockery of Dorset.' (Great sea-going misadventures already beckoned our Crusader). The second camp, this time in Ryde on the Isle of Wight, culminated in a 'motor-coach trip around the island' which, in the case of my father, who was reluctant to part with four shillings and sixpence, meant travelling pillion on a motor-bike which faithfully followed the coach; however, since my bicycling father had never ridden pillion before he was too busy clinging on to actually see anything.

Not that he minds; this Crusader-in-shorts, whether sat astride a motor-cycle or an over-turned table, can endure most ordeals. After all, he was no ordinary Crusader but what they called a Knight. And to win a Crusader Knighthood you had to attend (and I quote) 'one hundred consecutive Sundays,' a regulation that reveals a passion for calendar-watching which leaves for dead the Saturday-counting Masons. I shudder to think what happened if you attended ninety-nine consecutive Sundays and then missed one because, let us say, you forgot, or became ill, or were knocked down on the way by a stray, grey Bentley.

Fortunately, my father does not seem to have suffered any such catastrophe, though he was found guilty of chicken pox in the summer of 1944 and thus condemned to serve time in the school sanatorium – a sentence that elicited a kindly poem from JJFS. It is an ode to the 'strange disease' that the sick-room boy must endure even as 'We put up with bombs and shells / Doodle-bugs and siren-yells.' I am not sure what makes chicken pox a 'strange disease,' but it is not enough to vanquish our brave Crusader and thus, on October 29th 1944, he was duly granted his Knighthood and spiritual sword – a leather-bound, gilt-edged Bible originally forged, as it happens, in Oxford at the University Press. Embossed on its front cover is the Crusader Crest, a simple mock-heraldic crest partitioned into four by a central red cross; in the upper left-hand corner is a crown, in the lower-right is a helmet and, lying diagonally across the shield from bottom-left to top-right, is a sword. Beneath the crest, or shield is a motto now illegible and half-spirited away, as if in the process of being very slowly memorised; but I am told the motto is 'Looking unto Jesus.'

This Bible is still on my crumbling desk. And there the Bible lies, many of its air-thin pages oozing out as if dreaming of escape, of becoming unbound and separate sheets. Throughout, from Genesis to Revelation, my father had marked and coloured particular verses, hundreds of them; some with blue pencil, some with red: blue for commands and red for promises, a colour-code that makes this Bible an illuminated text. Indeed, you might say it is a printed book desiring to dissolve (as is the Oxford way) back into manuscript. And all the time the Kid is singing, in the rain, the show-stopping song of deconstruction – the song he calls *The End of the Book and the Beginning of Writing*.

As if to echo this toe-tapping number, there is some writing, by hand, on the inside of the Bible's frontispiece (the Book, if you like, is already dissolving). Here, even before the Book begins my father has scribbled chapter-and-verse for four short biblical texts (all Old Testament), each of which warns against the dangers of consulting the dead. You might say that I am doing this myself, but I can no longer hear you – I am dead to your cries. Besides, what *I* do is neither here nor there; the figure to watch is my father, and what this Bible reveals of my boy-father is that he was a Christian soldier marching as to war. He had enlisted for the greatest Crusade of all and was equipped with the full 'armour of God' – not only the sword of the spirit but the helmet of salvation and the shield of faith. These clanging metaphors, all of them, come from St Paul, in a letter he once sent, an open letter; it closes thus:

'Put on the whole armour of God, that ye may be able to stand against the wiles of the devil. For we wrestle not against flesh and blood, but against principalities, against powers, against the rulers of the darkness of this world, against spiritual wickedness in high places.'

My father knew these verses well, he had marked them in blue, and would have been reminded of them in the hour of his Knighthood. Now a young man, almost fifteen years old, he was armed and ready for invisible war. It was a strange war to be fighting when you consider that the world just outside Sutton Crusader Class was busy with so visible a conflict. Mind you, this war had itself become a holy war. Just four months before, on D-Day, June 6th 1944, General Eisenhower had waved goodbye to thousands of our bravest boys with the words, 'You are about to embark upon the Great Crusade.' My father knew all about Eisenhower's crusade; like all the boarders at school he had heard, in his narrow bed, the bomber-boys flying overhead. But my father was not flying with them – he was fighting on another front, a front somewhere else, somewhere in the Middle Ages, somewhere in Sutton, somewhere in Sussex, somewhere near hell. (Our beggar-boy once cried, 'I am the only Christian'). And there, somewhere, all alone, this only Christian would be singing the Crusaders' very own anthem. It goes like this (feel free to join in):

> The Lord hath need of me,
> His soldier I will be;
> He gave himself my life to win,
> And so I mean to follow him
> And serve him faithfully.
> So, although the fight be fierce and long,
> I'll carry on, he makes me strong.
> And then, one day, his face I'll see,
> And oh the joy when he says to me,
> 'Well done my brave Crusader.'

Eisenhower's war would be fought in camouflage fatigues and with bombers and tanks, but my father's battle was fought in big shorts and school-blazer and with shield and sword – somewhere in Sutton, in Sussex, near hell. He said: '666 . . . 666 . . . 666 . . . I am the only Christian.' After the long and perilous night of one hundred consecutive Sundays our brave Crusader had proved himself worthy of Knighthood. He was ready. And did he, I wonder, then see action? Did he actually encounter the Enemy? I am, first off, thinking of those cryptogogues, the 'Freemasons in high places.' Is it possible that, at the end, when in low places, my father was also thinking of them? He said and she wrote: 'He was grand – very. They were wearing purple – he came at me with a knife.'

Well, did he? Did he really? The voice from our well-padded lounge certainly said, 'They were cutting him'; but perhaps they were merely making as if to cut, making as if to cut, say, his tongue, to stop him telling – he said: 'the tongue.' That is, I gather, what sometimes happens in highly stylised abuse, the come-dancing school of harm. Or rather, that is how it is recalled, or imagined, or simply fantasised. This caveat is critical, for the well-choreographed ritual killer might always be merely imagined; though my father did once say: 'He was a real man.' And besides, the philosopher, he too seems to see a man with a knife:

I saw, he cries, *the hand raising the knife above me . . . the moment at which you . . . finally see your sacrificer face on.*

The philosopher, I admit, here speaks as a poet, as one that imagines he is Isaac looking into the loosened face of Abraham, his father and would-be assassin, the man who is coming at him with a knife. If so, the knife is raised above the Kid, gleams for an instant, but then is gone; for in the Bible, in this instant of death, a passing angel stays Abraham's desperate hand and screams, 'Do not kill!' Isaac is one boy that does live. The Kid, I admit, is a would-be Isaac, and so too my father – they share an Isaac-complex. It is a picture in their heads, and it is (above all) the dream of a victim. Please note (you must) that, as the Kid himself says, it is only when they *expelled me from school that I saw the hand raising the knife.*

The knife and its raising must, I know, be metaphor. But then, as my father used to ask, 'What's a metaphor?' or rather (because he thought it funny) 'What's a meta-for?' And he is right to ask. What is a metaphor for? What is the Isaac metaphor for? What is it for if it is not for saying what cannot be said? for doing what cannot be done? for experiencing what cannot be experienced – above all, death? Not quite your own, you can never be there when you yourself die, but you can be there for another's death.

So, how about being there for the death or near-death of a certain Maurice Blanchot, the writer who once sent a letter to our philosopher about the day in 1944 when he was made (so he says) to face a mock German firing-squad? The philosopher writes: it's *like a firing squad*. Or again, how about being there at the death of a four-year old girl called Heather Lamb, a pastor's daughter and the only child in the village nearest my father's school to have been killed by direct enemy action? My father, by the way, did once say: 'A lamb . . . I'll save you . . . I can't . . . Heather.' We have no idea where this came from.

I sometimes wonder if Heather Lamb saw the bomb on its way, out of the parted English dark, or if Maurice Blanchot imagined the bullet coming toward him, piercing the slow, occupied air. (*Death arrives, no? Not at its destination, okay, but it arrives, no?*). I suppose Monsieur Blanchot may well have imagined the bullet, even though it never arrived (. . . *it doesn't arrive*). I suspect, however, that little Heather did not see the bomb come down with the sky (. . . *it arrives for no-one*).

Either way, it is clear that neither man nor girl should have had to experience, all-alone, the event of death, or even near-death. Someone else should have been with them – should, indeed, have *been* them. Someone, in their place, should have died or so nearly died. That's the old law of Abrahamic sacrifice, the rule of metaphor, the sacrificial dream, the dream that I can live and die in your place, the dream that I, on your behalf, can see the bullet nearing, hear the bomb plummet.

This, I guess, was Isaac's dream, his bad dream, as he prepared to be sacrificed to his father's God. And, in Oxford, Isaac's dream is being dreamt yet again on that evening of April 25th 1951. In the cold

University Church, there is (as ever) *The Sleep of Prisoners*, and my father can still be found out there, in the dark, watching the prisoners play at Abraham and Isaac:

> **David:** . . . For our better freedom . . .
>   . . . I have to bind you
>   With cords, and lay you here on the stone's table.
> **Peter:** Are you going to kill me?
>   . . . Smile, father.
>   Let me go.
> **David:** Against my heart
>   . . . I must lay you down to sleep
>   For a better waking. Come now.

In mime he picks Isaac up in his arms and lays him across the front of the pulpit.

> **Peter:** Use the knife quickly . . .
>   Now, now, suddenly!
> **David:** *{The knife raised}* This
>   Cuts down my heart, but bitter events must be.

One day, forty years later, it finally lights upon the slow Crusader that he may have seen this night somewhere before. It was the day and the year I heard him say: 'Poor lad . . . tying him'; I don't recall what I said in return, but perhaps it was,

'Smile, father. Smile like you used to when, closing the bedroom door, you would say, "Goodnight sweet prince." And I would then fall down to sleep in front of a pulpit, safe in the knowledge that I was not however being consumed. Oh, smile father, smile and let us say together, you and I, Isaac and Isaac: "We look forward to a better waking."'

But our father could no longer smile, no longer smile at anything, not even at the thought of a better waking. His faith in this waking was elsewhere, misplaced, along with his keys; he knew it was around somewhere but we felt he could no more find it than he could wipe his nose, feed himself, or put his trousers on. He appeared to be quite without faith, quite without a Christian's hope. As we stood around and watched, he performed the slow movements of an Isaac who was not spared, the death of someone dying without viaticum, exactly as had been predicted way back in fortune-telling Oxford.

But then, in 1949, Oxford was accustomed to Isaacs who were not spared, boys for whom the angel turned up too late; hundreds of previous undergraduates had been sacrificed to war – they had come up, gone down, and then gone down for ever. It had happened once in 1914, and once again in 1939; so why not view the class of 1948 as anything other than yet more un-spared Isaacs? As our man in the seventeenth century, Hugh Trevor-Mercurius-Oxoniensis-Roper, observes: 'undergraduates . . . [are] but ephemera, like may-flies or midges.' Once HTMOR is back in the twentieth century, in 1952 to be precise, he confesses that his own may-flies, those he tutored himself, were subject to what he calls 'arbitrary acts of tyranny.' But how else should you treat may-flies, those who live only for a day? After all, why should Oxford undergraduates expect to escape all the perils and dangers of tyranny? This is the night we live in, even if we have an Oxford address; even here there are dangers. In 1953 HTR casually remarks that, 'Girls are being done-in and buried under floor-boards in ever-increasing numbers.' Perhaps my distracted father was thinking of this, or them, the day he cried, 'We couldn't get the air to her.' These are, I know, terrible words; but then my father's Oxford knew many terrible things. That's why, I think, my father was not surprised to see a boy being prepared for execution in the middle of the University Church; in those days in Oxford you expected a certain cut and thrust.

And this edge could still be felt by the Kid in the late 1970s, when he discovers that in Oxford the pencils are sharp enough to make you bleed. As the Hollywood Kid scans the Oxford book he comes across a still of Pythagoras: *bent just enough to write . . . the fine devil . . . is writing with . . . {a} grattoir (. . . {a} knife or scalpel).* In Oxford, it seems, philosophers come at the Kid with their knives. It's like when, he says, *they expelled me from school* – that's the first time he *saw the hand raise the knife above* him, and he sees it again every time they want to expel him again from school, from the academy, from Oxford. *Would they not,* he asks, *start all over, if they could, prohibiting me from school?*

CHAPTER ELEVEN

Fast Cars

In the end, the philosopher gave them what they wanted – he left. And the end begins when, on July 19th 1979, in that Bodleian reading room, he waits to be given the fortune-telling book.

I felt myself watched . . . the preparations were . . . lengthy . . . and for a long time I believed that I would not be given the thing. [And then] . . . all of a sudden . . . the small volume was there, on the table . . . . Finally I've got them, everything stands still, I hold the book open with both hands. If only you knew my love how beautiful they are. Very small . . . What a couple! They could see me cry.

I'm not sure who 'they' are, 'they' who see him cry. I once approached the French archivist and asked if it was he and his colleagues? Had they seen Derrida cry? 'No,' he replied, nodding. He then added, 'But I wish, I had.' Perhaps, then, it was old Plato and Socrates, perhaps it was they who had seen the Kid crying? We must be careful: this picture, this post-carded picture, can return (by post) our gaze; the Kid, he says, *the Oxford card is looking at me.*

I think this is why the Kid finally declares,

It was too much. I was stupefied, speechless . . . . In such moments I have to leave . . . {and giving} back the book . . . I took several steps in the street.

He says that he returns, later that afternoon and again the next day; but we who read with closed eyes, we know better. We know that, once on the red-hot pavement, just outside the Bodleian, the philosopher suddenly remembers that Oxford burns, and so takes to his burning heels and runs through the beautiful crowds as fast as he can. As he runs he is still somehow reading, though not books anymore: *. . . your love letters . . . I reread running in the street and I scream . . . like a madman.* The runaway philosopher is escaping Oxford, but not quickly enough; waving violent arms he stops a passing taxi, and leaps in thinking something like: 'Follow that car; any car.'

Closing my wide eyes still tighter, I imagine that the thinker is soon leaving Oxford just as he came, or says he came – in a taxi:

July 19th . . . I am in the station and I am going to take a taxi to Balliol where I see Alan again.

Alan himself (Alan Montefiore), once said to me, 'No! No! That's not quite how it was. I had collected Jacques from Heathrow and drove him all the way to Oxford in my own car.'

So: private car or taxi? That is the question. Indeed, for this philosopher, that is the only question; he says: *It is always a question of cars* – in fact, let us (he adds) *think that we have spent our life 'en voiture' . . . steering-wheels held with 4 hands . . . pursuits and crossings . . . and . . . routes that are lost in the night.*

Quick, stand well back, against that wall, as the Kid's get-away car hits the dark; with four hands on the wheel, this car is a beautiful hazard. There were four hands when Plato wrote, there were four hands when Adorno played piano, and now (at last) there are four hands again, four shaking hands. The philosopher asks, *Who is driving?* He clearly has no idea, and nor do I; all I know is that he is dangerous in a car. As his good friend Geoffrey Bennington once said: 'There's always something quite adventurous and exciting about being in a car with Jacques.' And even now, right now, Jacques (with another) is *driving like a madman. He says, We both had our feet to the floor. We were leaving everyone behind.*

This philosopher-on-wheels is, I dream, leaving behind everyone in Oxford; however, just before he has quite gone, he finds time to taunt every pedant in the city, crying aloud: *Guess the number of false citations in my publi-cations.* The Kid is desperate, he admits, *to provoke them . . . to expel me again.* No wonder the word *'scapegoat' comes back* to him. And no wonder he exits Oxford, and even now is speeding along the A40, as fast as HTR in his Bentley, and as careless as those army dispatch-riders that, in May 1944, took top secret D-Day documents from Oxford to London – so careless, in fact, that they failed to secure their paper burden, which flew like so many secret doves all over the silent road.

'Go out, we go out,' cried my father in distress. And so they did, he and his beloved; they too got out of Oxford, in that 1926 Morris Cowley, just as the June night of the Christ Church ball became a June morning, somewhere in 1951. The lovers were bound north for Woodstock, on the A44, *as at the first morning of the world . . . from the very first light of dawn.* Engaged to be married, they had, at the end of the long night's dance, slipped out of the House. The philosopher, he sings: *en voiture . . . I pass you and you pass me and the routes that are lost in the night . . . and waking upon the side of the road . . . .*

And waking, at dawn, like wonder-tramps, upon the side of the road to Woodstock, my father and his girl together beg the philosopher's well-thumbed question: 'An erit bonum ire extra domum vel non?'

So, is it? Is it good, this taking leave of the House? I think so. For I see the thirteenth-century answer to this thirteenth-century question even as I follow the philosopher out of the Bodleian. And as I follow, in ridiculous haste, I walk straight through a wall of books, priceless works all flying to either side of me like ten thousand D-Day doves, each one in love with absolutely nothing. Among them I see the very book I had been pursuing, cut open at the very page I had been pursuing; and, as we (the bleeding book and I) fly past each other, I see the words: 'Si iueris cum luco redibis.' Before I even have time not to understand, a passing Classicist sings, over his shoulder, this loving translation: 'If you,' he sings, 'shall have gone out, with money you shall return.' With money, with money, he says – so says, he says, the fortune-telling book.

I now see why, dream why, my father went out, one June morning; he somehow knew that if you go out you will return with money. And it was money that my father so often needed. In the faintest among voices, the beggar in our lounge once said, 'I haven't a lot of money.' That's partly why, upon leaving Oxford, he drove straight into the Atlantic, going so far and so fast that his Morris Cowley became first an upturned table and then, finally, a ship called RMS *Samaria*. He went away, to sea, for a year, all the while waiting at tables which, although not quite upturned, certainly danced with the sickening waves. He went away until with money he returned, money enough to be married.

But there was an earlier returning with money. That was in April 1951 when young Schad was called to the Royal Courts of Justice in the Strand to receive £15 of Savings Certificates. Having just turned the door of 21 he was finally entitled to compensation that had been awarded way back in 1932. This followed a faraway car-crash deep in the side of France, one summer holiday. For my father, the crash was never an actual memory (he was too young) and only ever the source of a mildly comic £15. But apparently JJFS, who was at the wheel at the time, wanted never to drive again; perhaps because both of his beloved boys were injured – not just my two-year-old father but my six-year-old uncle. Writing to my mother, in 1951, my father makes the mock-complaint that whilst his brother had received £50, 'all for a broken jaw,' he had got 'a measly £15 for concussion' and yet (he writes) 'I have since suffered I don't know how many vital repercussions.' My father jokes, but £15 would not be much if there *were*, in the end, repercussions; if the hell that shook in his head fifty years later were the hell that shook a two-year-old on a hard road in France.

I do still remember the day he did cry just like a two-year old; it was one Saturday afternoon. My mother has often said that my father never liked afternoons; he had used to talk sometimes of feeling 'afternoony.' But on this particular afternoon he felt far worse than that; for half an hour my two-

year-old father simply cried. Was this, I now wonder, that most particular
sound of a child in a French car-crash? the sound of an infant wailing on an
unremembered road? a voice recorded and replayed elsewhere in France just
three years later when *Jean-Pierre Derrida, the cousin, one year older . . . {is}
knocked down by a car in front of his home in Saint Raphael*?

The philosopher once slipped into one of his books a snap-shot of Jean-
Pierre, aged four or five, sitting safe on his mother's lap, as she (in turn) sits
safe on the front bumper of a large dark 1930s car. This child, Jean-Pierre,
went out of the house, but did not return enriched – there was no child to
return; this boy did not live. Had he done so, there may well have been
compensation, money with which he could return.

We must, it seems, return if we are to profit from the howling journey
out; there is no pay-back for those who do not come back. Or, at least that
is Oxford's secret medieval creed – 'If you shall have gone out with money
you shall return.' It is a creed that proves to be no more and no less than the
first law of capitalism: namely that there is no point or purpose in risking
the expense of departure unless you can guarantee a return.

My father, though, had no such guarantee. He and his intended, they
leave Oxford with no thought of return; they are off to breakfast on cham-
pagne in Woodstock, to declare their engagement, and then to be married.
As for the philosopher, he does not leave Oxford to be married but he is even
more determined to get out of the city on a one-way street; if only because
he could never endure a place which teaches only going out in order to
return. He is, you see, the reckless philosopher of the *absolute risk* that is
writing; he is the abandoned Kid, the one who wishes devoutly for *the
consummation, without return*.

So, intoxicated with this, let us go, you and I; let us go, each *driving like
a madman,* four hands gripping the wheel, four feet pressed to the floor. Let
us go anywhere, just the other side of everywhere, fast by nowhere. My
father once cried, 'Isn't there anywhere?' Perhaps there isn't, but we shall
only know if, like the philosopher, we get the hell out of somewhere. So,
quick, let's follow the philosopher-Jew wherever he wanders, even if it
means exiting Oxford on *an Italian highway* and heading for *the Italian border*
in a car bound for Northern France: in 1956 (he writes) *I went to Normandy
with that old car from 1930, my first car, and the first car owned by a student at
the École Normale . . . a Citroen C4.*

However far the Kid journeys out, this first-ever car, this original
student car, is always, I think, taking him back, back to the very academy
he so wishes to side-step. This thought hits me with the gentle force of
disaster when we find that he is speeding toward Herr Heidegger's university city: *this morning in Freibourg . . . he accompanied me by car.* This is, I think,

a dangerous place to visit, particularly in a car that takes the philosopher back to the 1930s; but he will take the risk, and so must we (you and I) who follow him. To be honest, though, I don't myself care where we go; I just want to get out of Oxford, out of England, out of this sick and living room. My father once said: 'They should let me go, they have no right to hold me here.'

So, like the philosopher, let us keep going, keep departing, *leaving everyone behind*; and even as we drive we shall do anything and everything, and all at once: we shall *eat while . . . driving . . . {and} while turning the radio dial*; we shall also be desperately making love: *. . . we love* (I say) *each other . . . in a car;* we shall even be senselessly writing: *write* (I say) *on the wheel or on the seat next to me . . . neither 'ideas' . . . nor sentences, but just words that come.* Writing as fast as we drive, let us find our *acceleration in the speed of angels.* God's speed, you might say.

It's like that evening in November 2001, the evening that followed the philosopher's lecture in (of all places) Loughborough, when the philosopher failed to make it to the pub on time; there, like virgins in a parable we waited and waited until finally the long-expected groom arrived, his beautiful head of white hair a halo of alarm. 'I am late,' he explained, and promptly sat down. After a long pause he added that, upon leaving his hotel, he had smartly turned the wrong way, got lost, and waltzed for twenty minutes before (he said) 'A man in a car, he picked me up and brought me here.' I now recall the following words from his long-before book: *I am going out to walk for a bit, I'll be back right away, probably I won't go far.* But in 2001 he did go far and may never have returned had it not been for an angel driving a car.

It was, I now realise, all like another wonderful story I found in the school magazine, my father's school. It is a forever-and-ever story from 1940 called 'A Hero Stepped Out,' the hero being a shadow known only as 'the Angel.' The story, in its beginning, has the Angel on the run, 'making a break for it' with a bombshell blonde. Our hero, the Angel, has just recovered the girl, or at least her unconscious body, from a gang of mobsters (Basher, Martino, and Hymie) who had strapped her to an iron chair and asked her long-forbidden questions. Having cut the girl until she was loose and slung her, cross-wise, over his shoulder, the Angel leaps into the driver's seat of his get-away car, a glorious Hispano-Suiza, and together they roar out into darkness.

So, let us go too, *en voiture . . . {on} routes that are lost in the night.* I dream, though, that I now hear my father, a famously cautious driver of famously cautious cars, a man who, when a passenger, was inclined to grip the sides of his seat in ill-disguised panic. I dream that he cries: 'Slow down . . . be careful . . . you will crash'; and I retort, 'Yes, indeed; but, if we do, with money we shall return. Don't you remember? the compensation? the £15? 1951?' But he doesn't remember; he is too concussed and was always, perhaps, a bit concussed. At Oxford he once got hit on the lid with a hockey ball and was subsequently voted, he would claim, 'The Chap We Would Most Like To See Hit On The Forehead With A Hockey Ball – Again.'

The ball did not, I fear, have the same wondrous effect as the bang on the nut that Stan Laurel received in that justly-neglected 1940 film *A Chump at Oxford*. Here, when an old college window comes down on his hilarious Yankee head, Stan immediately thinks and acts as if he were someone else – to be precise, as if he were one Lord Paddington, 'the greatest athlete and scholar in the history of Oxford.' When Albert Einstein subsequently turns up in Oxford (as he actually did in both 1931 and 1932) he is, it happens, having just a bit of trouble with his famous theory of relativity; so, good old Stan-cum-Lord Paddington kindly helps out the towering genius of modern physics, and is then himself duly lionised as a mighty intellect. This black-and-white epic of curved space and comic caper finally closes with the curmudgeonly Olly looking on and irritably declaring that, 'If it wasn't for that bump on his head, Stan would not know Einstein from a beer stain.'

Welcome to slapstick Oxford, my father's crash-bang-wallop Oxford. The trouble is, for the last years of his life, my father would not have been able even to recognise a beer stain; or indeed any of the stains that daily accrued on his shirt, trousers and bedding, as every day we tried to feed him, water him, and (above all) persuade him to shuffle a thousand miles to the nearest toilet.

With the cure of hindsight, I see that I should have just pushed him into a car that never stopped on a journey that never ended. Like the car he drove in August 1964 when he was well and I was just three and not yet 'John' but 'Johnny,' and we were migrating west (all of us), off on our summer holiday, crawling from Swindon to Cornwall in a beautiful grey-blue Mini van. It was rather wild in the back, back in the east, among us the four children, having no seat-belts; but then, we (the loose children) had no seats, nor indeed any windows – such things were luxuries, said my father. And so the four of us rolled around happily enough; or at least my three sisters did. I, for some reason, felt compelled to stand, leaning forward just against, or behind, the two front seats, poised over the gear stick; and there I stood all the way to Cornwall, in the rain, through a land still un-straightened by motorway, until in the final end (hypnotised by windscreen wipers which moved forever like two perfectly synchronised drowning hands) I fell upon sleep, still standing. There I stood, leaning westward, a sentinel dreaming of my own wakefulness, of how our finally reaching the sea *at the other end of the world . . . there, in the west* all depended upon myself.

As I now look again at that post-card from the thirteenth century I see that I had been playing the part of little Plato whilst my father was big Socrates, the man at the wheel. As the philosopher observes, *plato* [sic], *distinctly smaller, hitches himself up behind Socrates . . . and he drives, he drives.* The 'he' that drives is, I think, Socrates, but it could just be Plato, it's not clear; though that is the sharpened point, the question that wounds the philosopher whenever he looks at the picture – *Who's driving?* he asks. Is it the one that writes, that transcribes? Or is it the one that speaks, that dictates? I don't myself know and, to be frank, don't care. All that matters is that my father and I are somehow following the philosopher's car, pressing our feet to the floor and *leaving . . . behind* the lot of them – doctors, nurses, carers, counsellors, home-helps. We shall simply follow that car, that 1930 Citroen C4. But my father's grey-blue Mini refuses to go to Normandy; it is only and forever slow-bombing west toward the beloved sun (. . . *the more I go west, the closer you get*).

I am, however, beginning to notice that the man at whose shoulder I stand is beginning to drive ever more slowly, and soon is driving with *all the slowness . . . in the world.* Miles become days, become years, and my father ever-so gently shrinks even as I, the boy in the background, ever-so slowly swell. In the end, the car is drifting down the wrong side of the road, gradually coming to a halt; my father's forgetful hands fall from the steering-wheel, his heavy head drops to his chest, and now (right now) he seems to remember something or other. I quickly seize the lonely wheel, convinced my time has come; but though my foot is pressed hard to a grey-blue earth our Mini-van shall never keep up with a huge Citroën C4 which, again and again, goes screaming out of Oxford, overtaking, as it goes, first *Plato . . . the tram conductor* and then, at the very crown of Headington Hill, a 1929 omnibus that nurses, on its upper deck, one Angel Jack who is busy being born, again.

But enough of all this bookish traffic; just give me a car fast enough to follow the philosopher clean out of Oxford. Desperate to find such spinning wheels, I cruelly abandon the plucky Mini-van and run back down our road in Watford, a well-marshalled line of post-war council houses, a road where so often my father's fragile cars would insist on their own nervous break-downs. In my mind the road is now a psychiatric ward littered with all the improbable cars my father ever drove, borrowed, or envied. (*My father's car,* echoes our Kid). Seizing hold of my father, his frame still shrinking, I smuggle him into the first and oldest car – the 1926 Morris Cowley; but, try as I might, it never will finally leave Oxford. Having been made in Cowley, this tainted engine is a piece of Oxford wherever it goes, even bloody Watford. Slamming its rusting door, I run toward the second car my father ever bought, the one after the grey-blue midget; it is huge, beige, curvaceous and leather-seated, a warm mother of a car that he bought one grey-grey Swindon afternoon, a Saturday it was, in 1965. In this maternal spectre we will (I think) make our exit stage-left, until, upon approaching the beloved, I realise that she too is a child of Cowley – her gleaming badge says 'Morris Oxford.' Weeping with melodramatic rage, I tear violently through my father's letters, those written from Canada, until I find a reference to a car, any car; finally, I find him mentioning a brand-new Chrysler 1952 in which he was driven into Quebec when his ship was in dry-dock. 'At last!', I cry and, seeing this elegant Chrysler monster a bit further down our road, I put my father on my back, *the child that I am carrying*, and run to claim our prize. *I had been guided towards my father's car . . . by . . . guardian spirits*.

Once in the driver's seat I grasp the wheel and we are on our way out of Oxford. No-one can catch us now, not in the Chrysler, not as we leave behind the chasing city, the pursuing spires, and drive for thousands of nowhere miles, all the way to vanishing Canada. But, just as we hit the freeway north of Quebec, someone somewhere (a mystery-tramp at a phone-booth) happens to say that Chrysler was owned by a rich German family called Flick who, one fine day in 1997, would offer £350,000 to Oxford to found and fund a chair in 'European Thought.' The tramp then adds that the Flick fortune had derived, in large part, from Adenoidal labour-camps. Upon hearing this, the world's traffic immediately freezes, in mock-shock, as if astonished; the tramp, as if not astonished, slowly looks around at all the frozen cars, vans and lorries before nonchalantly remarking that the money was, in the very end, rejected – but only after protests.

So much for the Chrysler 1952, so much for my hopes of finally leaving burning Oxford and its empire. I stare at the dull, half-remembered road with its fleet of abandoned cars: the Morris Cowley, the Morris Oxford, and the Chrysler 1952, each one, in some way or other, forever marked with the stain of Oxford. All three I have considered, studied and examined. So: this must be it, the end – or so I fear, because the philosopher said that once there is a definitive reading of the Oxford car the end would come; *the one and true reading, will be* (he said) *the end of history*.

I drop to the pavement just outside our house and solemnly await the end. After a while, with no obvious signs of apocalypse (or at least not here in Watford), it slowly comes to me that the philosopher had not said 'the

Oxford car' but rather 'the Oxford card.' My alarm at this somewhat embarrassing mistake (*I still like him . . . the bad reader*) is swiftly overcome by my delight that the game is not yet up, that there is still hope.

Relieved, I rise to both my feet and recall the Angel, the one from the school magazine, the one in the speeeding 1940 Hispano-Suiza. Cradling my father (who is, by now, the size and weight of the girl the Angel rescued) I decide simply to ask him for such a car: 'Could he please, please get one for his little boy? . . . his only little boy?' My father's watery eyes roll back into his head, his drying mouth gapes open, and his breathing grows fitful; but he is still Daddy, he can still do anything. And so it is that my very own Hispano-Suiza is suddenly waiting for me, just down our road. Waving cheerily to bewildered neighbours, I lift my father tenderly into his seat, before taking my place at the wheel; we then disappear toward yet another and adjacent night.

Speeding somehow out of both Watford and Oxford, I push the car to its very limit, all the while screaming that we had 'made it,' that we had crossed the midnight border, and left behind quad, school, cloister, and living-room. Dad and I, Socrates and Plato, we had made it, we had entered the neutral dark. Exultant, I turn to the man beside me, just as the Angel (in the story) turns to the girl beside him. But neither the man nor the girl respond; they both look resolutely ahead, or rather down, or rather nowhere, for both are dead, long dead.

'It was now that he made the discovery that the girl he had been carrying was very very dead. For how long she had been in this condition the Angel did not know; it was certainly irregular for a respectable hero to find his future wife a corpse. Another glance at her face, however, was enough to convince the Angel that perhaps she was not meant to be his future wife at all. A dead heroine was bad enough; one with a pock-mark face and a long scar down her cheek was beyond a joke.'

It may not be funny, but the Angel still cannot stop to bury his dead; the mob are right behind him and he must drive on and never stop, even though this ugly-lovely girl grows cold and rigid beside him. With *Eurydice's death . . . Orpheus sings no more* – so sings the philosopher. But Orpheus-the-Angel, though song-less, drives on. And I too must carry on driving, carry on pursuing the philosopher who seems to know so much about the fatherly corpse beside me. And now, even now, I must pursue him through the fast streets of Paris – both him and his clown of a car, a car now stuffed full of torn-up letters.

I got there, he says, by car (always looking in the rear-view mirror to make sure no one was following me). The most beautiful letters in the world, more beautiful than all literature, I began by tearing them up on the banks of the Seine . . . and

. . . all those cops {flics} always on my path as if obsessed about my private life of which they know nothing . . . . I packed it all back in the car and in a suburb that I did not know, where I chose to wind up, I burned everything, slowly at the side of the road.

Later the Kid will remark (of this driving, this burning), *I swear to you, that it's true*; but I don't need his oath, I know it's all true because I am one of those who hound him. Obsessed as I am with the philosopher's life, I will forever chase his careering, four-wheeled archive. It is true, though, that he didn't see me in his rear-view mirror; so I shall steal his words and say to him: *you no longer knew that I was following you.* I had been invisible, mistaken for just another car on the streets of 1970s Paris, but herein lies the art of following – somehow to follow without following.

Besides, one will never see everything in a rear-view mirror; if one really wants to see what's happening it is necessary to turn round. But the philosopher won't do that, won't believe that; he has read too much Plato, too much of that famous 'Simile of the Lounge.' This is that parable according to which we (all humanity) are trapped in a living-room, stuck on the sofa and unable to turn our heads; on the television-set opposite us, just to the side of the mantel-piece and beneath the flying ducks, we see, in black-and-white, such things as, say, cafés and such people as, say, hairdressers or bakers, our whole tedious universe, in fact. However, these cafés, bakers and hairdressers are only the projected shadows of model-cafés or mere effigies of hairdressers and bakers which someone (with, it seems, nothing better to do) is holding up before a bright three-barred electric fire that glows behind us, behind the sofa. What we mistake for the whole world (says Plato) is no more than, say, a Masonic slide-show, albeit without a talk or indeed light refreshments.

We are, you might say, lounge-folk, confined to the sofa of existence – and that includes the Kid who, even as he tears through the infinite streets of Paris, mistakes his car for Plato's lounge; the Kid doesn't realise he can turn around and look, he thinks that in order to see who's following he can only ever look in his rear-view mirror. But then, I do suspect that our philosopher may be a little mad; after all, he clearly thinks that Socrates can drive a car – when the Kid looks again at his medieval picture-book, he is convinced that *Socrates . . . is writing on . . . a rear-view mirror.*

I am not sure what Socrates is supposed to be using in order to write on the mirror, but perhaps it is lipstick, like in the films and like in this book, the philosopher's book: *One day*, he says, *you will forget all the messages in lipstick on the little mirror in the bathroom.* These messages have, I think, been left by the Kid who does, in general, behave unusually in the company of mirrors. ('Hanging . . . the mirror,' said my father). What I mean is that if a mirror is there to give back your image the philosopher will write all over it in lipstick; but when a mirror is there to show whoever it is that hides behind you the philosopher looks only at his own Hollywood reflection. This 'old narcissist' (as he once called himself) confesses that *looking at yourself in the depths of the rear-view mirror, in an automobile that passes all the others, this is the most mysterious thing.* With respect, I will accept that it may just be 'the most mysterious thing' but, to be frank, it is also the most insanely dangerous thing. As is using your rear-view mirror to gaze at whoever she is that sits so seductively in the back: *while I was driving on an Italian highway . . . {I} was reading your tongue in the rear-view mirror.*

Driving like this, the philosopher is clearly heading for a crash, and he knows it – or rather, knew it: *never*, he says, *was an accident more probable*; *I was*, he says, *risking accidents in the car.* Indeed, *an accident* (he adds) *is always possible 'at the last moment,' it is the last moment.* He is right, an accident is always possible and, like the last moment, it's getting closer: *the countdown is accelerating, don't you think?* (The leper in our lounge cried: '6, 5, 4 . . . 3, 4, 5, 2'). And, as zero fast approaches, heavy as a dead man, the philosopher really does go mad, now positively longing for an accident, a deliberate accident. In his head he even has running the film of this accident-to-come:

It is very late . . . 7 hours in the car with the old film of the accident . . . I can hear them from here, 'we'll never know if it was on purpose that he threw himself against the tree and sent himself flying in the air . . . a car accident . . . never happens by accident.' The philosopher then adds, *I think that I made this film for myself even before I knew how to drive.*

Before the philosopher could ever drive he knew exactly how to crash, even knew exactly how to film the crash. Within the picture-house stuck inside his head, the philosopher is always the Kid, forever the film-star balletically skating on fragile celluloid ice, right to the end of his life, in fact more then than ever. *Derrida, the Movie* was made just two years before his death. He did, though, see it before he died. Indeed, he did, in fact, see you see it, but he feared he might not.

I will die without knowing . . . what you could have felt once the film had gone through. He adds the refrain, *our life, {it is} barely a film,* and then says much the same of his death: *I have just hung up, I am still lying on the floor, nude: of no interest, this suicide, if you don't first pass them the film.*

The film of the philosopher's life, what he calls his *cinemato-bio-gram,* will not conclude (he now fears) with anything as dramatic as a man in a car who, with the speed of stolen light, hits a tree and sends himself spinning in the air. (That sounds like someone else). No, the philosopher now fears he may die nude and lying on the floor – dare we say: nude and lying in an operating theatre, in a hospital in Paris? That, they say, is how the real film ended, on Friday October 8th 2004; that, they say, is how he went away, and the curtain came down.

Writing to my mother from Oxford, in November 1950, my father remarks: 'It has not stopped raining since you went away.' He is right, it hasn't; but he has more to say, adding that 'It Has Not Stopped Raining Since You Went Away' would be 'a good name for a film' – a film, presumably, about someone standing in the rain alone (. . . *they have all gotten out of the train, I am alone. I miss you*). The movie now showing is a motionless movie about someone going nowhere; someone has rain on his face and is standing, up there on the platform.

It's like the film they showed on VE-Day at my father's school – *Ghost Train*, a comedy (they said) starring Arthur Askey, Will Hay and Richard 'Stinker' Murdoch. The film depicts a night lost and stranded at a haunted railway station in the middle of a very English nowhere. It is May 8th 1945 and the film now showing is a train now standing, is the world now standing, standing around, warless and pointless. In Oxford they stand and watch a well-stuffed dummy perched on a burning bush; at my father's school they sit and watch big-hearted Arthur stuck on an empty platform.

The warless world-at-night is stuck, stuck somewhere near twelve. It is not, though, alone for the post-war air is thick with ghosts, real ghosts: in May 1945 the train now standing is a real ghost train in a real ghost film. This film is a Pathe Newsreel and its ghosts are all naked, and many had once arrived by train.

In the train, even before the departure . . . you appeared at the other end of the corridor . . . It went away so fast, I would have liked to kiss you . . . on the platform, right next to the track. This goodbye scene, so like an old film, it haunts. And films they do that, especially the bad ones.

Our man from Brussels, Paul de Man, he knew this and said so, one day in the 1970s: 'I forget bad movies,' he remembered, before then adding: 'although certain scenes . . . haunt me like a bad conscience.' Paul did not name these 'bad movies' or indeed these 'certain scenes.' And neither did my father; so, perhaps he too was, in the end, pursued by a movie, a victim of the flicks. One day, near the end, he said: 'It's time to turn in, the film.' Nearer still (to the end) he said: 'Everybody talk, the film.' The late-late film, the last to be shown, was a talkie, a film in which Here Came Everybody, everybody talking.

It was a film, I think, being played to the unlikely soundtrack of a thousand cartoons, a soundtrack my father began recording on May 10th 1951. On this day, just after lunch, my father is standing on a platform at

Paddington; that night he slips the afternoon into a small white envelope, writing that,

'I missed my train at Cheam and therefore also my connection to Oxford; so, whilst waiting at Paddington for the next train, I went to a newsreel which included a new series of cartoons featuring a character called Bugs Bunny, with the voice of Mel Blanc.'

The weak scholar pays almost strong scholarly attention to cartoonic detail, to the voice of one who could not be seen. Mr Mel Blanc was a Jew who gave his voice away, not only to Professor B. Bunny but to all the good folk of 'Toon Town' – from Tweety Bird and Porky Pig, through Yosemite Sam (the one with the guns), to Sylvester-the-Hyphenated-Cat and dear Daffy Duck . . . *the sacred . . . does leave us laughter, thank God.* Mr Blanc, they all said, was the 'Man of a Thousand Voices,' an un-seeable star in a cartoon sky. He was everybody talking, 'everybody talking, the film.'

And everybody did talk when the Oxonian on Paddington Station, so soon grown old, once again is stranded, and once again the newsreel is running, this time behind closed eyes. The philosopher looks at him, across the room, and says: *under your eyelids . . . there is something like a film.* I dream, to my astonishment, that my Oxford father hears this voice, voice number one-thousand-and-one. The Oxonian nods agreement; Oxford says 'Yes' – 'Yes, it is all a film.'

Oxford has said this before; it was when, in 1922, a Balliol undergraduate called George Edinger disguised himself and then arrived in Oxford, claiming to be Professor Emil Busch of Frankfurt University; he then proceeded to address a packed Town Hall on the topic of 'Freud's System of Psychology.' Professor Busch concluded his spectacularly fraudulent lecture with the ingenious claim that, in general, human personality should, on the whole, be seen 'against a mental background yet to be defined, a screen on which,' he said, 'the figures of our mental cinema move.' This revelation was greeted with astonished approval, and Busch returned to the station surrounded by enthusiastic Oxonians all eager to learn yet more about the film in their heads. They could see that he was right, could so readily see it. After all, they lived on a film-set, since in Oxford a camera-crew is always shooting someone somewhere; usually in a quad, a lane, or cloister, but just as often in someone's head, someone like my father.

His head was certainly a film-set, and flea-pit too, an Oxford flea-pit. He knew these flea-pits well; as an undergraduate he regularly saw films, even if no-one else saw them with him. (*It's cold in this hotel, I miss you*). In January 1951 he writes to my mother,

'I went to the flicks just once last week, and went alone. I saw *The Wooden Horse* (a film about three POWs tunneling their way out and escaping to neutral Sweden). It was very fine, though I missed having someone to whom I could complain about the lack of a full supporting programme.'

This solitary filmgoer meant to say: 'It's cold in the cinema and I miss you' – cold and lonely.

One slow day in the living room he said, 'They all went away and left me.' Yet another slow day he added, 'It's cold.' He is right, in his head it is as cold as Plato's lounge, and what passes before him, under his eyelids, are lonely shadows, shadows that he thinks are real. He thinks they are real because that's what the thousand voices say, the cartoons in his head. So, I shall shake him even though he is dead, and say:

'Don't be fooled – you're only looking at shadows, just reflections in your rearview mirror; this car, this lounge is under Plato's spell.'

CHAPTER TWELVE

Secret Marriage

Quick, let us be quick, you and I – and yes, I mean you (*whoever you are, my love*). It is time to crash this bloody cinema, time to hit a wall, a tree, even a passing train; just brace your beautiful frame. For *we, my angel, we love each other . . . in a car*, above all in a fast and abandoned car; hand in hand as we speed out of control, all the while getting closer, loving ever more finally and desperately. They, the others, just don't realize that *this story . . . this children's story, is a love story and is ours . . . from the very first light of dawn.*

Don't, though, be fooled; this is the light of disaster, of terminal illness; but it is still a light to be desired, for *this is the disaster on the basis of which I love you.* Disaster is the one condition of our love. We are, you see, like those who love because they are in hell; like young, naked and perfect strangers who fall in love even as they shuffle towards the gas. But, let us not go there; we cannot. Instead, let us say simply that our love courts disaster even here in everyday hell, everyday Balliol:

. . . going back up the stone stairs, I asked myself what we could have done in order to love each other in 1930 in Berlin when, as they say, you needed wheelbarrows full of marks just to buy a stamp.

Here, in Oxford, our love flirts with disaster because, above all, it is impossible love; as impossible as buying a stamp in Berlin. And what makes love so impossible in Oxford is that here almost no-one is there to witness love, not a soul. Almost no-one sees my father proposing to my mother in the midsummer night of Christ Church, June 1951. Again, almost no-one sees Angel Jack marrying a dying Jewess in March 1957 in a bed-side ceremony in Churchill Hospital. Yet again, almost no-one sees Adorno marking his marriage in September 1936 to a living Jewess with a private lunch at Magdalene College. And absolutely no one sees the philosopher in the Bodleian being asked by a woman librarian to read aloud the Bodleian oath: *You can see the scene. We were alone in her office. I understood better the marriage ceremony.*

This, or rather these, are what the philosopher calls *our innumerable secret marriages,* our secret Oxford marriages; secret because impossible, and impossible because secret. There is something about the home of impossible loyalties that makes us marry in secret, out of sight, in near-silence.

The philosopher, it is true, does insist that '*I love you*' *cannot be . . . read with lowered voice, like the Oxford oath*; but how else do you get married if you are forever trapped in the Bodleian? Or if you are made to queue in hell?

But, stop! Why talk of love now that the philosopher is dead? or rather, is finally dead, for his death had been coming for some while, had been on the cards; like when, on *May 6ᵗʰ {1998}, 'someone'* (he says) *. . . post{s} on the web . . . the news of my death after a serious car accident in California . . . . I pinch myself . . . what if it were true?* Now, though, that it is true, now that the Kid really has crashed his car (as it were), he can, at last, remove the seat-belt, step from the wreck and, for the very first time, turn his brilliant head. Finally, he can look behind him and see for himself, without a mirror, who exactly has been following him all this time. For some while I have been thinking that, *I . . . will catch up with you* (you the philosopher and) *you will turn around and I will be there*, and now this moment has come. It comes as I hear the boy in the living room plead: 'Turn, turn . . . turn, turn.' And the philosopher, now a free man, replies: *I am slowly turning around toward you, you are smiling.*

Smiling? Am I smiling? Well, only if my father is smiling, and that I doubt. We did, however, keep saying to him 'Smile, father' (like in the play) and perhaps, by a miracle that is secret to the philosopher, he does. And my father would certainly be smiling if, somewhere, it were October 1944 and he were still a Sutton Crusader, and they (his fellow Crusaders) were still all singing: 'And then one day His face I'll see / And oh the joy when He turns to me . . . .'

But again, I say 'Stop!' This is bloody nonsense. In the lounge, in his head, there is no joy, only fear, purest fear – my father says: 'It's nasty, he's turning, he's looking.' So, who is turning to face him? Who's face is it? The philosopher is in no doubt; he says, very deliberately, that it is *the master who is looking at you.* Pausing, I turn to the boy with the patient look; he nods and, like young Echo, cries: 'It was the Master!'

But which Master? School Master? Masonic Master? College Master? Or his Lord and Master, that Jesus of his? The philosopher has in mind Master Heidegger, but my father sees yet another master making fast and straight toward him; it is that Master called Hell. I know, because it is April 1951, he is in the University Church, and the pulpit is occupied by a soldier called Peter who is saying:

> Hell is in my father's head
> Making straight toward him . . .
> . . . He sees the air
> Streaming with imagined hordes

And conjures them to come.
. . . But what is
A little evil here and there between friends?

What indeed? What, indeed, is a little evil? a little evil between friends, friends in school, friends in Oxford? Well, I shall tell you what it is; it is (in my father's head) the face of Hell making straight toward him. He said: 'It's nasty, he's turning, he's looking.'

CHAPTER THIRTEEN

Hastings

'Staring!', he added, 'staring, they all went away.' And the philosopher does not look surprised; instead, he looks as if he had always expected to see this staring, livid face. In fact, I now think it was precisely in order to see this face that the philosopher had, all his life, been writing. He wrote, you might say, this face-toward: *it was*, he tells himself, *enough to write to prepare the moment . . . at which you will . . . finally see your sacrificer face on.*

The philosopher is sure that he will finally see the face of his killer. He is sure that Isaac will finally see Abraham, that son will see father, that face will come to face. So I look straight ahead, right into my father's elsewhere eyes, his very pupils, desperate to see the face that is there reflected. My father responds (if that is the word) by looking up, in my direction, and I recall the time he said, 'He came to me with a knife.'

My father now looks beyond me, as if someone else were in the room. Looking around the ill-named lounge, I see no-one; or at least no-one wholly new – only a man who, now I think about it, may have been in the room before. (*We have never yet seen each other. Only written.*) He is an old man, on the whole; tall, though slightly bent, and very thin; he is, in short, a tangle of angles. And it is, perhaps, a Friday. *I hadn't noticed that it was a Friday the 13th.* The crown of his head is bald but he has intense tufts of hair as well as a pointed beard which, though elegant, looks like a thwarted attempt at disguise. From time to time he raises a wonderful hand, his long fingers stretched as if to reach out and pick up something small. With his other hand, his left, he nurses a book; he is, I think, *the old man who remains the last to read himself, late at night.*

This old reader of the night is wearing plus-fours, has glazed buckles on his worn-out and theatrical shoes, and is busily thinking. I fancy that he might be drunk, or perhaps dead.

'So, who are you, again?', I ask.

The man hesitates, as if unsure, as if he has quite forgotten; but then everything seems to come back to him at inhuman speed, as almost a shock.

'I am,' he breathes, 'the very late, very great and spectacularly infamous Aleister Crowley, known to the *Daily Mail* as "The Wickedest Man in the World." But what care I for praise?'

(He says and she writes, 'He was grand – very.')

I must be looking bewildered, since the Wickedest Man adds, as if it would help, 'I was equally well-known for always signing my letters simply as "666".' This does not help me, though it does seem to catch my father's attention who looks hard toward the corner of the room and then, as if merely recalling a telephone number, mutters: '666.' The Wickedest Man is not perturbed by the echo, simply adding:

'I have also styled myself as 'Perduabo' (which means, by the way, 'the one who endures, or lives on'). It is a somewhat awkward soubriquet, I appreciate; so you may call me "Master Therion," or (if you wish) simply "The Beast."'

I thank him, even as my father says (and she writes), 'You beastly . . . .' Coughing nervously, as if to drown my father, I offer the wicked man a cup of tea. He looks a little surprised at this, even slightly insulted; but I nervously mention the possibility of some 'devilish' biscuits, though I have no idea what I mean. He visibly relaxes and eases back into one of the gaudier of our armchairs, and composes himself to tell the Wickedest Story in the World.

'I once, you know, moved to within just thirty miles of your father and his school; that was back in January 1945 when I became a resident of the so-called town of Hastings.'

He pauses and then, agitated, cries: 'Bloody Hastings! a place and a name forever manured, thanks to 1066, with the stinking ordure of English defeat. It was a frightful, tedious place full of little people such as dentists, traffic wardens, and the Hastings Winkle Club – all huddled together pretending that finally they had something to do with victory, with that war being won just across the Channel. This sublimely pointless town was called a seaside resort, but during the war it was simply a last and desperate resort.'

I smile at this, but he simply continues.

'And there, there, for almost three mortal years, I lived, and partly lived; until a day, very late in 1947, when I completely died.'

I adopt what I feel is an appropriately mournful expression. He looks grateful, almost touched. Then, with a sudden cheerfulness, he is off again:

'I was, I should explain, the honoured guest of one Mr Vernon Symonds who, with his dear wife, ran a genteel but cultured and enlightened guest-house called "Netherwood."' Mind you, though broad-minded, the house had its limits, or perimeters. We, the caged, could not, you know, do simply as we willed. The 'House Rules,' as typed out on a piece of paper skewered to the dining-room wall, included such injunctions as: "Guests are requested not to tease the ghosts" and "Guests are requested not to cut down the bodies from the trees." Bloody rules!'

He says and she writes: 'Picture this house.'

I don't think the Most (or Mostly) Wicked One hears my father's interjection, for he adds without a pause: 'It was a very fine house – a large, elegant and gabled property set, albeit very loosely, within four acres of garden and shrubbery.'

He says and she writes: 'There were no neighbours.'

The man they called 'the Beast' now seems to hesitate as he sips from his tea and looks in vain for his biscuits; he then resumes: 'I believe, though, that dear Netherwood is now demolished – I have no idea why. The house, perched on a road known simply as 'The Ridge,' high above Hastings, commanded quite stunning views. From this Victorian eyrie one could see the whole bloody town, not to mention Beachy Head, the sea and the ruined castle.'

He pauses again as if he is being made to think twice by the word 'castle.' He then graciously thanks me for his tea and (had they ever arrived) his biscuits. I cannot help but feel that such politeness is not what one expects of an Enormously Wicked Man. I put this to him.

'Ah but you see,' he replies, 'my move to Netherwood was my final move and I was very nearly seventy. At that age, one's most wicked days are behind one, or some such place. All that beastliness and sex-magick, it can't be kept up forever. I was, in the end, just too old. And now I am too dead. Besides, it is so very easy to lose your Satanic edge at the English sea-side.'

I nod, as if this were a common observation.

'Particularly,' he continues, 'when you are being looked after so well. Mr and Mrs Symonds were, you see, the most generous of hosts; particularly kind was dear Mrs Symonds, or "Johnny" as we all, for some long-dead reason, would call her.'

He says and she writes: 'Johnny, Johnny, Johnny.'

The Beastly Wicked Man looks round as if, this time, he has heard someone; he looks a little distracted, but then resumes his apology:

'I am afraid the world's favourite Beast grew somewhat domesticated. Breakfast at ten, followed by a walk in the garden; then, if the weather was benign, I would sit with my face upturned towards the Sussex sun, my idling hands open and lifted. If the weather were inclement, the Beast would slouch towards Hastings for amusement – very often the Chess Club, just occasionally the Theosophical Society, though never the Hastings Branch of the Limbless Men's Association or, indeed, a quarterly meeting of the National Council of British Embalmers. Yes, all this and less was happening in my time at Hastings; which makes me grateful for the fact that I could always go for a drive with that good friend of rough beasts, Mr Watson the grocer.'

He says and she writes, 'Went in a car.'

The wicked man pauses as a car happens to ghost past at this moment; he then adds, sorrowfully: 'Some days, however, the Beast would not leave his cage.'

He says and she writes, 'Do it in the house in private.'

I cannot hide my disappointment at the humdrum quality of the Beast's final days, so he quickly seeks to assure me that, even in bloody Hastings, he maintained certain standards of inhuman wickedness:

'On arrival,' he says, 'I made a point of choosing room number 13.'

My father turns his head and counts rapidly: '6, 7, 8, 10, 13'; he then stops.

'And every night, summer or winter, I would stay awake eating sardines laced with curry powder.'

Sardines and curry powder leave me still unimpressed, but I don't think the Beast is taking any notice of me now.

'When reading every night, clean through the dark, I always injected a little heroin.'

My father suddenly cries: 'No cocoa.'

The Beast seems, just for a moment, to hear, replying: 'No, no cocoa – just heroin. A little outside the law, I know, but the local constabulary was, in general, very understanding of great wickedness.'

He says and she writes, 'We must tell the police. Arrest him.'

'Oh, yes, the Hastings "Boys in Blue" were very understanding, even when I would alarm the occasional holiday-maker on the promenade with my usual greeting-cum-injunction – namely: "Do What Thou Wilt Shall Be The Whole Of The Law." Otherwise, my alarming days were largely over, though I did once seem to disquiet poor Miss Clarke the housekeeper; it was the day she entered my room only to be astonished to find that, despite our living in "an age of continued rationing" (her very words), I would appear to have boxes of chocolates stacked from bloody floor to ceiling. These, I explained, to this good but simple woman, were merely loving gifts from loving friends across a shrinking Atlantic.'

'So . . . is that it?' I ask. 'Have you nothing more to confess?'

He concentrates hard, as if desperate to recall something really wicked.

'Well, I did once worry dear Johnny when I expressed a keen interest in seeing the latest feature-film to come to the Ritz, our local picture-house; *The Wizard of Oz* the film was called. I had thought, by the title, that it might be to my recondite taste, but apparently not. When I suggested to Johnny that I might go along she said something about my possibly frightening the many children that would, apparently, be in the cinema.'

He says and she writes, 'It isn't for children.'

I want to smile at the *Wizard of Oz* anecdote, but the Wizard of Hastings (*'each village had its sorcerer'*) doesn't seem to see anything funny; so we fall, both of us, very silent. And as we fall so the day goes low, the defeated sun wanders off, the streetlights think about coming on, and the headlamps of passing cars project the Watford road onto our wallpapered cinema . . . *our small private cinema.* Just outside a boy on a broken and borrowed bike goes in circles, as if skating the wet pavement that gleams with the reflected light of a shop window.

I pull the curtains and find myself asking: 'So, did you never do anyone any serious harm?'

He looks amused, and is about to answer when the phone rings. He suggests I answer. It continues to ring, and as it does so he raises one thin hand and holds it there, in the air, as if about to pick up the receiver, or reach toward an invisible chess piece. When the phone finally gives up ringing he says, 'Do you mean: did I ever actually sacrifice a child?'

My eyes say yes. He looks mildly embarrassed, then shakes his head as if I have, in fact, flattered him. 'I don't know, I can't recall.'

'But in court, in 1934,' I protest, 'under cross-examination, you were asked "Do you believe in blood sacrifice" and you said "Yes."'

'Mmm,' he said, before remarking, as if *à propos* nothing, 'You do realise that the world was destroyed by fire on March 20th 1904?'

'We do, though, seem still to be here.'

'Ah, but that is only according to the Initiated Doctrine,' he declares, with a smile.

I shake my head and start again, saying 'But this believing in blood sacrifice, you did say "Yes" in court, didn't you?'

He nods and smiles again.

'And, when asked if you would say that human sacrifice is best, again you said "Yes."'

He looks down at his buckles as if hunting for an old reflection, though not his own. He then stares somewhere and says with sudden and terrible earnestness:

'Well it is. Your Jesus knows that.'

He looks solemn, almost bowing his head. But I am not to be silenced by any act of piety; instead, I pick up his book *Magick in Theory and Practice*, a book that no British publisher would touch when first written, back in 1926. Opening the quiet, cloth-bound book at a very particular page, I read aloud to the Beast his own words:

'"A male child of perfect innocence and high intelligence is the most satisfactory and suitable victim."'

As I look up from the book I see he is looking accusingly at his own shadow, silhouetted on the wallpaper. Then, with all the seriousness of a shadow he says,

'That was rhetoric – something that had to be said.'

'And is it something that had also to be done?'

I show him a footnote, one where he claims to have carried out 'this particular sacrifice on average about 150 times every year between 1912 and 1928.' Again he is silent, seeming to count something else, anything else; then, as if taken by a fit of concentration, he declares:

'Many more are sacrificed in our not infrequent world wars.'

I am about to interrupt but he will not be stopped.

'Besides, without the possibility of murder what would a witless writer like you have to scribble about? You would have no story were it not for death, cruelty, and anguish. Without these friends of mine, without the gravity of hurt, your writing would be weightless. You feed on heavy corpses.'

My father stirs. I hope he has not heard these words. He then says (as she writes), 'Standing on the dead.'

The Great Beast does not speak again; he does not need to. I think, in fact, that he may have left the room, perhaps gone off with Mr Watson. My father still does not look up; but the philosopher now speaks for him, saying, very simply and very slowly: *You terrify me.*

My mother nods and, turning to me, cries:

'You see! Of all the shadows in the day, who should be just thirty miles from the school but him, that man.'

'Yes,' I reply, 'but it would be madness to insist on an unproven link between a boy in a school and a beast in a cage.'

'But didn't both have Masonic connections?'

'True.'

'And Sussex, wasn't it once known as the Devil's Playground?'

I am not listening anymore, but she is right. In January 1944 the local newspaper carries a cheerful report on a talk given by a Mr F. R. Williams to the Women's Institute on the theme of 'Sussex Folk Lore.' Apparently, the assembled women were informed that, 'judging by the place names alone, the devil has been busy in Sussex.'

Enemy planes may be kissing the sky over their heads and spies sleeping open-eyed under their beds, but the good women of Sussex still find time for entertaining devils. ' . . . *all the ladies had their fortunes told {and} the possessed ran through the fields; playing at who had seen the devil.*' And, according to Mr Williams, the easiest way to see the devil, at least in Sussex, was by running seven times round one particular moor-land tree, at which point, apparently, the Father of All Darkness would obligingly appear with a bowl of soup.

I remember now that my father once said, 'Who held this bowl?' Another day, he said: 'Seven. You're next.' But I shall move on and take my investigation elsewhere; after all, Hastings's very own Satanist-in-Residence had long been in retirement and, besides, he preferred to be served rather than to serve. Long gone, I think, were his days of hanging round remote moor-land trees with bowls of fast-cooling soup; he was now too busy deriding the Winkle Club, going for drives with limbless grocers, and pushing wood at the local chess club.

It is true that in 1946 the town of Hastings saw a few more corpses than most places – sometimes they had just fallen from the cliffs, like the eleven-year-old boy called Cecil who was found on May 22nd; and sometimes they had got washed up on the beach, like the so-called 'woman in black' discovered on February 12th (with a full set of false teeth in her handbag), or the headless man they uncovered on November 30th with nothing to identify him save a laundry mark on his shirt ('K175,' by the way). But these were just 'deaths by misadventure' – none of which could ever be dragged to the door of our Beast, not even the baby boy called Marcus who was found dead in his perambulator on June 3rd. ('Her baby,' he said, 'was dead.') This too was declared a misadventure. So, as I say, I shall move on. I will.

But I cannot, not quite. And it is, strangely, because of the chess; or rather because, in March 1947, my father's school magazine includes a report of the 22nd Annual Hastings Chess Congress, an international tournament held, as ever, in the White Rock Pavilion at the very end of the year. *Let us say the last or next to last day of a given year.* And in the given year of 1946 the congress was, almost certainly, attended by the Most Wicked Man in Hastings; we know because he refers to it in a letter.

'At the Chess Club we are having,' he writes, 'a great "do" . . . at Christmas.'

And a 'great do' it was, deep inside the White Rock. The terrible winter of 1946–47 was threatening to make white rock of the whole town, and thus very few risked the icy promenade; but inside the sea-front pavilion each room was warmed with famous masters making their famous moves. These were masters with towering names, like Yanosky, Columbek, Tartakower, and Abrahams. Gerald Abrahams, by the way, 'represented English Jews' at the tournament and was famous for what was known as 'Abrahams' Defence.' So there, in Hastings, the masters gather for their horizontal battles and murderous moves.

And, lest we forget, chess *is* a game for killers, particularly so soon after the war. This is there for all to see in the book of the tournament. It was written, in 1947, by H. Kmoch and L. Prins, and I find the book astonishing; for it is quite clear to me that it is not really about chess at all. It is,

I think, a fragmented version of *my* book, *this* one, the one you are kindly reading right now; for what I find in Kmoch and Prins are endless bits and pieces of this weightless work of mine. It is here and there, like shrapnel, in a hundred cruel and twisted phrases of chess-match analysis, phrases like: 'the queer position,' 'the threatening and killing,' 'the death-sentence,' 'the decisive liquidation,' 'the martyrdom of the doomed,' the 'buried alive,' the 'hampered Bishops,' the 'shortening agony,' and, not-quite-finally, 'the execution'. This smashing-and-mirroring of my poor book is all but completed when Messrs Kmoch and Prins together write, 'Now the day is over.' All that remains is for K and P to report 'the sacrifice of a pawn' and observe that someone in the watching crowd cries: 'Now I recognise Abrahams again!'

Last night I dreamt that this figure in the crowd was none other than my boy-father. I do not know if he was there, among the party from his school, but it is possible; he was certainly a keen player of chess. And it is clear that schoolboys were very much a part of the event, clear too that they mingled with the senior players. According to the school magazine, a previous winner of the tournament, one Sir George Thomas, was 'unable to resist a friendly game with some of the schoolboys in the lower sections.' For men of a certain age, temptation is always difficult to resist, face to face with the young, and just pieces of wood between them.

The boy in our living-room once said: 'Game . . . Can I play? Let the man start. It's my turn. He said, "Your turn."'

CHAPTER FOURTEEN

Sacrifice

The boy, when himself a man, tried to teach me how to play chess and take my own turn, but he, or rather I, failed miserably. I cannot endure any game that has more than three rules and, besides, I was impatient, unable to live through the long silences between my father's moves, as he would purse his lips, narrow his eyes, and look so inward that I would begin to think he had grown ridiculously sad. It's easy to get the wrong end of silence, across a motionless board, waiting at a table, face-to-face with nothing or no-one between the two of you; or rather, with no-one but a ghost who loves with doomed and impossible loyalty.

I am not completely sure who this spectral lover was. I used to think it was the Mayfly who was married for a day in Paris. But in these my declining years I think it was the philosopher, or even that hero of his, Franz Kafka, another man whose love was always stillborn. To Milena he wrote, 'When you say you love your husband so much . . . that you can't leave him . . . I believe it.' Kafka is right, she will not leave her husband and that is why, I think, in another letter to Milena, he wrote: . . . *on the great chessboard {I} am . . . a piece that does not exist and, therefore, cannot participate in the game.*

These are words that the philosopher steals; he too wants to say that he does not quite belong to the great chessboard, to the great world of Kings and Queens, a world mad with the madness of public marriage – such a world (he wants to say) is not for those of us who marry in secret, in the shadows. No, not quite our world, though very nearly; since we who marry darkly and impossibly will, in the end, be killing each other like pawns. *It is to hell that we have destined each other.*

We, the impossible lovers, condemn each other to exquisite destruction. Each to the other is an Abraham, killing out of love. Or at least that's our defence, Abraham's defence. Like the Kid, we say, *Right here I kill you . . . you . . . whom I love.* And that is why the Kid, I think, was always writing toward the day he would see, face to face, his own killer – his own beloved assassin. Look, look again at how the Kid once said to himself, *It was enough to write to prepare . . . the moment at which you will . . . finally see your sacrificer face on.*

My father said: 'He's turning, he's looking.' And even as this enigma turns, even as he looks, the Crusaders in Sutton are singing, 'And then one day his face I'll see.' That day is approaching, is near; but the face, says my father, is 'nasty.' He says this even as one of the prisoners in Oxford is whispering, 'Hell is in my father's head / Making straight toward him.'

Hell, I now fear, is also in the son's head, making straight toward *him*. And Christopher Fry has seen this, which is why he writes about Isaac as well as Abraham:

In mime, Abraham picks Isaac up in his arms and lays him across the front of the pulpit.

Peter: Use the knife quickly . . .
      Now, now, suddenly!
David: *(The knife raised)* This
      Cuts down my heart, but bitter events must be.

The knife is gracefully raised, delicately lifted; and there is, for a moment, the sharpest silence – in Oxford, in Sussex, in Algiers, in a Paris hospital. It is a silence between face and face.

Then quickly, now suddenly, in Christopher Fry's Oxford, Corporal Joe Adams appears 'as the dream figure of the Angel' and cries this:

'Hold you arm. / There are new instructions. The knife can drop / Harmless and shining.'

The knife can fall, Isaac is not to be killed; we are not to get our long-awaited murder. But we never do; in the Bible the boy is never quite killed. For, just as Abraham is about to slit open the belly of his own son, even in that instant, he is shown a ram caught in a thorny thicket – and an angel then telegraphs Abraham telling him to knife the beast instead. It was all, in a way, just as Abraham had predicted: 'Dear Isaac,' he had said, 'God will provide himself a lamb.' In my father's Crusader Bible, his paper sword, these words are marked with red pencil, a red as red as lamb's blood.

So: new instructions, different orders – but, please never forget, there is still a ram to be killed. The amount of killing (let us measure it) is constant. You may escape the knife, but another will have to die, standing in your shoes. Don't forget, therefore, the ram caught in that crown of thorns. Indeed, this ram, the one who dies for you, could yet turn out to be a child.

This truth is revealed to all by dear Thomas de Q.; it is when he is advancing that astonishing thesis that all genuine philosophers will, at some point, either be murdered or at least come very close to being murdered. This leads Thomas de Q to relate a story apparently known only to himself regarding the near-murder of Immanuel Kant. The mighty Kant, we learn, was once just about to be murdered whilst undertaking his daily walk; however, at the very last moment, his would-be assassin thought again:

'An old professor, he fancied, might be laden with sins. Not so a young child. On this consideration, he turned away from Kant at the critical moment, and soon after murdered a child of five years old.'

A child in exchange for a philosopher – a fair deal, I suppose. Jacques Derrida certainly seems to think so; for he nods a 'Yes' and cries, again: *to the devil with the child, the child the child.* And why not? Why not kill the child rather than the philosopher? I fear the murderer may well have been right in thinking that a professor would be full of sin; and if Professor Kant wasn't a man of sin before, he is now – now that a child has died in his very boots.

So (thanks to TdQ) again we have new instructions; but this time the child does die, this time the boy does not get to live. These are not, of course, the instructions that Abraham heard, or said he heard; nor are they the instructions staged again in Oxford in 1951. So, the question is this: which new instructions have been wired to the world? The instructions to kill ram instead of child; or child instead of philosopher?

The answer is a slow train coming; so slow that there is time for some among us to say that it does not matter, to say that both arrangements have the same weird effect on the way you, I, we, might die. Both arrangements (they will say) mean that, whereas (once upon a time) I might have died my own death, now I will only ever die someone else's. *I am dead*, repeats the Kid, *of a death that is no longer my own. We know,* says the Kid, *that . . . we are going to die for one another.*

Death, I think, is not a fine and private place, it is not a living room of my own; it is, I see, a fine but public place, a waiting-room full of perfect strangers – namely: the one I die for, the one who dies for me, and the one who comes to kill me. And this one, the one with the knife, will ensure that I am not so much killed as, let us say, 'sacrificed.'

Let me put it this way: the one who holds the knife above me is not my killer but my sacrificer; and thus I am told not to condemn him – the philosopher says: *the moment at which you . . . finally see your sacrificer face on, {you are} not to accuse him.* I cannot believe this; how can I avoid accusing the man with the knife? How can I not accuse him as our faces close across the room, the theatre, the church, the gas-chamber? But the philosopher says again, 'Do not accuse.' And he adds (or so I have dreamt) the following: that I may just die the kind of death that gets another off the butcher's hook; for instance, if I am to be shot then the bullet that rips through my empty brain cannot be used to kill someone else. In this respect, it is possible that I may yet die for another, in another's boots.

Indeed, according to the Kid, this is not just a possibility, it is in fact an order; these are the new instructions – instructions I am to obey whenever I die, and instructions I must follow, to the letter, on the day that I kill. My killing is to be a reversal of killing, an act in defiance of killing. Welcome back to Purim, to Esther's new instructions, Esther's *counter-order*, the one which (says the Kid) *is 'written to revoke'* . . . *{Haman's} order of extermination* – the order to exterminate the children of Israel, every one of them. Esther's counter-order is that the people of Persia should be killed instead, all seventy thousand of them. Though *the bearded . . . old man dictates the horror* Esther rewrites the horror, re-orders the order. Hers is a counter-killing, a killing against killing.

And the philosopher stands and applauds, even encourages, crying yet again: *give fire its due, light counter-fires in order to stop the progression of a blaze, avoid a holocaust.* So (if I have got this right), according to the Kid's new diktat, we are to fight fire with fire, holocaust with holocaust. To be honest, I had always thought that one holocaust was enough, far more than enough – but not for the philosopher. *I am*, he says, *still dreaming of a second holocaust that would not come too late.*

CHAPTER FIFTEEN

Elijah

This, I think, is why the Kid returns to Oxford, to the city that dreams, that burns; he seems to see somewhere in Oxford a second and counter holocaust, a fire that will be counter-fire. . . . *back to Oxford . . . this summer . . . the great burning of us.* The philosopher has chosen well; Oxford, we know, is good for burning. Up here they fight Luther's fire with Roman fire, and do so until Protestant bodies curl, crack and melt; here too they fight Adenoidal flames with English flames, asphyxiating a rag-doll Hynkel high in the night. This is Purim Oxford, a buried, reserved but angered Oxford, and one which is seen again a year later on October 16th 1946 in that room in Corpus Christi when the Jews gather to read aloud the book of Esther even as, in Nuremberg, Haman Goering and his Adenoidal sons are about to swing among invisible flames. Indeed, I think these condemned boys overhear the Oxford Jews – for, out of purest nowhere, with the rope laced around his neck and the ground about to give beneath him, one of the damned, Julius Schtreicher, screams: 'Purimfest 1946!'

I should not like to be thought pedantic but the hanging man is not, strictly, correct. Purim fire never falls upon old October. Purim burns in the Spring; that is when Jewish minds turn to counter-fire and that is when, in 1888, a great scholar (both weak and strong) called Claude Joseph Goldsmid Montefiore feels it is high time to write upon Purim. It is an essay for the *Jewish Chronicle* in London; but Claude, although a cross-hatched Anglo-Jewish theologian, was a pure Oxonian; this Balliol alumnus had recently been asked to give Oxford's annual Hibbert Lectures, and will do so in 1892. Claude, you might say, never really left Oxford – as many have said, it is not easy to find your way out of the Oxford forest. And, in fact, I think Claude is still deep within the wood when Jacques Derrida first climbs Balliol's endless stone steps; for Claude, as you will have foreseen, is the grandfather of Alan, Derrida's Oxford host. (. . . *the grandfather is present*, he whispers). Inspector Derrida is getting warmer, his host is a ghost, a Purim ghost, a donnish after-image of Jewish counter-fire.

That fire, though, was barely a fire, a Purim that was barely a Purim, for Claude saw many dangers in Purim – 'Purim Difficulties' is the title of his essay. This ancient carnival of rough pleasure and shadow-killing was too much for such an English Jew, a man who once defined himself as an 'Englishman of the Jewish faith.' But then Claude dies in 1938, too early to see the evil Haman finally have his terrible order carried out. Had Claude lived on to watch, open-mouthed, Haman's pan-European bonfire he may well have seen fewer difficulties in the Purim mirror.

Claude may, in fact, have become a very different man, a man to be found, I dream, at the bottom of a whiskey glass; indeed, after six million shots he may have even become that solemn and intense Oxford drunk whom the Kid meets outside Balliol, by the phone booth on Broad Street. It is foolish, I know, but I have often dreamt that this scholarly beggar is Claude. You see, the Kid sees the beggar as both *the Englishman* and yet also a Jew – that's why the Kid *surnamed him Elijah.* And what keeps me dreaming this dream, impossibly believing that the beggar somehow is Claude Montefiore is this: that he wants so desperately to meet his grandson's guest, the caged philosopher who shares so completely Claude's fierce fascination with Purim.

. . . *small, red, paned booth in the street, under a tree, a drunk was watching me the whole time and wanted to speak to me; he circled around the glass cage . . . with a solemn air . . . the imperious beggar . . . with whom I communed intensely through the pane.*

Whatever it is that they communicate, whatever is being smuggled through the thin Oxford glass, Jew to Jew, it is enough to kindle fire; for, that night, in Derrida's sleep, Elijah the beggar-man is *rubbing his new pencil against a box of matches and was in danger of burning.* Right by the Broad Street phone-booth is a one-man Purimfest, a human counter-fire doing his drunken best to burn against burning. Here and now, the holocaust movie is (in a way) countered, reversed, rewound – *rebroadcast, a sinister play-back.* This, I think, is what the philosopher means when he says he is *dreaming of a second holocaust that would not come too late*; he is dreaming again of a counter-holocaust.

But they won't be coming back, or at least not this way, not the people of ash. Besides, we can't count backwards, we can't count downhill from six million to zero; we can barely make the leap from one to zero. Not even in Oxford could we light such counter-fires; not even if all the books in all the libraries in Oxford were to burn; not even if the whole dammed fire began with the *imperious beggar* setting himself alight. His fire is finite fire; what we need is a beggar so imperious that he burns forever, burns without however being consumed.

This way lies the beggar Jesus, the tramp my father followed, and never more closely followed than when the Crusaders of Sutton sang on that Sunday afternoon in a wartime autumn. They sang that one day he would see his Jesus, the one who 'has need of me,' whose 'soldier I will be,' and the one who, in the end, at the last, 'will say to me: "Well done my brave Crusader."' These are the words our Christian soldier believed he would hear when he made it across the coldest border of all; and once there, over there, he would call it 'Heaven,' that far and blind side of the track.

This, though, is resurrection hope, the hard hope of my father. It is not, I say, a hope shared by our philosopher. I say this out-loud, alone at dawn in Oxford, half-wishing that the philosopher would somehow overhear and contradict me. There follows a silence, or at least no sound save that of singing from a tower. But then, of a sudden, I hear the Kid's wild voice (and I have the words before me, here in this book): *I am*, he says, *fomenting a resurrection*.

'What!', I cry, 'You a philosopher and Jew, how can you be singing wild resurrection songs?'

Looking in my direction, he says (and these are, I swear, the very next words in his book): *Had you finally encountered him, Elijah? You were right nearby, you were burning.*

I think, for a moment, that the philosopher is talking to me; I then think he must be addressing Elijah. I am now not sure; but, whichever it is, 'Elijah' is his answer to my impertinent resurrection question, an answer that takes the cryptic form of a secret Jewish name. 'Elijah' is both his own secret Jewish name and the beggar's secret Jewish name, but above all it is resurrection's secret Jewish name. The philosopher makes this clear in another place.

I expect, he whispers, *the resurrection of Elijah . . . the name from which I expect resurrection.*

Even as he says this the philosopher glances at the Bible oozing on my desk, he also gesticulates wildly toward a bare upper-room. In this room, on an unmade bed, the prophet Elijah has laid himself over the hardening corpse of a widow's son, and there Elijah breathes a kiss to his open-mouthed God. Elijah then comes down, down the stone stairs, with a boy who is no longer dead. 'See,' he says to the widow, 'the boy liveth.'

But does he? Can we really believe in the resurrection of Elijah? I am myself a widow's son and I am not so sure, certainly not so sure as the philosopher who expects so very much from the name of Elijah.

'So, is there,' I ask, 'is there really a resurrection?'

At this, the philosopher looks down, and suddenly looks very old, very thin, very pale, just as he does in those final cancer-kissed photos, the pictures that were taken less than two months before he was. These pictures illustrate an interview he did for *Le Monde*, an interview in which the dying Kid imagines a very particular scene – he imagines that

Someone, you or me, comes forward and says "I would like to learn to live finally."

To this, the Kid replies, *No, I have never learned to-live. To learn to live that must mean to learn to die, to accept absolute mortality* – and this, he implies, is a stone step too far.

The Kid then walks out into silence, the door being open. He had always said we were *to leave the door open*.

But in, and out, of the silence someone somewhere remembers the Kid's secret name; he has, they say, a secret answer to the question of resurrection, the question of the widow's son. The answer is an open secret, an answer scribbled lovingly onto a thousand postcards. (*Listen – tenderly I am going to tell you*). As always, however, the Kid's handwriting is impossible to read; and besides, each and every postcard is signed and counter-signed with fire. There is, I think, nothing to read save unreadable fire. That is why my shaking hands are burning.

But the philosopher, he just whispers again, *Had you finally encountered him, Elijah? You were right nearby, you were burning.*

I say, 'Yes, and *"I am burning"* still, I am still right nearby.' Then, like a burning boy in a dying room, I say, 'Help me.' *Help me.*

No help, though, is coming; for he is gone, gone now. Quite gone. He is not here.

Appendix

My mother's transcript of what my father said, February 1992–
January 1996.

February 28th 1992
The dog!
Black . . . an axe . . . a cup

March 1st 1992
A sword
I couldn't sing
[*As if singing*] Amen
Pray . . . pray
Sermon
Last thing he said . . . German
Oh . . . it was upside down
Horrible, horrible, horrible service
Oh, the book
. . . you had to pull them up
He said so
It's happening now
Dirty meetings

March 2nd 1992
Game – turn over – cards
. . . speaking
The book
Satan

March 5th 1992
Peace
Not to tell

March 6th 1992
All lovely things
A hammer

March 11th 1992
Can I play?

March 18th 1992
{Extremely distressed} Heavy . . . sighing . . . turn, turn
That's the place!
Out of this door . . . I can't guard you
Horrible . . . horrible
Please, please . . . I can't, I can't
Too much . . . the boys
She *died!*
She died
Oh, oh, oh, someone take me out
Many men, different prayers
You haven't turned!
The dark
Who is there?
Dig a hole . . . just to say the word . . .
Dig there . . . quick, get clean
The door . . . smash it . . . horrible, oh . . .
Place it in the right place
Can you come? You must be careful
Let the man start, he's playing now and he's not going to get us
I can't . . . oh . . .
Where did she go?
. . . and the hearts . . .
No . . . never
Oh no
Please, please, please, please – burns
Police
Come back, come back, come back
Stop stop stop don't don't
You silly woman
Cold cold cold
No . . . no . . . no . . .
Do it in the house in private
Carry it out
I couldn't do it I tell you
Oh, oh, oh.
And the end came
Kill cats

What is the date?
Who held this bowl?
Out – stop the music
Now get out
Singing at a time like that!
Keep out of it . . . oh . . .
Don't do it . . . don't do anything

March 19th 1992
Went in a car . . . in a garden
He was just a little lad
A little boy
Tell about it . . .
He didn't want to touch
6 7 8 9 10 11 12 13
When he did it to you he would be good
Two nights
Those games, card games
There were no neighbours
He sang. I could never stick with him
It's time to turn in
The film
No no no no
I believed
Knives
I'll come back if I can
{Extremely distressed} The little lad
I didn't want to read

March 20th 1992
Book. Incantations
Don't read.

March 21st 1992
The clock!
I can't, please please please
The brains, kill, quick
There's money here . . . I wanted to help
Behind me . . . I can't help anymore
I felt ill
You can't pray with them

The head . . . look out everybody!
Playing . . . 6 . . . 4

I am the only Christian
Two other men
He came back
To get to church . . . to burn

The girl
Oh oh oh oh oh
I threw it down
Please . . . before she takes it
This one is a new person.
Please, please
Horrible
She . . . on the cross, alive

[*Very distressed*] ME . . . ME

You must come up and sip it
The floor was awash
Preserved
You've got to see if you want to do this
I can help him over the wall
The cross
I know where to get blessed, the cross
I'm sorry . . . taken away
Pray for ———— to tell . . . [*he repeats an inaudible name*]
The police pushed you on
———— fell over
I couldn't drink anything
[*Distressed*] Kill . . . oh oh
He couldn't do it . . . please please
Turns, no, no.
Poor lad – oh oh ooooh
Turned it, tying him
It all goes, please please
People outside
Pull it in the bath, three of them, the basins
Don't let me get . . . [*an inaudible name*]
[*Distressed*] Take it out, take it out

Go . . . go . . . we go home

3 4 5 2 . . . who don't know, awful
Everywhere . . . I . . . gone . . . no . . . never
Pile . . . he pulls them off
Turn . . . touch
That's worse
In the occult game . . . help them

March 22nd 1992
A lamb
I'll save you
Isn't there anywhere?
No, no, the tail – no no
The little lad . . .
Tattoo . . . no
The cross, no, others . . . oh no!
No, no, alone when she . . .
Tattoo, oil, tar
Take them, tell
The girls, let them, poor girls were driven falling
Turned, oh
No, God
I will try, yes
The line in the machine
Ding dong. The clock

All right then, we'll go
. . . definitely not, get up, yes
Best thing is to get out and stay out
Everybody talk, film.

March 24th 1992
Turn . . . turn
Taking me! . . . tattoo, come forward !
No !
Pray for the help
Dirty meeting

. . . I am tiny

March 26th 1992
[*Very distressed*] She . . .

I can't, I can't do it
Sirs, help . . . no!
I'm not standing on it – crying –
Think, think, *please, please.*

They are due to the big thing, and they don't

March 27th 1992
[*Very distressed*] Oh, the poor lad . . . tried to help . . .
They were only *little*
I couldn't take it
[*Incredulously*] Laughing!

Look at the *little* ones.

Never do it . . .
It was a girl who was bruised . . . beaten
He said, 'Your turn'
Oh . . . horrible, horrible
No, no, no . . . I didn't want to come . . .
A sword . . . turn, turn
Don't, don't, don't!
[*Wailing*] You can't, you can't!
Come on, tell it.
Who's coming? Here he comes.
Oh, my body, oh, oh.
[*Wailing*] Terrible
Don't want, don't want
Not you . . . not you, you . . . no, no!

Play – six, five – no . . .
Four . . . *please*
[*Wailing*] Kill him! Deadly!
[*Screaming*] Take it out!
[*Shrieking*] You can't my body – splits

March 28th 1992
. . . and then we carry on with the torch . . .

I haven't got a lot of money . . . . but help
4, 3, 10 . . . how many numbers
A little church . . . I don't want to go to sing

March 29th 1992
The worst day so far, intermittent screams all morning; tears all after-noon
How to help him?
He's naming *me*!
You can't eat it!
The children . . .
Little girls . . .
We have to tell

March 30th 1992
As yesterday, he woke screaming
It's my turn!
I can't, I can't eat it
Tattoo
Young men turn to do it –
You can't do it
You can't do it – oh poor lad . . .
The last time
This is the place where . . .
Poor lad . . . only one little lad . . .
The last time
This is the place where . . .
Poor lad . . . only one little lad . . .
He's dead!
That little boy . . .
I saw him bring him out screaming . . .
His poor mum
Two deaths –
5 . . . 5 . . .
He was hanging
Chairs and a plank
I had to get him down!

March 31st 1992
He woke up crying but not so loudly
Help him . . . he can't help it!

Burying
I *couldn't* pray
Please, please
I didn't . . . he wanted to come
[*Very distressed*] His mother
Oh, *poor* little lad
He couldn't . . . I can't, I can't.
You couldn't catch . . . *poor* lad
She was a nurse!
Devon.
The little calf.

April 1st 1992
They wouldn't believe me
They won't listen
They said, 'You'll have a lovely time'

April 3rd 1992
It was a ruse
. . . oh, a baby
Mother . . .
[*Screaming loudly*] You can't . . . you can't

You beastly . . .

Turn . . . trying to sink . . .
We can't start.
What are you doing?
That's what they do!
Fifteen people.

April 4th and 5th 1992
In the water . . . I don't want to . . . never, never

After this he was almost silent until March 1993

March 1993
Get it off!
He was grand – very
Heavy, burning
Turn, turn

[*Very distressed*] It burst
I can't, I can't, I can't, I can't, I can't . . .
Down, down, turning, turning
I couldn't

She had a little table
They were wearing purple
He came to me with a knife.

April 1993
Death.
They said they'd kill us
  . . . and then come back.
Give him a hand . . .
Where are you going?
No . . . not
Bang!
Here we are
Turn
Come
Take it, take it
———— and ————-
Open, good
This one
Is it here?
Oh, you can't do it!
It was here – where is he?
———— hiding
They're whipping him!
A coffin
I was to blame . . .
Wicked

It was empty, it was empty, it was empty

Oh the poor boy!
The heart.
[*Very distressed*] Oh, the poor girls
I couldn't, I can't.
The poor boy.

She died . . . the girl died
Run.

Poor thing!

My hand!

He's sinking, sinking!

The body – a man

May 1993
The door

The lock – it's strong
Pull!

Six!
Everybody
I beat him

It's ringing, the bell
Burn
A cord
He's not kicking!
Help him!

There was nobody else
He had a mask
No, don't go!

It's not for children!

They were singing up there
John, the next one
They're gone

He was a *big* man

The bell is ringing

The dog died

Who is missing this morning?

Sick all over it

He's coming down the corridor

Tonight!

No – I'd never tell

So, we don't fight
[*Very emphatically*] We must tell the police

June 1993
Guns.
Hide her!
Cover him up

It was the sergeant!
A very big man
I didn't hurt the little boy

The sea
The band
The boy
Turning, turning
Get him in

Hanging –
I said, 'Turn on the light, you can't see anything'
They were kicking him
Just shut the door
666

I had to hold her head
Tattoo . . . .
They threw the bird

September 1993
[*Almost chanting*] Knocking
Here he comes!
You're working for him
The hands
Jennifer and Heather
He's coming from Exeter
Torquay
A birth
Hold her!
They're kicking him
Two men
We couldn't get the air to her
Hold her down
I can't – I can't
I wanted to help
It was ———
He left me here
The sea – the boy –
[*Very distressed*] One at a time
Mother – don't make me stay

October 1993
I must telephone
He's murdering *me*!
Staring
They all went away and left me

A dead one

She said I'd have to sing
He had a sword
Bells ringing
The clock
They buried the dog
The sea – the sand
The sailors helped us

They all went away
I'll have to rescue . . .
The hand . . . there it is!

He was sinking

Saved him
They were cutting him
[*Screaming*] Johnny – Johnny
 . . . girl,
Dig, dig, in a cellar
Save her

November 1993
Legs
Hands
Trunk
Buried in the sand

Hanging

Legless

Hear her, hear her, hear her

November 14th 1993
On Sunday
Tomorrow
He was wearing uniform
[*Imitating a drum*] Pom-pom-pom
I hear her
Quickly, quickly –
Down, down, down.
Hear her, hear her
When he realized . . . .
Pray, pray

November 15th 1993
He's barred!

November 17th 1993
In the army –
They threw me on the floor

November 21st 1993
You're coming with me

November 23rd 1993
On Monday, in the evening
Hear her, hear her

November 24th 1993
I heard him cry

Standing on the dead

Children

Be careful!
See her – it's cold
Hear her, hear her, hear her, hear her . . .

It was a tragedy

Would you like to play?

December 3rd 1993
The boy – they're kicking him
I've got to go – 'hit him!'

You can't leave her! They took turns
They're holding her. Go home and lock the door
Hear her, hear her, hear her, hear her . . .
No cocoa

December 23rd 1993
He ran away – I saw him
Hear her, hear her, hear her, hear her . . .

December 24th 1993
Arrest him

I couldn't kill her

December 28th 1993
Never, never, ever
I walked off

December 29th 1993
It burst!

January 1994
I had to drag her –
He knows how –
Can you help her?

January 10th 1994
He attacked me
He hit me

January 12th 1994
She gave birth –
The baby!

January 14th 1994
Digging – I can't
A female

January 15th 1994
Down the stairs
Dark – horrible
Hear her, hear her, hear her, hear her . . .

January 17th 1994
A bad smell –
He was in a mood

I had to see the dead boy

January 18th 1994
The poor boy!
666
I don't know why she sent for me
Down, down, down
Hear her, hear her, hear her, hear her . . .

January 23rd 1994
The boy had a knife
It was lonely feeling

January 24th 1994
Tell my mother about the teacher
Don't make me go back mother
It was lethal

He was hanging there, they were
Kicking him

Hear her, hear her
He thumped her
[*Very distressed*] Singing signing

January 28th 1994
He'll kill you!

I'll save you

I couldn't kill him

No you can't

January 31st 1994
He left me there
I can hear her, I can hear her, I can hear her, I can hear her . . .

February 3rd 1994
A procession
He was a real man

We'll help you
[*Very distressed*] The fire!!
Burned!

February 6th 1994
Shoot!
They were drugging him
Waking up

I didn't kill the girl

February 7th 1994
[*Very distantly*] Hear her, hear her . . .
I'll go and get her
Hot
Oh – you can't burn!
I'll tell!

September 9th 1994
I feel . . .
Looking . . .

September 11th 1994
Fighting

September 12th 1994
He was whipping

. . . I heard

The covers – the man.

It's nasty –
He's turning
He's looking

September 13th 1994
Kicking her
Laughing
Pray
Horrible – see her

September 16th 1994
Help her . . . hear her
Clapping . . . hear her
Birth

September 17th 1994
Cross – martyr
All he wanted

September 22nd 1994
There's nobody there
Don't drown

September 23rd 1994
Three

September 24th 1994
Three
Come and help her
Singing!
Coming
Kill yourself
Hear her, hear her

September 26th 1994
Hear her
Cut it
Picture
His house

September 28th 1994
Get her down!

September 29th 1994
They killed her
I hear her
At school
Come *on*!
Number
They're coming!

October 1st 1994
I never hurt her

October 7th 1994
Three things

October 8th 1994
My bed!
Failure . . . be careful

They play

October 9th 1994
The children
Staring!

October 20th 1994
Pray
Kill her
My gun
Two girls
I can't
[*Emphatically*] The second time
I can't . . . I can't

October 22nd 1994
We'll help you

October 23rd 1994
I must, I must.

October 29th 1994
Stare
Next
Hear her, hear her, hear her, hear her . . .

November 2nd 1994
On the train
Hanging
The mirror
Help me
We'll help you
Hear her . . . hear her
We must help
He'll kill
Kill kill!
Seven
You're next

November 3rd 1994
No! . . . you can't do that

The writing, the mirror
Don't shoot!

November 4th 1994
My mother
Kill
I'll tell you
The woman
The master killed
Hell fire
Laughing
Save her save her

November 5th 1994
My mother
I saw her
Anybody!
Hold him

November 6th 1994
The man killed her

November 7th 1994
Horrible . . . horrible
Her hands . . . her hands
He writes above the door
I'll tell her
'We want you'
He was pushing
Horrible . . . horrible
I'm going to hide

November 9th 1994
You can't kill her

November 10th 1994
Biting, biting

November 11th 1994
Her hands
Hanging

I saw her

November 16th 1994
Kicking me
Don't tell
Down, down
Prayed

November 19th 1994
It was her heart
Tell her, tell her, tell her, tell her, tell her, tell her

November 24th 1994
[*Very distressed*] It burst!

November 25th 1994
Burned

December 5th 1994
Kicking her

December 14th 1994
When I realised . . . not joking!

December 17th 1994
A gun

December 20th 1994
The baby!
Burned
Horrible horrible

January 1995
Still very distressed, many nightmares. During the day still saying 'hear her' and 'help me' but not much else

February 1995
As above

March 1995
As above, but at the end of this month a further period of extreme despair,

severe nightmares, loud shouting and sleepless nights. He once said very clearly 'A murderer' and then 'Burned'

April 15th 1995
We're not to say
Leave her *alone*!
A murderer!

April 19th 1995
See me
Don't say
I don't like it.

April 24th 1995
He ran away

April 25th 1995
She might see me

April 28th 1995
You don't know
666 666 666 666 666 666 666

May 1995
Singing
Mother mother mother mother
666 666 666 666 666 666
Nobody – help me
Purple
They're kicking her
Singing
The clock

June 8th 1995
I rescued it
I punched them
Don't say

July 6th 1995
Her baby was dead

July 16th 1995
They hated her
Help us

July 17th 1995
You can't eat it

August 4th 1995
Trapped
No-one helped me

August 5th 1995
Fire – singing
Clapping

August 6th 1995
They're kicking her
Burned

August 12th 1995
The tongue

September 14th 1995
Don't kill her
Help her

September 20th 1995
When I saw her

September 22nd 1995
We had to see her
Fire

September 23rd 1995
Cross
Purple
They gagged her

September 27th 1995
Hanged hanged
666 666

October 6th 1995
Her hand
I'm sorry
I saw her
Kicking

October 7th 1995
Ringing
Sing
Running running
Down, down
Run
666
I saw
Let's shout
Burn burn

October 8th 1995
She was the first
Singing
Gosh, the seal
Hanging
Her hand

October 10th 1995
Singing
I saw you
He made me
With him
Sinking
Duck
Quick

October 16th 1995
I saw
Kicking
Hang

October 18th 1995
Killing
Singing

Not singing!

October 21st 1995
We had to
I saw it

October 29th 1995
The gun
The sand
Looking
Burn, burn

November 3rd 1995
In a mirror
666 666 666 666 666 666 666
Quick, quick
Hear her, hear her, hear her, hear her . . .

November 4th 1995
Down, down
Dig, dig

November 6th 1995
He hid

November 10th 1995
Hear her hear her
Kill – gun

November 12th 1995
Kicking

November 16th 1995
Nobody knew

November 19th 1995
He killed the girl
I caught her
Bang

November 23rd 1995
Anybody!
Her hand
666 666 666 666 666 666 666 666 666

November 24th 1995
Her hand
Burn
Kill her

November 29th 1995
I saw him
The gun
Tell her
Tell, tell

December 5th 1995
This time
Pretends
Little
2 2 2 2 2 2 2 2
He said
He said
I'll tell

December 9th 1995
Kicking her
666
Come on – help her

December 18th 1995
Running running
I saw her
I heard her

January 6th 1996
Her hand
Fire
See her, see her
Help her, help her

January 8th 1996
I saw it
Sinking
Her hand her hand

January 15th 1996
Sand
Sinking
666

January 20th 1996
666
Coming

Notes

'I am citing, but as always rearranging a little; guess the number of false citations in my publications . . .'

JACQUES DERRIDA

I 'si puer vivet'

1   The 'book,' as I misname it, is 'Envois' which is, more properly speaking, part of Jacques Derrida, *The Post Card: From Socrates to Freud and Beyond*, tr. Alan Bass (Chicago: University of Chicago Press, 1987) / *La Carte Postale: de Socrate à Freud et au-delà* (Paris: Flammarion, 1980). In the notes that follow all quotes are to this text, unless otherwise stated; in each case I shall give the page reference to the English translation first.

230 / 246.

143 / 156.

78 / 86.

96 / 106.

77 / 86.

191 / 206.

148 / 161.

Letter to the author, May 28th 1999.

2   167 / 181.

135 / 148.

87 / 97.

77 / 85.

3   167 / 180.

All references to the words my father spoke in his final years are as transcribed by my mother. This transcript appears in the Appendix.

210 / 225.

247 / 265.

21 / 25–6.

4   143 / 156, 43 / 49.

25 / 29–30.

115 / 126.

82 / 91, 144 / 157.

33 / 38, 112 / 123.

It is said, very elegantly, by Peggy Kamuf, as a footnote to Jacques Derrida's 'Biodegradables: seven diary fragments,' tr. Peggy Kamuf, *Critical Inquiry* 15.4 (1989), 848, n. 19.

246 / 263.

5 68 / 75, 143 / 155.

190 / 205.

254 / 272.

Ms. Ashmole 304, Bodleian Library, University of Oxford. To learn more about the author of the fortune-telling book see Suzanne Lewis, *The Art of Matthew Paris* (Berkeley: University of California Press, 1987) and Francis Wormald, 'More Matthew Paris Drawings,' *The Walpole Society* 31 (1946), 109–12.

218 / 233.

225 / 241.

47 / 55.

223 / 239.

3–4 / 7–8.

6 It was Matthew Arnold who said this – see Matthew Arnold, *Selected Prose*, ed. P. J. Keating (Harmondsworth: Penguin, 1970), p. 130.

15 / 20.

7 216 / 227.

217 / 233. It is true that the 'you' who is predicted to one day enter the Duke Humfrey Room is, by virtue of the verb form, feminine in the French original; however, Derrida goes out of his way to warn us against believing in such grammatical signs and wonders: 'Letters,' he writes, 'are always post cards: neither legible nor illegible, open and radically unintelligible (unless one has faith in "linguistic," that is grammatical, criteria: for example to reach the conclusion from the fact that I say "It's nice that you are back [*revenue*]" that I am certainly writing to a woman' . . .).' (79 / 88).

109 / 120.

211–16 / 227, 208 / 224.

96 / 106.

I visited the Duke Humfrey Room on Tuesday, 22nd March 2005.

8 209 / 224.

84 / 93.

9 216 / 227–8.

223 / 239.

174 / 188.

173 / 187–8.

210 / 226.

14–15 / 19.

10 *The Letters of Mercurius* (London: John Murray, 1970), p. 6.

The Collected Writings of Thomas de Quincey, ed. Davis Masson, 14 vols (London A. & C. Black, 1889–1890), xiii.24.

Gervase Fen, also an amateur sleuth, is a fictional character in a series of novels by Edmund Crispin. Lord Peter Wimsey is another amateur sleuth and fictional character, in his case in a series of novels written by Dorothy

L. Sayers, including *Gaudy Night* (1935) which is set in Oxford. Detective Chief Inspector Morse is a fictional character in a series of Oxford-based novels written by Colin Dexter, many of which were adapted for television between 1987 and 2000.

I revisited Oxford at the very beginning of August 2005, which happened to coincide with the filming of *Inspector Lewis*, a spin-off from the *Morse* television series, featuring the actor Kevin Whately as Lewis. The one-off episode was screened in 2006.

11   Faith Wolseley, *Which Way Came Death?* (London: John Murray, 1936), p. 33.

Ibid., p. 329.

Ibid., pp. 343, 152.

14 / 18.

12   248 / 266.

School Magazine LXXXIX (December 1947).

13   33 / 38, 80 / 89.

233 / 250.

This remark regarding a condom has always been a vivid part of my memory of 'Envois'; however, every time I re-read it I fail to find the actual quote. I suspect I must have dreamt it.

252 / 269.

28 / 33.

15   Christopher Fry, *Three Plays* (London and New York: Oxford University Press, 1960), p. 182.

Ibid., p. 187.

Letter to my mother, April 1951.

Ibid., March 1951.

223 / 239.

16   Letter to my mother, March 1951.

17   122/134.

William Shakespeare, *Henry V* [1599], ed. Gary Taylor (Oxford and New York: Clarendon Press, 1982), IV.iv.76.

211 / 227.

Ms Ashmole 304, fol.43v. I am very grateful to the Bodleian Library for kind permission to quote from the fortune-telling book here and elsewhere in my book; and I am especially indebted to Dr. Bruce Barker-Benfield, of the Bodleian, for kindly transcribing this particular extract. Dr Daniel Ogden of the University of Exeter very kindly helped me to translate it.

2   A Sleep of Prisoners

18   Fry, *Three Plays*, p. 197.

William Shakespeare, *Hamlet,* ed. Harold Jenkins (London: Routledge, 1957), V.ii.364–5.

Ibid., V.ii.363.

Geoffrey Bennington and Jacques Derrida, *Jacques Derrida* (Chicago: University of Chicago Press, 1993), tr. Geoffrey Bennington, p. 328.

111 / 122.

39 / 45.

19   Fry, *Three Plays*, pp. 184, 187–9 (slightly adapted).

20   Karl Marx, 'The Eighteenth Brumaire of Louis Napoleon,' in David McLellan (ed.), *Karl Marx: Selected Writings* (Oxford: Oxford University Press, 1977), p. 25.

School Magazine LXXXVI (December 1943).

Ibid., LXXXVII (March 1944).

Ibid., LXXXIV (June 1941); LXXXIII (October 1940); LXXXVI (December 1943; LXXXV (December 1942); LXXXIII (October 1940).

Ibid., LXXXVI (December 1944).

21   Ibid., LXXXVI (July 1944).

108 / 118.

22   *School History* (2001), p. 194.

Ibid., p. 191.

School Magazine LXXXVIII (September 1945).

248 / 265.

117 / 128.

23   115 / 126.

National Archives, WO372/19.

School Magazine LXXXVIII (December 1945).

223 / 239.

19 / 24.

24   My father died on Friday, October 25th 1996.

167 / 181.

25   43 / 49.

See James T. Richardson, Joel Best and David G. Bromley (eds), *The Satanism Scare* (New York: Aldine de Gruyter, 1991).

55 / 62.

80 / 89.

Local Newspaper, September 8th 1943.

26   Ibid., July 11th 1945.

33 / 38.

See Ewen Montagu, *The Man Who Never Was: World War II's Boldest Counter-Intelligence Operation* (New York: Oxford University Press, 1953); Ronald Neame (dir.), *The Man Who Never Was* (Twentieth-Century Fox, 1956).

61 / 69.

51 / 58.

Bennington and Derrida, *Derrida*, pp. 314–15.

3   XX

27   Fry, *Three Plays*, p. 202.

B. Harrison (ed.), *The Twentieth Century* (1984) in *The History of the University of Oxford*, 8 vols (Oxford: Oxford University Press, 1984–94) .

See Nigel West, *MI5 British Secret Service Operations, 1909–45* (London: Bodley Head, 1981), p. 142.

28   *The Oxford Times*, May 11th 1945.

My account of the exercise is based on Bruce Montgomery's own description. I have, at times, used whole phrases and half-sentences from this brilliant account – see 'Hitler Over Oxford,' *Oxford Today* (2001) 13.2.

See A. L. Rowse, *Shakespeare's Sonnets: The Problems Solved* (London: Harper and Row, 1964).

29   237 / 254.

30   For a good account of the role of Oxford dons within the Secret Service, see West, *MI5*, p. 161.

Gilbert Ryle, *Collected Papers*, 2 vols. (Bristol: Thoemmes, 1990), 1.223.

See Anthony Kenny, *A Life in Oxford* (London John Murray, 1997), p. 15.

31   J. D. Mabbott, 'Gilbert Ryle: a Tribute' in Gilbert Ryle, *Aspects of Mind*, ed. René Meyer (Oxford: Blackwell, 1993), p. 224.

177 / 191.

See 'Emmet Cole Interviews John D. Caputo', <www.themodern-world.com/features>.

Charles Chaplin (dir.), *The Kid* (Charles Chaplin Productions, 1921).

Charles Chaplin (dir.), *The Great Dictator* (Charles Chaplin Productions, 1940).

Kirby Dick and Amy Ziering Kofman (dir.), *Derrida* (Zeitgeist, 2002); for a full transcript of the film see *Screenplay and Essays on the Film, 'Derrida'* (New York: Routledge, 2005).

69 / 76.

14 / 19.

Derrida refers to this 'icy consternation' in Jacques Derrida *Without Alibi*, tr. Peggy Kamuf (Stanford: Stanford University Press, 2002), p. 127.

32   36 / 42.

247 / 264 (adapted, though only slightly).

154 / 167.

218 / 234.

70 / 78.

Gilbert Ryle Papers, Linacre College, University of Oxford. I am grateful to Linacre College for kind permission to quote from these papers both here and elsewhere in my book.

Simon Glendinning (ed.), *Arguing with Derrida* (Oxford: Blackwell, 2001), pp. 52–3.

Gilbert Ryle, 'The Thinking of Thoughts: What is *Le Penseur* Doing?' in Ryle, *Collected Papers*, 2.480–96. The lecture was given at the

University of Saskatchewan; I am grateful to the University's archivist
and Professor David Crossley for establishing the date of the lecture.

I am indebted to the Maison Française for this information (email correspondence, June 27th 2005).

33 Ryle, 'The Thinking,' p. 484.

6 / 10.

169 / 183.

This trip to London is recorded in David Wood (ed.), *Derrida: A Critical
Reader* (Oxford: Blackwell, 1992) p. 258; it is not, though, recorded in
the long inventory of Derrida's academic trips that appears in Catherine
Malabou and Jacques Derrida, *Counterpath: Travelling with Jacques Derrida*,
tr. David Wills (Stanford: Stanford University Press, 2004), pp. 289–94.
This inventory does not mention a trip to Oxford in either 1967 or 1968.
See Ms. Eng. misc. d. 937, Bodleian Library, University of Oxford.

131 / 143.

34 Professor Montefiore kindly allowed me to interview him on March 1st
2005.

177 / 191.

Ryle, 'Thinking,' p. 484.

35 45/ 52.

42 / 48.

70 / 78.

For an excellent account of post-war hostility toward continental philosophy within the British analytic tradition in general and Oxford in
particular, see Simon Glendinning, *The Idea of Continental Philosophy*
(Edinburgh: Edinburgh University Press, 2006).

Interview with Montefiore, March 2005.

Gilbert Ryle, 'The Theory of Meaning' in Max Black (ed.), *The Importance
of Language* (Ithaca: Cornell University Press, 1962), p. 150.

36 113 / 124, 243 / 260, 98 / 108, 218 / 234.

244 / 261.

243 / 260.

98 / 108.

See J. C. Masterman, *The Double-Cross System in the War of 1939 to 1945*
(New Haven: Yale University Press, 1972), p. 143. For full list of double
agents' code-names see West, p. 242.

I should confess that Ryle does use 'Fido' as a philosophical exemplum
before the war; though not famously.

Ryle Papers.

37 Ryle, *Aspects of Mind*, p. 206.

C. S. Lewis, *Broadcast Talks* (London: Geoffrey Bles, 1942), p. 28.

The Oxford Times, June 10th 1977.

173 / 187–8.

See the story 'The Silver Blaze' in Conan Doyle, *The Memoirs of Sherlock*

Holmes, ed. C. Roden (Oxford: Oxford University Press, 1995).

Derrida, *Without Alibi*, p. 127.

38   See A. J .P. Taylor, *A Personal History* (London: Hamish Hamilton, 1983) p. 139.

See A. L. Rowse, *All Souls and Appeasement* (London: St. Martin's Press, 1961).

247 / 264.

55 / 62.

W. H. Auden, *Collected Shorter Poems, 1927–1957* (London: Faber and Faber, 1966), p. 142.

4 Silences

39   Ryle, *Collected Papers*, 1.224.

The Dog It Was that Died is a play by Tom Stoppard first performed on BBC Radio 4 in 1982.

My account of Adorno's Oxford years is based primarily on: Lorenz Jäger, *Adorno. A Political Biography*, tr. S. Spencer (New Haven: Yale University Press, 2004); Stefan Müller-Doohm, *Adorno* (London: Polity Press, 2004); Theodor W. Adorno and Walter Benjamin, *The Complete Correspondence* *1928–1940*, ed. Henri Lowitz, tr. Nicholas Walker (Cambridge: Polity Press, 1999); Evelyn Wilcock, 'Adorno's Uncle: Dr Bernard Wingfield and the English Exile of Theodor W. Adorno 1934–8,' *German Life and Letters* 49 (1996), 324–38; and Gerard Delanty (ed.), *Theodor W. Adorno*, 4 vols. (New York: Sage, 2004), 3.344–57.

See Müller-Doohm, *Adorno*, p. 180.

40   A. J. Ayer is cited in ibid., p. 190.

80 / 89.

Müller-Doohm, *Adorno*, p. 193.

73 / 81.

Gilbert Ryle, review of Martin Heidegger's *Sein und Zeit* in *Mind* XXXVIII (1929), 364.

92 / 102.

41   Jäger, *Adorno*, p. 88; see also Delanty, *Adorno*, 3.347.

See Müller-Doohm, *Adorno*, p. 199.

Irene Roth, *Cecil Roth: Historian Without Tears* (New York: Sepher-Hermon Press, 1982), p. 145.

The stunning and chilling phrase 'chosen of the Chosen' I have borrowed from Geoffrey Hartman.

159 / 172–3.

42   188 / 203.

See John Felstiner, *Paul Celan: Poet, Survivor, Jew* (New Haven: Yale University Press, 1995), pp. 244–5.

155 / 168.

141 / 153.

Heidegger, quoted in Thomas Sheehan, 'A Normal Nazi,' *New York Review of Books,* January 14th 1993.

In exploring Heidegger's controversial years I have drawn, *inter alia,* upon Richard Wolin (ed.), *The Heidegger Controversy: A Critical Reader* (New York: Columbia University Press, 1991); Hugo Ott, *Martin Heidegger, A Political Life,* tr. Allan Blunden (London: HarperCollins, 1993); Rüdiger Safranski, *Martin Heidegger: Between Good and Evil,* tr. E. Osers (Cambridge, MA: Harvard University Press, 1998).

Safranski, *Heidegger,* p. 232.

Ott, *Heidegger,* p. 247.

43   60 / 68.

Felstiner, *Celan,* p. 287.

196 / 211.

31 / 36.

Derrida writes: 'the presumed subject of the sentence might always say, through the "supplement," more, less, or something other than he would mean' – Jacques Derrida, *Of Grammatology,* tr. Gayatri Chakravorty Spivak (Baltimore: Johns Hopkins University Press, 1974), pp. 157–8.

44   Ryle Papers.

Ryle, review of *Sein und Zeit,* p. 370.

77 / 85.

Ralph Glasser, *Gorbals Boy at Oxford* (London: Pan Books, 1988), pp. 59–60.

For details of the vote see Wilcock, 'Adorno's Uncle,' 333.

45   David Walter, *The Oxford Union: Playground of Power* (London: Macdonald, 1984), p. 94.

10 / 14.

I am grateful to Dr Christine Ujma of Loughborough University for pointing this out to me.

These words form part of an additional *envois* that appears on the back cover of *The Post Card.*

225 / 241; Derrida is here citing Neil Hertz citing Freud's *Civilisation and its Discontents* (1930).

46   Oscar P. Wood and George Pitcher (eds), *Ryle: A Collection of Critical Essays* (London: Macmillan, 1971), p. 8.

35 / 40 (bold indicates italics in the original).

See Peter Gay, *Freud: A Life For Our Time* (London: J.M. Dent, 1988), p. 629.

Michael Ignatieff, *Isaiah Berlin: A Life* (London: Chatto and Windus, 1999), p. 123.

47 / 54.

Alan Montefiore, 'Jacques Derrida: A Tribute,' *The Philosopher's Magazine* 29 (2005), 33–5.

15 / 19.

47   J. C. Masterman, *An Oxford Tragedy* (London: Penguin, 1933), pp. 87, 31, 177.

Ibid., p. 26.

Ibid., p. 36.

48   For full text of this address see Wolin, *Heidegger*, pp. 29–39.

Details of the Rectoral ceremony are drawn from Ott, *Heidegger*, pp. 151–3 and Safrinski, *Heidegger*, pp. 242–4.

Ibid., p. 248.

Wolin, *Heidegger*, pp. 29, 34–5.

Isaiah Berlin refers to Fraenkel's Oxford appointment in a letter written in December 1934 – see *Flourishing: Letters of Isaiah Berlin* (London: Chatto and Windus, 2004), p. 112.

J. C. Masterman, *To Teach the Senators Wisdom, or An Oxford Guide-Book* (London: Hodder and Stoughton, 1952), p. 274.

49   Ryle, 'Autobiographical,' in Wood and Pilcher, pp. 9–10.

Ryle Papers.

Ryle, 'Autobiographical,' in Wood and Pitcher, p. 14.

Ibid., p. 9.

50   Ryle, *Collected Papers*, 1.241.

5   Freiburg

51   170 / 184.

177 / 191.

Oxford Tragedy, p. 30.

52   As quoted in the 'Translator's Introduction,' to *The Post Card*, p. xi.

65 / 72.

66 / 74.

190 / 204.

53   189 / 203.

For full details and text of this interview, see Wolin, *Heidegger*, pp. 91–116.

188 / 203.

54   12 / 16.

173 / 187–8.

14 / 19.

Derrida mentions this secret name in Bennington and Derrida, *Derrida*, pp. 96, 185–6.

55   Minutes of the Oxford University Jewish Society, January 26th 1946 – Ms. Top. Oxon d. 488/1, Bodleian Library, University of Oxford. I am very grateful to the Bodleian Library for kind permission to quote from these Minutes both here and elsewhere in my book.

See Freda Silver Jackson (ed.), *Then and Now: A Collection of Recollections* (Oxford: Oxford Jewish Congregation, 1992), p. 20.

12 / 16.

56   See Adorno and Benjamin, *Complete Correspondence*.

See Evelyn Wilcock, 'Adorno in Oxford 1: Oxford University Musical Club,' *Oxford Magazine* (1996) 11.

See Momme Brodersen, *Walter Benjamin: A Biography* (London: Verso, 1997).

33 / 39.

See Franz Kafka, *Letters to Milena*, ed. Willi Haas, tr. T. and J. Stern (London: Secker and Warburg, 1953).

32 / 38, 35 / 40.

57   OUJS Minutes, May 22nd 1938.

Ibid., October 29th 1939.

See David M. Lewis, *The Jews of Oxford* (Oxford: Oxford Jewish Congregation, 1992), p. 77; for a summary of the debate see *The Oxford Magazine,* February 4th 1943, pp. 164–5.

OUJS Minutes, June 19th 1946.

194 / 209.

OUJS Minutes, November 23rd 1946.

82 / 91.

OUJS Minutes, January 26th 1946.

123 / 135.

58   OUJS Minutes, April 26th 1947.

For photo see Rowse, *All Souls and Appeasement*, p. 40.

OUJS Minutes, June 7th 1946.

Ibid., May 7th 1949.

Ibid., November 10th 1944; the marginalia is signed by 'F. D. K.'.

6   Esther

60   I have taken the word 'foresuffered' from T. S. Eliot, *The Waste Land* in *The Complete Poems of T. S. Eliot* (London: Faber and Faber, 1969), page 69.

204 / 220.

61   152 / 165.

158 / 172.

Home Office, Registered Papers – HO 144/6158, The National Archives, Kew. <http://www.movinghere.org.uk/deliveryfiles/pro/Aliens_Act_1905/0/3.pdf>.

62   15 / 20.

21 / 26.

189 / 204.

Home Office, Aliens Department, Internees Index – HO396/78/134, The National Archives.

64   Exodus 3. 2.

See HO 144/6158, National Archives. I am grateful to Dr Kevin Brown,

St Mary's Hospital Trust Archivist, for giving me permission to quote this letter.

230 / 246.

65   Robert Wise (dir.), *The Sound of Music* (Robert Wise Productions, 1965).
71 / 79.

Bennington and Derrida, *Derrida*, p. 19.

66   71 / 79.

72 / 80, 75 / 83.

222 / 238.

For an excellent guide to the cultural history of the book of Esther see Jo Carruthers, *Esther Through the Centuries* (Oxford: Blackwell, forthcoming).

216 / 232.

127 / 139.

182 / 196.

67   24 / 29.

OUJS Minutes, October 16th 1946 and October 19th 1946. < http://www.geocities.com/dr_b_goldstein/kever.htm >.

68   MS 179, Parkes Library, University of Southampton.

69   Glasser, *Gorbals*, p. 183.

245 / 262.

I have filched the phrase 'tramp in flames' from my Lancaster colleague Paul Farley; it is the title of his most recent collection of poems – published by Picador in 2006.

222 / 238.

220 / 236.

29 / 34.

70   See *Oxford University Calendar* (Oxford: Oxford University Press, 1958), p. 798 n.1.

<http://judaism.about.com/library/2_holocaust/testimonies/bl_eunger.htm>.

Paul Johnson, *A History of the Jews* (London: Weidenfeld and Nicolson, 1987), p. 508.

Quoted in Cathy Caruth, *Unclaimed Experience: Trauma, Narrative, and History* (Baltimore: Johns Hopkins University Press, 1996), p. 24.

71   *School History*, p. 198.

Wolseley, *Which Way Came Death?*, p. 16.

School Magazine, LXXXVIII (March 1946).

Ibid., LXXXV (March 1942).

Which Way Came Death?, p. 180.

72   Paul Celan, 'Death Fugue,' in Paul Celan, *Selected Poems*, tr. Michael Hamburger (Harmonsdworth: Penguin, 1996), p. 65.

I allude, of course, to J. S. Mill's famous definition of poetry – see his essay 'What is Poetry?' in Thomas J. Collins and Vivienne J. Rundle (eds), *The*

Broadview Anthology of Victorian Poetry and Poetic Theory (New York: Broadview Press, 1999), p. 1216.
School History, p. 198.

7   'They Weren't Really You Know

73   *School History*, p. 206.
        School Magazine, LXXXVII (March 1944).
        138 / 150.
        Bennington and Derrida, *Derrida*, p. 173.
        97 / 107.
74   128 / 140–1.
        School Magazine, LXXXIX (September 1947).
        Local Newspaper, September 8th 1943.
        186 / 200.
        School Magazine, LXXXIX (March 1947).
75   See Walter Benjamin, *Illuminations,* ed. Hannah Arendt, tr. Harry Zohn (London: Fontana, 1992), p. 253.
76   The judge is quoted at <http://www.spartacus.schoolnet.co.uk/2WWcrime.htm>.
        Local Newspaper – March 1st 1944, March 24th 1944.
        57 / 64.
        The majority of psychiatrists find it hard to believe, often for extremely good reasons – see, for example, James T. Richardson, Joel Best and David G. Bromley (eds), *The Satanism Scare* (New York: Aldine de Gruyter, 1991); Elizabeth Loftus and Katherine Ketcham, *The Myth of Repressed Memory: False Memories and Allegations of Sexual Abuse* (New York: St Martin's Griffin, 1994); and Robert A. Baker (ed.), *Child Abuse and False Memory Syndrome* (New York: Prometheus Books, 1998). Just a few, though, do (on occasions) believe: see Martin A. Conway (ed.), *Recovered Memory and False Memories* (Oxford: Oxford University Press, 1997); and Valerie Sinason (ed.), *Treating Survivors of Satanist Abuse* (London: Routledge, 1994).
77   74 / 83.
        See Diana Serra Cary, *Jackie Coogan: The World's Boy King* (New York: Scarecrow Press, 2005).
        13 / 18.
        School Magazine, LXXXVII (July 1944).
        Which Way Came Death?, p. 89.
78   26 / 31.
        12 / 16.
        Letter to my mother, April 1951.
79   Ibid., February 1952.
        219 / 235.
80   26 / 31.

Roger Bacon *Secretum Secretorum cum glossis et notulis : tractatus brevis et utilis ad declarandum quedam obscure dicta,* eds. Robert Steele and A. S. Fulton (Oxonii: E Typographeo Clarendoniano, 1920).

Ibid., p. xxi.

169 / 183.

81   Gilbert Ryle, 'Heterologicality,' in Margaret MacDonald (ed.), *Philosophy and Analysis* (Oxford: Basil Blackwell, 1953), p. 46.

Mabbott, 'Tribute,' p. 224.

Ben Rogers, *A. J. Ayer: A Life* (New York: Grove Press, 1999), p. 252.

82   Gilbert Ryle, 'Conscience and Moral Conviction' in MacDonald (ed.), p. 157.

Ryle, *Aspects of Mind*, p. 137.

School Magazine, XCII (Summer Term 1950).

129 / 141.

Gilbert Ryle, *The Concept of Mind* (Harmonsdworth: Penguin, 1949), p. 310.

8 The House

83   I visited the school on June 9th 2005.

John Richard Schad's termly tutorial reports, Christ Church, Oxford University, 1948–51.

84   See Richard Davenport-Hines (ed.), *Letters from Oxford: Hugh Trevor-Roper to Bernard Berenson* (London: Weidenfeld and Nicolson, 2006), pp. xiv, xviii.

Robert Harris, *Selling Hitler: The Extraordinary Story of the Con Job of the Century* (London: Pantheon, 1986), p. 225.

This book is more usually known as *The Last Days of Hitler* (London: Macmillan, 1947).

Hugh Trevor-Roper, *The European Witch-Craze of the Sixteenth and Seventeenth Centuries* (London: Pantheon, 1969).

85   Termly reports, July 1949.

45 / 51.

252 / 269.

171 / 185.

217 / 233.

86   Trevor-Roper, *The European Witch-Craze*, pp. 38–9.

Ibid., p. 96.

C. S. Lewis, *Screwtape Letters* (London: Geoffrey Bles, 1942).

87   *School Magazine,* LXXXVI (December 1943).

Letter to my mother, June 1949.

Ibid., February 1951.

167 / 181

See Cecil Roth, *The Jews of Medieval Oxford* (Oxford: Clarendon Press, 1951), p. 97.

245 / 262.
88   Letter to my mother, May 1951.
        69 / 77.
        Letter to my mother, May 1949.
89   Ibid., June 1950.
        Ibid., November 1950.
        219 / 235.
        A. J. Ayer, *Part of My Life* (London: Collins, 1977), p. 193.
        Lord Dacre Papers, Box 13, Christ Church, University of Oxford; email
        from Judith Curthoys, College Archivist. I am grateful to the Literary
        Estate of Lord Dacre of Glanton for kind permission to quote from these
        papers.
        Letter to my mother, May 1951.
90   Jacques Derrida, *Specters of Marx: The State of the Debt, the Work of Mourning,
        and the New International* (London: Routledge, 1994), p. 14.
        237 / 254.
        Ryle, *Aspects of Mind*, p. 211.
        Letter to my mother, May 1951.
91   13 / 18.
        114 / 126
        135 / 147.
        121 / 133.
        50 / 57.
        As painted by William Frederick Yeames (1835–1918) in 1878.
92   Shakespeare, *Hamlet,* II.ii.168.
        Judges 5.20.
        Bennington and Derrida, *Derrida*, pp. 265–6.
93   208–9 / 224.
        211 / 226–7.
        See Bennington and Derrida, *Derrida*, p. 334.
        This astute person was Dr Sarah Wood, of the University of Kent. The
        others at the meal were: Dr Kevin Mills, Professor Christopher Norris,
        and Professor Nicholas Royle.
        This better friend is Jean-Michel Rabaté; the conference was held at Paris
        7 in 2003.
94   180 / 194.
        Trevor-Roper, *Letters from Oxford*, p. 64.
        Bennington and Derrida, *Derrida*, p. 211.
        Ibid. p. 277.
95   See David Lehman, *Signs of the Times: Deconstruction and the Fall of Paul de
        Man* (New York: Poseidon Press, 1991), pp. 188–9.
        For facsimiles of all the articles, see Werner Hamacher, Neil Hertz, and
        Thomas Keenan (eds.), *Wartime Journalism, 1939–1943 by Paul de Man*
        (Lincoln: University of Nebraska Press, 1988).

Quoted in Lehman, *Signs of the Times*, p. 173.

Le Soir, October 28th 1941 in Hamacher *et al.*, *Wartime Journalism*, p. 158.

Ibid., p. 45.

See Jonathan Culler, '"Paul de Man's War" and the Aesthetic Ideology,' *Critical Inquiry* 15 (1989) 779.

Lehman, *Signs of the Times*, p. 164.

9 Stolen Evening

96   See Lehman, *Signs of the Times*, p. 190.

97   Emmanuel Levinas, *Proper Names*, tr. Michael Smith (Stanford: Stanford University Press, 1997), p. 4.

Jacques Derrida and Maurizio Ferraris, *A Taste for the Secret*, tr. Giacomo Donis and David Webb (Cambridge: Polity, 2001), p. 52.

Michael Payne and John Schad (eds.), *life.after.theory* (London: Continuum, 2003), p. 49.

98   See Lehman, *Signs of the Times*, pp. 191–7.

Payne and Schad, *life.*, pp. 3–4.

99   See Geoffrey Hartman, *The Longest Shadow: In the Aftermath of the Holocaust* (London: Palgrave, 1996), p. 15. To learn much more of Hartman's life see *A Scholar's Tale* (New York: Fordham University Press, forthcoming). Geoffrey Hartman visited Loughborough University on December 12th–13th, 2004.

148 / 160.

100   *See* <www.angelfire.com/space/u_line/dupondt.htm

183 / 198.

Derrida, *Without Alibi*, p. 127.

See Lehman, *Signs of the Times*, pp. 179, 175, 197.

101   See ibid., p. 197.

Jacques Derrida, *Memoires for Paul de Man*, tr. Cecile Lindsay *et al* (New York: Columbia University Press, 1986) p. 126.

Hugh Trevor-Roper, *The Philby Affair: Espionage, Treason, and Secret Services* (London: Kimber, 1968), pp. 38–9. 'C,' by the way, was otherwise known as Sir Stewart Menzies, then Chief of MI6; see Christopher Andrew, *Her Majesty's Secret Service* (London: Viking, 1986), p. 462.

102   Trevor-Roper, *Letters from Oxford*, pp. 145–6.

'I used to think, 'writes Trevor-Roper, 'that historical events always had deep economic causes, I now believe that pure farce covers a far greater field of history' (ibid., p. 58).

See Lehman, *Signs of the Times*, p. 187.

Paul de Man, *Allegories of Reading: Figural Language in Rousseau, Nietzsche, Rilke and Proust* (New Haven: Yale University Press, 1979), p. 293.

103   See Trevor-Roper, *The Last Days of Hitler.*

See Trevor-Roper, *Letters from Oxford*, pp. 211, 184, 183, 184n, 60.

Ibid., p. 95.

Ibid., p. 184.

Ibid., p. 177.

104   David Irving was imprisoned in Austria from February to December 2006.

See Mark Weber, 'David Irving: Intrepid Battler for Historical Truth,' *The Journal of Historical Review* 13.1 (1993). This is a misquotation of a review of Irving's book *Hitler's War* which HTR wrote for *The Sunday Times* on June 12th 1977. What HTR actually wrote in his review was that 'No praise can be too high for his [Irving's] indefatigable scholarly industry'; the rest of the review was largely critical.

105   See Harris, *Selling Hitler*, pp. 510–20.

Private letter to HTR, 20th May 1983, Dacre Papers, Box 375.

Quoted in Andrzej Warminski, 'Introduction to Paul de Man,' *Aesthetic Ideology* (Minneapolis: University of Minnesota Press, 1996), p. 1.

10   High Places

107   See Carol L. Marks, 'Thomas Traherne and Hermes Trismegistus,' *Renaissance News* 19 (1966), p. 119.

248 / 265.

207 / 222.

For an interesting study of the relationship between Freemasonry and public schools, see P. J. Rich, *Chains of Empire: English Public Schools, Masonic Cabalism, Historical Causality, and Imperial Clubdom* (London: Regency Press, 1991).

108   Ryle, *Collected Papers*, II.161.

See *School Magazine* LXXXIX (March 1947).

109   Wolseley, *Which Way Came Death?*, pp. 43, 16.

Ibid., pp. 9, 329, 78, 184.

See *School History*, p. 171.

Wolseley, *Which Way Came Death?*, pp. 94–5.

School Magazine LXXXVI (July 1943).

180 / 194.

110   *School Magazine*, LXXXVI (December 1943).

Ibid., LXXXIV (June 1941).

Ibid., LXXXIII (October 1940).

111   Ibid., LXXXVI (December 1943).

109 / 120.

22 / 27.

112   195 / 210.

113   36 / 42.

228 / 245.

250 / 267.

219 / 234.

207 / 223.

169 / 183.
137 / 149.

114   Letter to my mother, June 1951.
       Ibid., June 1952.
       137 / 149.
       Georgette Derrida died on December 5th 1991. Her final illness is treated
       extensively in Derrida's long confessional text, 'Circumfession' –
       Bennington and Derrida, *Derrida,* pp. 3–315.
       Ibid., p. 262.

115   *School Magazine* LXXXIV (June 1941).
       228 / 245.

116   52 / 59.
       99 / 109.
       216 / 232.
       Lynn Haney, *Naked at the Feast: A Biography of Josephine Baker* (London:
       Robson Books, 1996), pp. 146, 148.
       170 / 184.

117   228 / 245.
       170 / 184.
       See Haney, *Naked at Feast*, p. 221.
       216 / 227.
       60 / 67.

118   Ephesians 6.17.
       Bennington and Derrida, *Derrida*, p. 124.

119   Letter to my mother, August 1950.

120   Derrida, *Of Grammatology*, p. 6.
       Ephesians 6.11–17.
       See Dwight David Eisenhower, *Crusade in Europe* (Baltimore: Johns
       Hopkins University Press, 1997).

121   Bennington and Derrida, *Derrida*, p. 300.
       The story of Abraham and Isaac appears in Genesis 22. 1–14.

122   Blanchot sent the letter on July 20th 1994, exactly fifty years after the
       mock-firing squad – see Jacques Derrida 'Un témoin de toujours' (an
       address Derrida gave at Blanchot's cremation on Feb 24th 2003) –
       <http://www.jacquesderrida.com.ar/frances/blanchot.htm>.   Blanchot
       also wrote about the mock execution in a narrative called *The Instant of
       My Death* (1994).
       She was killed in February 1943 – see *History of the Village* (2001), p. 373.
       248 / 265.

123   Fry, *Three Plays,* p. 192.

124   Anon., *Mercurius Oxoniensis*, p. 64.
       Trevor-Roper, *Letters from Oxford*, p. 81.
       Ibid., p. 133.
       211 / 227.

88 / 97.

11 Fast Cars

125   209 / 224–5.
         93 / 103.
         210 / 225.
         197 / 212.
         208 / 223.
126   Interview with Alan Montefiore, March 2005.
         115 / 127.
         200 / 215.
         46 / 52.
         Derrida, the Movie – DVD extra titled 'Friendship.'
         44 / 50.
         162 / 176.
         89 / 99.
         88 / 97.
         138 / 150.
         See West, *MI5*, p. 142.
         101 / 111.
         200 / 215.
127   Ms. Ashmole 304 fol. 39 v; I am grateful to Dr Barker-Benfield for trans-
         lation.
         Bennington and Derrida, *Derrida*, p. 248.
128   Jacques Derrida, *Writing and Difference*, tr. Alan Bass (London: Routledge,
         1978), pp. 257, 270.
         93 / 102, 43 / 50.
         Derrida and Ferraris, *Taste for the Secret*, p. 42; Bennington and Derrida,
         Derrida, p. 343.
         188 / 203.
129   162 / 176.
         43 / 50.
         101 / 111.
         163 / 176.
         44 / 50.
         Derrida visited Loughborough University on November 9th–11th 2001.
         127 / 139.
         School Magazine LXXXIV (June 1941).
130   Letter to my mother, November 1949.
         Alfred Goulding (dir.), *A Chump at Oxford* (United Artists, 1940).
         See Jan Morris (ed.), *The Oxford Book of Oxford* (Oxford University Press,
         1981), p. 368.
131   163 / 177.
         17 / 21–2.

168 / 182.

135 / 148.

17 / 22.

This bus plays an important part in the story of C. S. Lewis's conversion – see C. S. Lewis, *Surprised by Joy* (London: Geoffrey Bles, 1955), p. 179.

34 / 40.

42 / 49.

34 / 40.

132   Letter to my mother, April 1952.

See *The Times*, 14th April 1997. The £350,000 endowment was offered by Dr Gert-Rudolf Flick, grandson of the Nazi sympathiser Friedrich Flick. Friedrich Flick was an adviser to Heinrich Himmler and used 48,000 slave-labourers, mostly Jewish, to help him build Germany's richest industrial empire. About 40,000 slaves, whom he obtained from concentration camps, died in appalling conditions. He was jailed for seven years in 1947 but freed in 1950.

115 / 127.

133   4 / 8.

20 / 25.

33 / 38.

134   Malabou and Derrida, *Counterpath*, p. 102.

162 / 176.

This simile is easily confused with 'The Simile of the Cave' – see Plato, *The Republic*, tr. H. D. P. Lee (Harmonsdworth: Penguin, 1955), pp. 278–86.

119 / 130.

Derrida, the Movie.

60 / 67.

93 / 102

162–3 / 176–7.

87 / 96.

127 / 137.

177 / 191.

233 / 250.

68 / 76.

136   Letter to my mother, November 1950.

167 / 181.

Walter Forde (dir.), *Ghost Train* (Gainsborough Pictures, 1941).

181, 183 / 196, 197.

Paul de Man, *Blindness and Insight* (London: Routledge, 1983), p. xii.

137   Letter to my mother, May 1951.

See Jerry Beck and Will Friedwald, *Looney Tunes and Merrie Melodies* (New York: Owl Books, 1989).

176 / 190.

90 / 99.

See Morris, *Oxford Book of Oxford*, pp. 350–1.

180 / 194.

Letter to my mother, January 1951.

Jack Lee (dir.), *The Wooden Horse* (Essex Films, 1950).

12 Secret Marriage

139   223 / 239.

101 / 111.

112 / 123.

When talking of falling in love on the way to the air that kills, I am indebted to a brilliant-terrible prose-poem by Steven Cohen.

10 / 14.

The dying Jewess is Joy Davidman – see Roger Lancelyn Green and Walter Hooper, *C. S. Lewis: a Biography* (London: Collins, 1974), p. 268. The living Jewess is Gretel Karplus; as Adorno writes, on September 13th 1937, 'the marriage took place in truly total privacy on the 8th – and in Oxford, where my friend, [Redvers] Opie, invited us to lunch' – Adorno and Benjamin, *Complete Correspondence*, p. 208.

208 / 224.

219 / 235.

140   238 / 254.

Malabou and Derrida, *Counterpath*, pp. 278–9.

120 / 132.

166/ 180.

190 / 204.

Fry, *Three Plays*, p. 182.

13 Hastings

142   Bennington and Derrida, *Derrida*, p. 300.

68 / 75.

167 / 181.

My portrait of Aleister Crowley and 'Netherwood' is very largely based on John Symonds, *The Great Beast: The Life and Magick of Aleister Crowley* (London: Macdonald, 1951); Kenneth Grant, *Remembering Aleister Crowley* (London: Skoob Books, 1991); and Rodney Davies, 'The Last Days of Aleister Crowley' at <http://www.21stcenturyradio.com/articles/03/ 1001231.html >.

199 / 214.

144   There are regular references to these clubs and societies in the *Hastings and St Leonard's Observer*. It is well known that Crowley was a member of the Chess Club; I am only guessing that he attended the occasional meeting of the Theosophical Society. The embalmers met in Hastings just

once during Crowley's time – see *Hastings and St Leonard's Observer* April 6th 1946.

146   97 / 107.

179 / 193.

See Tim Tate, *Children for the Devil: Ritual Abuse and Satanic Crime* (London: Methuen, 1991), p. 101.

The Master Therion [aka Aleister Crowley], *Magick. In Theory and Practice* (New York: Castle Books, 1991), p. 95.

147   Ibid., p. 95, n. 4.

38 / 44.

For some details (albeit inevitably limited) of Crowley's Masonic affiliations see Kenneth Grant, *Remembering Aleister Crowley* (London: Skoob Books, 1991) and Tate, *Children*, pp. 96–7.

Local Newspaper, January 6th 1944.

97 / 107.

148   *St Leonard and Hastings Observer* – May 25th; February 16th; November 30th; June 7th.

School Magazine, LXXXIX (March 1947).

169 / 183.

I should confess that the letter (see < http://www.billheidrick.com/tlc1995/tlc0895.htm#ps3>) is dated October 1st 1945 and so refers to the 1945–46 Congress; however, if Crowley, a member of the chess club, attended in 1945–46 there is good reason to think that he also attended in 1946–47.

See < http://en.wikipedia.org/wiki/Gerald_Abrahams>.

149   H. Kmoch and L. Prins, *Hastings Conference 1946–1947* (Sutton Coldfield: Chess, 1947) pp. 40, 69, 71, 66, 39, 51, 59, 63, 52, 69, 72, 35.

School Magazine, LXXXIX (March 1947).

14   Sacrifice

150   Kafka, *Letters to Milena*, p. 162.

222 / 238.

155 / 168.

33 / 38.

151   Fry, *Three Plays*, p. 192.

Ibid., p. 193.

Genesis 22.8.

152   Thomas de Quincey, 'On Murder,' p. 35.

55 / 62, 148 / 161.

153   71–2 / 79–80.

222 / 238.

24 / 29.

15   Elijah

154   173 / 187–8.

See Robert E. Conot, *Justice at Nuremberg* (New York: Carroll and Graf, 1983), p. 506.

See Elliott Horowitz, 'The Rite to Be Reckless: On the Perpetration and Interpretation of Purim Violence,' *Poetics Today* 15 (1994), 16.

231 / 247.

155   Claude Goldsmid Montefiore, 'Some Old Fashioned Opinions and Reflections about the Jews: A Die-Hard's Confession' (October 22nd 1935) – Ms 108/4, p. 22 (Parkes Library, University of Southampton). I am very grateful to the Parkes Library for permission to quote from this lecture.

10 / 14.

11 / 16.

225 / 241.

156   230 / 247.

Bennington and Derrida, *Derrida*, p. 303.

Adapted very slightly from Kings 17.17–24.

Jacques Derrida, *Apprendre à vivre enfin: Entretein avec Jean Birnbaum* (Paris: Galilee / Le Monde, 2005), pp. 22, 24.

157   127 / 139.

32 / 37.

23 / 28.

164 / 178.

Index